new york

English Pea Soup, Lobster Crème Fraîche (page 109)

HAWKSWORTH

THE COOKBOOK

by

CHEF DAVID HAWKSWORTH

WITH JACOB RICHLER & STÉPHANIE NOËL

PHOTOGRAPHY BY CLINTON HUSSEY

appetite
by RANDOM HOUSE

CONTENTS

CHEF PHILIP HOWARD

David Hawksworth was one of those names that cropped up from time to time early on in my life at the Square restaurant in London. It could have simply been the fact that he was a rarity in the UK: an ambitious young chef from Canada. Whatever the case, he was here, working hard and spending considerable time in some of the finest kitchens in the land.

Those were the good old days when the finest kitchens tended to be very similar in their output, and the elite restaurants they created, with two and three Michelin stars, all served beautifully crafted and mostly classical French cuisine. It was a hugely important era in the evolution of cooking in this country, and the world, and David showed wise judgment to come and be a part of it. The truth is, he did more than that: he placed himself at the heart of it, in the knowledge that there is no replacement for good old-fashioned hard work. David earned his stripes in some of the toughest kitchens in England and in doing so he has those wonderful cooking techniques and classical flavours well and truly etched onto his hard drive. He spent many years learning his trade, honing his craft and understanding flavours, and, I am sure, quietly developing his own ideas that he would put to good use in time.

His stint at the Square was the beginning of the end of his time in London. I can't recall exactly how the appointment came about, but I'd guess it was his desire to come and see first-hand how a restaurant of considerable reputation managed to serve 1,000 covers a week, not only consistently but also without neglecting its primary purpose of being a high-achieving business. For my part, it was a joy to have someone of David's abilities walk into the kitchen and help keep the ship steady during those relentlessly busy years. I respected the fact that he knew exactly what he was doing and where he was going. I knew that he was on a journey, and his career would be one that I would watch with interest and expectation, in equal measure. Indeed, that proved to be true.

David's path once back in Vancouver was exactly as I expected. Armed with a wealth of knowledge, experience, and expertise, and with a well-earned air of quiet confidence, he was an unknown entity perfectly equipped to show the city exactly what his vision of a truly great restaurant should be. Hawksworth Restaurant became just that. It's not just a restaurant serving very good food. It is a rare entity where everything comes together to produce something that is so much more than the sum of its parts. It's about the restaurant experience that David has put together, one that keeps guests coming back not only because they have eaten some world-class food, but because they had such a great time doing so! That's special.

Nightingale, his next venture, has shown he has the capacity to create a wonderful dining experience in a more casual environment too. Consistency is key, and he has the ability to operate successfully in both restaurant markets. He's a chefs' chef, too, and an industry man through and through. He's at the heart of all that is good in the trade in Vancouver, and he has my utmost respect for that.

David has reaped the rewards of his hard-earned efforts. In this very fine book, you now have your hands on the recipes created through those efforts. I know for certain that you will not regret investing in this book—and the knowledge of this chef.

HAWKSWORTH
RESTAURANT

JACOB RICHLER

Back when we were getting started on this cookbook, David and I set off for a week together in the UK. Our plan was to retrace some of the formative steps of his early culinary career in London and Oxfordshire, to catch up with some of his old workmates who were still in the trade there, and—if we had time—double-check that English beer was still okay.

So, early one evening in March 2018, as David was boarding the direct overnight flight to London from Vancouver, I was gathering strength for my journey from Toronto to London with a quick stop at what was then the newest Canadian restaurant to bear the imprimatur of the Hawksworth Restaurant Group: Air Canada's Signature Suite at Toronto Pearson International Airport Terminal 1. To be clear, this is less a restaurant than it is a private club for the airline's long-haul business class travellers. But it's a good one: I snagged a crostini with peperonata and white anchovy from the buffet and a flute of champagne from the open bar and settled in on a bar stool for a considered look at the menu—which is unburdened by prices, and aims high.

The sablefish with bacon-scented gelatin-strained dashi was tempting—but then, I'd had it before, when David served it at his 2013 event at James Beard House, in the West Village, New York City, and I'd helped out in the kitchen for a story for *Maclean's* magazine. So I read on. In my mind's eye—or ear—I imagined David making the case for ordering something light and easily digestible that would have you feeling healthy as you dozed off on that long flight. So uncharacteristically, I went with his vegetarian option: a salad of crisp English pea falafels, with roast cherry tomatoes, pea shoots, and salsa verde. Then, suddenly fearful that my sentence for good behaviour would be to wake up ravenous halfway across the Atlantic, I quickly added a starter of seared foie gras on toasted pain perdu with chopped pistachios and braised cherries.

To come clean, the foie gras wasn't merely for insurance. It also felt like the right way to start this particular voyage—because nearly 20 years previous, it was over a plate of foie gras that my journey with David got started.

It was January 2001. I was the Toronto-based food columnist and restaurant critic for the *National Post*. And while on a quick assignment in Vancouver, on my way out to dinner at another restaurant, I had stopped in for a quick glass of wine at a month-old restaurant on Granville Street called Ouest. I'd never heard of its chef, didn't know that he was locally raised and fresh back from a decade in the UK working for some of the best chefs I knew of. But I liked the look of the room with its handsome cherry-wood bar, and after a quick look at the menu, decided that it would be a good idea to order up a quick parfait of foie gras to tide me over until mealtime.

The slice of foie gras and chicken liver mousse was presented unlike any I had seen before. Instead of being served with the expected mound of diced gelée on the side, the terrine was sitting on top of a shallow, glossy pool of the stuff, set on a chilled plate. And the terrine itself was not framed by the usual thin layer of pork back fat, but instead, with a whisper-thin edging of cold butter. I liked this stark, minimalist presentation—and the unctuous texture and Madeira-enriched taste of it, more so. After a second mouthful I realized that I had a problem: I did not want to leave Ouest for my dinner reservation elsewhere; I wanted to stay right where I was and keep tasting as many dishes as possible. Because that terrine was perfect.

I've been writing about food and restaurants for close to 25 years, and—trust me—these epiphanic encounters with perfection do not occur frequently. When you get lucky like that, you come back for more. As often as you can manage it. So I did—and over those meals at the short-lived Ouest and its much longer second act as West, David's cooking was for me an ongoing and considerable source of pleasure. So much so that even though I've long since disposed of my notebooks from that era and have no photos to look back on (my restaurant reviewing days were in the pre-smartphone era), I can still easily recall many of the dishes that moved me.

A small cube of pressed braised belly of wild boar, its richness perfectly offset by the acidity of the mound of confit tomato it was perched on. Sea urchin served in its shell, doused in a foamed fennel-scented fish velouté. Implausibly delicate pumpkin ravioli, their filling accented with almond, dressed in sage butter. Cylinders of sturgeon wrapped in a jacket of crisp prosciutto, roasted à point, and paired with shaved ceps. Seared, braised veal tongue, curled on the plate with capers and miniature brioche croutons.

At the time, cooking like this changed the Vancouver culinary equation drastically, for it brought into the city's midst for the first time a style directly connected to what was happening in the best restaurants in the UK. Which was then the most interesting fine dining happening *anywhere*. Like many of the chefs at the forefront of that culinary revolution (Pierre Koffmann, the Roux brothers, Raymond Blanc, Marco Pierre White, etc.), that cooking was fundamentally French. As it played out in the UK though, it was less constrained by tradition and far more inventive than anything happening across the Channel—while giving up none of the discipline. Back in Vancouver, in David's hands, the same culinary thinking combined French tradition and cutting-edge technique with a highly attuned seasonality to the best local ingredients, and arrived at a new and uniquely sophisticated West Coast cuisine. And then, as with all great cooking, his style evolved and continued to grow while staying true to its roots.

That is the essence of great cooking. Not reinventing the wheel—but appreciating what it does well already, and maybe tweaking the tread pattern on its tire to make it do the job even better. The best culinary ideas never go away. They linger. But they also must constantly be readjusted to suit the trends and fashion of the times. And the cooking we enjoyed during our trip to the UK, from London or out in Great Milton, Oxfordshire, at Le Manoir aux Quat'Saisons, was a case in point. What we ate there was still rooted in classicism, but prepared in a manner far less rich than it was in the early 90s. "Oooh, that's half a pound of butter, right there," David had said to me one evening back in Canada, as we sat in his office, looking over old UK menus. I was admiring the classic dishes I missed eating. David was doing math: in this case, butter content of lunch for one at the Canteen, if you started with the parfait de foie gras, followed with a risotto, and then moved on to cod viennoise, and any of several desserts.

It would be hard to do that in London now. And totally impossible at Hawksworth Restaurant, where a Hawksworth dish today is in all its details so very different from the early days at West. It's far less rich, less French, more Asian, brighter, more easily digestible, far less derivative, more colourful, and more assertively David's own.

But his plates of now and then have much in common, too. Namely, their checklist of culinary essentials: balance in flavour, texture, and acidity; the right number of things on a plate; flavours that show through with clarity. There is finesse in abundance, but no flashy pyrotechnics; his cooking makes its point with quality and balance. Which is to say that his culinary values have not changed, but they are differently expressed. They are the values imbued not just by getting great training, but by paying enough attention to understand, process, and remember the best of it—and having the good sense to know when to stay on and learn more and when to move on.

For smart young chefs, there is a story included in this book that more than hints at how to manage a career. How to make the most of great experience, and how to judge that the time is right to set out on your own, on what terms, and how to turn that culinary brand into something more than a single great restaurant (as in several restaurants, and a full-on diversified culinary business that runs the gamut from cafés to airport lounges serving up top-quality seared foie gras). For the rest of us, who just want to enjoy good food and cook it better, this book is a treasure trove of fantastic recipes. Recipes that reflect the whole range of David's remarkable culinary career. Some of them are easy; many are not. But whether you want to make the Nightingale pizza or the game terrine, every single recipe here is generous with the professional kitchen's secrets and tips. For cooks of every manner of ambition this book is a major asset, and overdue. I hope you enjoy cooking from it—and okay, looking at the pictures—as much as I do.

— J.R.

CHEF DAVID HAWKSWORTH

This is my first cookbook with my name on the spine, and it spans my whole professional career. We selected the recipes on the basis of quality—but also for range. I've included a few from my early career in the UK in the 90s because they informed so much of what I did afterward that; to me, their significance never fades. There are others from my early days at Ouest (then renamed West) that I thought really captured a moment. A few others date back to the early days at Hawksworth. Most are from our current repertoire—at Hawksworth, at Nightingale, and at Bel Café. So the cooking here represents a lot of different styles.

But even though cooking always evolves, ingredients go in and out of style, techniques change, and what we understand about eating well and healthily changes how we cook, a lot of things remain the same. Those are the lessons I learned first-hand in my early years working for some great, pioneering chefs—from Marco Pierre White at the Canteen, to Raymond Blanc at Le Manoir aux Quat'Saisons, and Philip Howard at the Square. I learned that a good dish always has balance in its seasoning, acidity, and textures, and always has a harmonious—not distracting—mix of ingredients on the plate. If you understand that, and the importance of classic old-school techniques, you get what makes great cooking—whatever its style.

My style has changed a lot over the years. The journey from when I first made my mark in Vancouver at Ouest with my idea of a new West Coast French cuisine, to the lighter, more multicultural idea of fine dining I now put forward at Hawksworth and the Californian-Italian–inspired vision of Nightingale has been a long one. And it would not have been possible without the key players I've been lucky enough to have on my team. They know who they are and how grateful I am for their contribution.

In some ways, I count on them more, and push them harder than ever before. Sure, I drove my brigade really hard when I was in the kitchen every day, directing traffic from the pass. But nowadays I demand even more of them in an arrangement that's tougher for me, too: I have to trust them completely to execute my vision, to my standards, even when I'm not around. No one can be everywhere at once, and I'm no exception. I also like to travel; it's a great source of ideas. These days if I'm cooking somewhere at night it's usually at my house, for my family. Or maybe I've just gone fishing.

In the pages that follow you'll find recipes and stories from all the places that are so important to me. I hope you like them nearly as much as I do.

NOTE ON THE RECIPES

If you bought this book just for a good read and to look at the pictures, that's okay—I hope you enjoy it. But my hope is that you will cook from this book too, so before you get started, I want to share a few words of advice. To begin, note that these recipes span a large range of difficulty. Some of them are a walk in the park. Others even the most gifted home cook will find challenging—at least when it comes to finding the time. Some of these recipes are long, with different parts sometimes happening simultaneously, and some require advance preparations, so read through from start to finish before you tackle them.

As a general rule, the recipes from Bel Café are the easiest and the quickest. Those from Nightingale will be a step up in required skill set, but ideal for casual home entertaining because they are conceived to be served family-style on sharing platters, just as we do at the restaurant. And then there are the more challenging dishes of the fine dining realm, primarily from Hawksworth but also from earlier days at West and a handful from my formative years in some great kitchens in the UK.

These recipes are restaurant dishes, and we decided early on that while most restaurant cookbooks simplify and streamline their lists of ingredients and method to make them easier to manage for the home cook, we wanted to share the recipes as close as we could to how we make them. There are lots of great classic techniques here that should not be ignored and mustn't be forgotten. They are the building blocks of great cooking. And I wanted to share them, rather than underplaying their importance, dumbing down our food, and leaving you to wonder why, when you followed all the steps so carefully, your finished dish still didn't taste anywhere near as good as it did when you last ate it at one of our restaurants.

That said, feel free to take a shortcut here and there. You don't need to bake your own focaccia to serve grilled with our fish soup, or roast your own duck just to use it in our Peking duck salad, or even toast and grind your own za'atar to sprinkle on our grilled broccolini. You can usually find a good substitute. But for those who want to go to the trouble—or just know how to go about it—I wanted the information to be there.

For the ingredients, unless otherwise stated, you should assume I use organic where possible and:

Butter is unsalted

Carrots, garlic, potatoes, parsnips, onions and shallots are peeled

Cream is heavy

Eggs are large

Flour is all-purpose

Herbs are fresh; parsley is flat-leaf

Juice is fresh and strained

Milk is whole

Olive oil is extra-virgin

Pepper is cracked black

Salt is kosher

Sea salt is Maldon

Sugar is granulated

The recipes in this book are the ones we use in the restaurants, adjusted for domestic scale. So I will end with one last note about measurements: in the professional restaurant kitchen, we are metric and work in grams. Grams are precise. Grams are reliable: unlike volume, weight never changes with ambient conditions like temperature and humidity. So if you want to tackle these recipes properly, I cannot recommend any single piece of kitchen equipment more strongly than a digital metric kitchen scale. But nonetheless, for home cooks more comfortable with scoops and measures, we have included conversions that are as accurate as we could manage.

A DAY IN THE LIFE

8:00AM   No breakfast at home today. Just a quick cup of black coffee, a few words with my son Heston as Annabel hustles him out the door to school, and off to Hawksworth for my bi-weekly checkup on breakfast service.

8:45AM   Hawksworth. Breakfast is our red-headed stepchild. Front-of-house staffing costs are ridiculous. We've got a hostess, a floor manager, a barista, and waitstaff who can only handle 20 covers each. Every customer wants substitutions in set menu items, and the servers do what's easiest for them—not the kitchen—and roll over. I've got cooks who could hardly put their pants on at 6 a.m., and now they're reading order chits with lists of substitutions as long as their arm: "Full English, sub toast, sub bacon, sub sausage, add avocado, add smoked salmon, add greens." It's making the kitchen crazy, and we have to fix it.

10:00AM   Hawksworth Group boardroom, in the Hotel Georgia Tower. PR meeting.

First up: The application deadline for the 2020 Hawksworth Young Chef Scholarship is coming up. Our social media, the $10,000 prize, and the prospect of a *stage* at any restaurant you want is driving a lot of requests for application forms. Every year we get more and more from all across the country.

Fundraising and awareness dinners paired to the regional competition heats we hold are helping, too. And we've finally figured out a way to take all the past scholarship winners to Peru. I've always been fascinated by the place. I mean with the Japanese influence, and the Chinese and African, too. All those incredible, unfamiliar ingredients. And the fishing! The Peruvian tourism commission is all over it. They're covering our hotels and restaurants. And with my work with Air Canada, well a lot of how they pay me is in points, so we can cover airfares. Decision: If this works, and we pull it off, we have to make social media hay with it. Let's scale back on awareness dinners, and milk this trip.

Next up: We've got foreign media reps eating at Hawksworth on Sunday night; the writer is allergic to wild mushrooms, and the kitchen and front of house must both be briefed. Also tell Chef that there are eight hockey players coming in on Thursday. Better explain to him that they'll eat salad and protein but no bread. And they'll drink water. And have no dessert.

What else is coming up? We've got a weekend-long pop-up at Whistler starting Friday with 155 guests, plus a private dinner on Saturday for the Whistler Mountain Ski Club. On March 20, we launch a new menu at the Air Canada Signature Suite; Stéphanie and her team have to be in Toronto for the 19th. New Air Canada inflight recipes are due on April 1. The catering website needs new photography. Dress for Success wants a donation item. Next? I'll be in London during the finals for the Roux Scholarship, the inspiration behind HYCS. Can I get in? Not for much of it. It's a closed event. They're only letting me in for part of the evening, and alone. "That's a shame," Annabel says. "I feel like you're trying to do good things, and they should help you . . ."

"Have you actually met any chefs from the UK?" The meeting adjourns in laughter. Then accounting arrives with an inch-thick stack of cheques for me to sign. Isn't there a more modern way to deal with this?

11:30AM Hawksworth kitchen is gearing up for lunch service. I scan the service notes on the notice board. Table 70 likes tap water with ice and lemon and doesn't like his cutlery touched—put it at the top of his place setting and leave it be. Host's wife at table 31 hates cucumber and halibut. There are four adults with one child at table 72. That child is ten; do not offer high chair, please. At table 42 we have a customer who won't tolerate nigella or sesame or any other small seeds in his food (not an allergy—he just doesn't like the way they get stuck in his teeth). There is a crab allergy at table 51, and the host of table 30 claims an allergy to sparkling water. The customer at 60 will order a burger and substitute his fries for a half order of same, with a half order of salad—be sure to accommodate, it's why he comes. At table 205, the host never, ever eats beans. And the loyal breakfast customer at table 86 is returning for the first time since he snagged his pants on an old chair; be doubly accommodating.

In the kitchen near the pass, my chef de cuisine is hunched over a computer, working through breakfast items, looking for simplifications and efficiencies. I skim his draft menu. He's streamlined it all right. There's a small plates section, a classical egg dishes section, and side dishes, too. The play is to build your own breakfast, not take away and fiddle with what's already there. But what's this braised thing? Put "braised" on breakfast menu, and people will run.

"It's the new steak and eggs," Chef says. "We've been using striploin, and it's killing us. It costs us too much, we can't charge enough, people want a bigger portion." The solution promptly appears on the pass: braised, smoked brisket on grits, topped with two poached eggs. "The cut is good. We might take it further, go softer. We want fresh corn in the grits."

"Fine," I reply. "Just don't call it braised. Call it pastrami, grits, and eggs."

12:30PM Lunch at Nightingale, second floor. I sit overlooking the pass, exchanging occasional words with the team. A plate of gnocchi with Roquefort cream sauce comes out. "When's the tomato sauce coming back on the gnocchi?"

"Next week, Chef."

"Good, I like that one better."

2:30PM   Hawksworth, chandelier room. Airport strategy meeting.

The Air Canada private lounge at YVR is opening in two weeks, in the middle of March. It is basically a knockoff of the Toronto lounge, but maybe a bit better. And our new concept, Hawksworth Kitchen, opening in domestic departures, is on track for after the summer. The kitchen is designed. With a pizza oven. We're just planning a beautiful 200-odd seat restaurant at the airport. Nothing to it! The airport operators need to do some of our basic food prep but we've tightened all the processes up quite a bit. We supply the recipes, they follow them, and we supervise. And all the key people are going to be ours. We get to decide who the chef is going to be, who the front of house manager is going to be. We talk about the menu: "Let's keep the food light and fresh. Nobody wants to eat fettucine alfredo before getting on an airplane, right? Well, maybe I did when I was 17. Never mind. What's next on the menu, Stephanie? What have you got?"

4:00PM   Stop in at the commissary kitchen, Kitsilano. Review the prep list for the weekend pop-up at Whistler. Meet with our catering chef, to review the menus for the dinner event tonight at the Permanent, on West Pender Street: duck rillettes with stone fruit and grilled sourdough, then grilled striploin with braised beef, lobster mushrooms, roast carrots, charred scallions, red cabbage, and pommes purée. Substitute chinook salmon for anyone who doesn't want red meat. Sous-vide the fish at the commissary; hold it at temperature on site in the steam oven—it's foolproof. For dessert, dark chocolate mousse with cherries.

5:00PM   Hawksworth Restaurant again. Review some new flatware from Legle. Pass through the bar, greet some dinner guests, work the dining room.

7:30PM   The Permanent, West Pender, check in on the catering event. The duck rillettes are on the table as I come in. I head straight down to the kitchen.

10:00PM   Back home at last. I've missed Heston; he's already in bed. Time for a glass of wine in front of the TV, maybe. Or not. Annabel is still up, sending emails. And there are some work issues we need to discuss. Neither of our days is quite done, yet. H

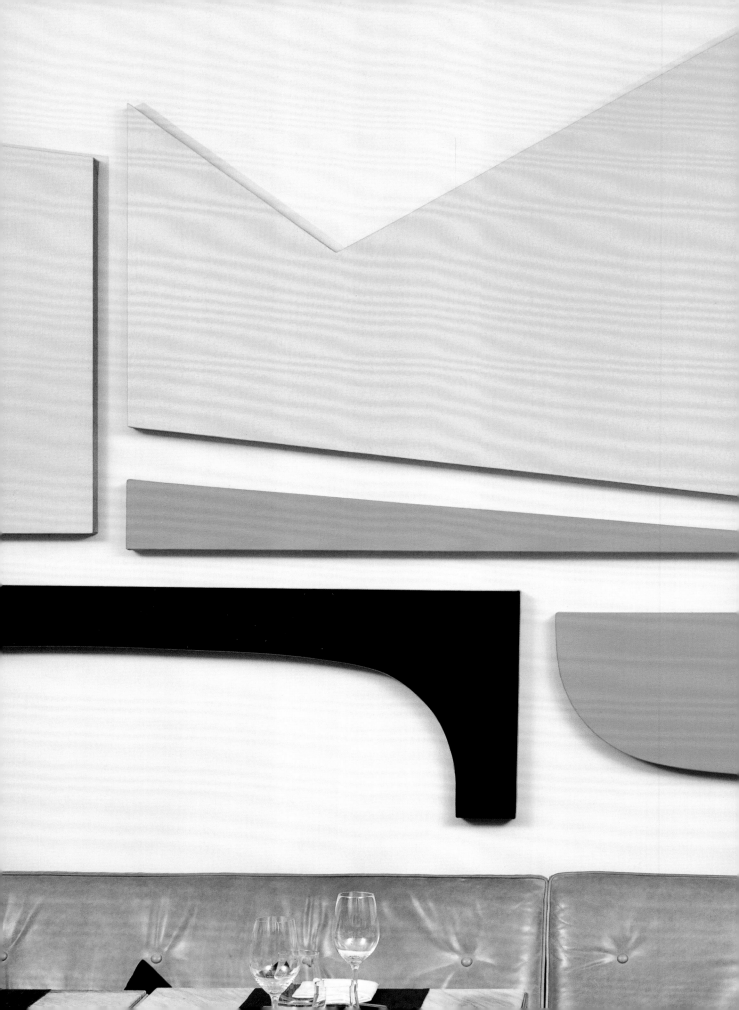

STARTERS

SUNGOLD TOMATO TOAST, WHIPPED RICOTTA, MACERATED PLUMS

Serves 6

(photo on page 183)

This is a showcase for our main Nightingale supplier, Zaklan Heritage Farm, which provides everything for this recipe but the ricotta (and the toast). We intensify the flavour of the tomatoes by roasting them slightly, and macerate the plums with balsamic vinegar. Tomato, plum, whipped ricotta, and fresh fennel seeds combined make these crostini a really potently flavoured appetizer.

INGREDIENTS

Macerated Plums

3 plums

30mL (2 Tbsp) balsamic vinegar

1 sprig rosemary, stem removed, finely chopped

Whipped Ricotta

250g (1 cup) ricotta

45mL (3 Tbsp) cream

30mL (2 Tbsp) yogurt

Toast

4 cups sungold cherry tomatoes

15mL (1 Tbsp) olive oil

Pinch salt

Pinch sugar

3 large slices pain de campagne (French sourdough), cut in half

Fennel seeds, for garnish (optional)

PLUMS

Cut the plums into small cubes or wedges. Combine with the balsamic vinegar and rosemary. Leave to macerate for at least 20 minutes and up to an hour.

RICOTTA

Combine all the ingredients in a mixing bowl and whisk until fluffy.

TOAST

Preheat the oven to 230°C (450°F).

Toss the cherry tomatoes with the olive oil, and season with salt and sugar. Transfer to a baking tray and roast until blistering and golden brown, 5 to 10 minutes.

Toast the pain de campagne under the broiler until golden.

SERVE

Spread a generous layer of whipped ricotta over the warm toast and top with roasted cherry tomatoes and macerated plums. Garnish with fennel seeds.

KOREAN FRIED CAULIFLOWER

Serves 6

About five years ago I took the team to a hot yakitori place in Sheung Wan, Hong Kong, called Yardbird. The chef there—Matt Abergel, who's from Calgary—complained to us that one of his dishes was so popular that he wanted to take it off his menu, just to get people to try something new. So of course we had to order some. It was called Korean Fried Cauliflower. When we got home, we developed our own version and put it on the bar snack menu at Hawksworth. Then we added it at the Air Canada lounges in Toronto and Vancouver. Matt never did get it off his menu at Yardbird: it's still on today.

NOTE

This recipe calls for an ISI gun. If you do not have one, just use sparkling water in place of cold water and keep the mixture in the bowl.

INGREDIENTS

Korean Chili Sauce

30mL (2 Tbsp) canola oil

7 cloves garlic, minced

100g (1 cup) sliced scallions, green parts only

250g (1 cup) gochujang (Korean chili paste)

125mL (½ cup) rice vinegar

50g (¼ cup) brown sugar

50mL (3 Tbsp) light soy sauce

40mL (scant 3 Tbsp) mirin

Tempura Batter

500g (3½ cups) rice flour

3g (½ tsp) baking powder

2.5g (½ tsp) baking soda

3g (1 tsp) salt

500mL (2 cups) ice-cold (or sparkling) water (see Note)

15mL (1 Tbsp) sherry vinegar

15mL (1 Tbsp) sesame oil

15mL (1 Tbsp) grapeseed oil

Cauliflower

1 large head cauliflower, in bite-sized florets

Rice flour, for dredging

2L (8 cups) canola oil

Salt

Sesame seeds, toasted, for garnish

Micro cilantro, for garnish

Lime wedges, for garnish

KOREAN CHILI SAUCE

Heat the canola oil in a pot over medium heat. Caramelize the garlic until fragrant and golden, about 1 minute. Add the scallions and sweat until wilted. Add all remaining ingredients and simmer for 10 minutes. Blend until smooth in a blender or Vitamix. Do not strain.

TEMPURA BATTER

Mix together the rice flour, baking powder, baking soda, and salt. Add the water, sherry vinegar, sesame oil, and grapeseed oil and whisk until smooth, but do not over whisk. Pour into an ISI gun and charge the gun with 3 cartridges (see Note).

Continued . . .

CAULIFLOWER

Bring a pot of salted water to a rapid boil. Blanch the cauliflower for 1½ minutes. Drain and dunk in an ice bath. Drain again and pat dry with paper towel.

In a large stainless-steel bowl, dredge the cauliflower in the rice flour until fully coated. Gently shake to remove any excess flour. Transfer to a clean stainless-steel bowl.

Squeeze some of the tempura batter out of the ISI gun, enough to cover the cauliflower completely. Roll the cauliflower in the batter to fully coat them.

Heat the oil to 175°C (350°F) in a pot large enough that it is not more than half full.

Fry the cauliflower in batches until crispy and golden brown, 4 or 5 minutes. Transfer to paper towel to soak up excess oil. Season with salt and immediately toss with the prepared chili sauce. Make sure every piece is nicely covered with sauce.

Transfer to a serving plate and garnish with toasted sesame seeds, cilantro, and lime wedges.

HAWKSWORTH COOKBOOK

STEAMED DUNGENESS CRAB

Serves 6

The first time I went crabbing I was maybe ten years old, and it was in West Vancouver. I had one of those flat traps where you shred some chicken, drop it in the trap, launch it, and wait. When I pulled it back in, sure enough, there was a crab. I brought it home and my mother was horrified. But she cooked it for me. My first hunter-gatherer moment!

NOTE

In this recipe you have the option of boiling your crabs whole, or cutting them up and steaming in sections. When you're cooking crab, try using fresh seawater—it has the exact right salinity to it and reinforces that sea flavour you're looking for.

INGREDIENTS

3 large Dungeness crabs (about 900g–1.4kg/2–3 lb each)

Salt

1 recipe Garlic Butter (page 312) (optional)

1 recipe Cocktail Sauce (page 313) (optional)

1 recipe Tartare Sauce (page 313) (optional)

COOKING WHOLE CRABS

Fill a very large pot with fresh seawater (or mix 60g/¼ cup of salt per 3L/12 cups of fresh water) and bring to a boil. Immerse the crabs in the water and bring back to a boil. Boil for 6 minutes per pound. Remove the crabs and allow to cool naturally (don't put them in ice water) so the meat stays nice and dry and keeps its great flavour.

COOKING CRAB SECTIONS

Alternatively, cut up the crabs before cooking. Start by using your fingers to remove the abdomen (also called the apron)—it is the flap of shell on the underside of the crab. Remove the outer shell (also called the carapace) from the back of the crab by sticking your thumb into the hole exposed by removing the abdomen and lifting up firmly. The shell will detach from the body with some guts attached. Discard the shell.

Remove and discard the leaf-like, spongy gills from either side of the body. Rinse out the greenish-brown guts from inside the crab. Break off and discard the mandibles, which are the mouthparts at the front of the crab. Turn the crab upside down, grip it on either side, and place your thumbs underneath near the midline on the back where the shell used to be. Push up with your thumbs and pull down with your hands to crack the crab into two sections. The crab will crack easily along its centreline.

Fill a large pot with a tight-fitting lid with 2.5cm (1 in) of seawater (or stir 15mL/ 1 Tbsp of salt into fresh water). Place a steamer rack inside of the pot and bring the water to a boil. Place the crab sections on the steamer rack, cover the pot, and bring back to the boil for about 1 minute. Reduce the heat to medium-high and steam until the crab sections are cooked through, 6 to 8 minutes.

SERVE

Serve the whole crab (for people to pull apart themselves) or the crab sections with melted garlic butter, cocktail sauce, or a tartare-style sauce for dipping, or even just a squeeze of lemon.

SQUID, PEANUT NAGE, NASHI PEAR, CRISPY PORK & CHILI VINAIGRETTE

Serves 6

On my first trip to Thailand four or five years ago, I was bobbing around on a fishing boat south of Phuket in the Strait of Malacca when I was served an incredible dish of roasted fish with green curry and peanut dressing. Those flavours stayed with me. Since I love squid, when I got home, I put them together for the Hawksworth menu. I gave the squid a Thai marinade and a quick sear, and combined it with a peanut nage and a nashi pear salad.

NOTE

The peanuts should be soaked in water 24 hours before making the nage. The squid will take on a lot more flavour if it's marinated the night before.

INGREDIENTS

Squid & Marinade

510g (18 oz) squid bodies (not tentacles), skinned and gutted (ask your fishmonger)

250mL (1 cup) canola oil

100g (⅔ cup) minced ginger

½ bunch scallions, green parts only

Crispy Pork & Chili Vinaigrette

300g (1⅓ cups) diced cured pork, such as pancetta, prosciutto trims or end pieces, or slab bacon

300mL (1¼ cups) canola oil

50g (5 Tbsp) minced ginger

7 cloves garlic, minced

65g (¼ cup) tomato paste

50mL (3 Tbsp) soy sauce

45mL (3 Tbsp) Sriracha-style chili sauce

Peanut Nage

1L (4 cups) chicken stock

145g (1 cup) peanuts, toasted and soaked in water for 24 hours, then drained

60mL (¼ cup) low-sodium soy sauce, plus more as needed

1 small knob (2.5cm/1 in) ginger, peeled and roughly sliced

½ stalk lemongrass

75mL (5 Tbsp) lime juice

Fish sauce, to taste

Honey, to taste

Garnish

50g (⅓ cup) peanuts

2 gai lan stems

20mL (1⅓ Tbsp) canola oil

Sea salt

1 nashi pear (also known as Asian pear), thinly sliced

Micro cilantro

Continued . . .

SQUID &
MARINADE

Insert a knife into the pocket of the squid and make a long slit, from the inside, from the wide opening down to the pointy end. Open it up like a book. Without cutting all the way through the squid, use the tip of a very sharp knife to create parallel diagonal lines from end to end, about ½ or ¾ of the way through the squid flesh. Make sure the cuts are on the inside of the squid because squid curls from the inside out. Cut the squid into 7cm (2¾ in) squares. Place the squares in a large, shallow dish.

Combine the oil, ginger, and scallions in a food processor and pulse until smooth. Spoon over the squid, cover, and refrigerate overnight, at least 8 hours.

CRISPY PORK
& CHILI
VINAIGRETTE

Using a meat grinder, grind the cured meat, or use a food processor to dice the meat very, very finely.

Heat 100mL (7 Tbsp) of the oil in a skillet until smoking and add the cured meat. Cook at medium-high temperature, stirring often until it is completely crispy, about 5 minutes.

Heat another skillet with 100mL (7 Tbsp) of the oil until smoking. Add the ginger and garlic and cook at medium-high temperature, stirring often until golden brown, about 2 minutes.

Combine the pork with the garlic and ginger and stir in the tomato paste, soy sauce, chili sauce, and the last of the oil. Simmer for 5 minutes. Remove from the heat and allow to cool.

PEANUT NAGE

Place the chicken stock, drained peanuts, soy sauce, ginger, and lemongrass in a pot. Simmer over low heat for 1½ hours. Discard the lemongrass and ginger. Strain the nuts from the liquid and reserve the liquid.

Use a blender to purée the nuts with some of the reserved liquid, adding a little at a time (you may not need it all), until it has a creamy soup consistency. Season with the lime juice, fish sauce, and honey to taste. Adjust the seasoning with soy sauce as needed.

PREPARE THE
GARNISHES &
SERVE

In a small sauté pan over medium heat, toast the peanuts until fragrant, about 1 minute. Remove them from the pan and allow to cool, then chop coarsely.

Bring a pot of water to a boil. Add the gai lan and cook until bright green, about 1 minute. Remove from the water and allow to cool, then slice into julienne pieces.

In a heavy-bottomed or cast-iron frying pan, heat the canola oil over high heat. Sear the squid in batches, scored side down, until golden brown and curled up, about 3 minutes. Do not overcrowd the pan. Transfer to paper towel to absorb excess oil. Season with sea salt and generously cover with most of the pork vinaigrette.

Place a spoonful of peanut nage on each of 6 serving plates and position the squid on top. Garnish with a little more of the pork vinaigrette, and the nashi pear, gai lan, peanuts, and micro cilantro.

YELLOWFIN TUNA, DUNGENESS CRAB, PASSION FRUIT SAUCE, SQUID INK CRACKERS

Serves 6

When I was working for Bruno Loubet at Isola we did a seabass dish with the fish boned but whole, stuffed with panzanella salad, then roasted in the wood-burning oven. That idea of a salad inside a fish really appealed to me, and it lingered. So at West I came up with this really light, West Coast riff on the idea, with a thin sheet of raw tuna wrapped around a brightly acidic, crunchy salad, and a little fresh brioche or baguette standing in for the day-old Tuscan bread we used at Isola. The tennis-ball–sized sphere is an interesting look.

NOTE

If you cannot find squid ink, make the cracker recipe without it; the compromise is one of colour more than flavour. Squid ink is a wonderful way to add a dramatic black colour to other dishes, like pasta. Prepare the semi-dried cherry tomatoes ahead of time if you like; they will last in the fridge for up to a week.

INGREDIENTS

Squid Ink Crackers

200g (1 cup) jasmine rice

2.5L (10 cups) water

30mL (2 Tbsp) squid ink

1L (4 cups) canola oil

Crab & Tuna Spheres

3 slices brioche or baguette

30g (2 Tbsp) butter

360g (12½ oz) yellowfin tuna loin, about 5–6cm (2–2½ in) in diameter

½ cucumber

1 orange

½ fennel bulb

1 small green jalapeno, deseeded

450g (1 lb) Dungeness crab meat

1 recipe Semi-Dried Tomatoes (page 311)

10g (¼ cup) chopped chives

1 lemon, juice

50mL (3 Tbsp) olive oil

Salt

Passion Fruit Sauce

1 passion fruit

200mL (¾ cup) orange juice

20mL (1⅓ Tbsp) lime juice

15g (1 Tbsp) sugar

25g (¼ cup) sea buckthorn berries (or coarsely chopped mango)

300mL (1¼ cups) grapeseed oil

½ bird's eye chili, deseeded

½ small shallot, finely chopped

Pinch salt

Olive oil

Sea salt

SQUID INK CRACKERS

Rinse the rice under cold running water until the water runs clear.

In a heavy-bottomed pot, combine the rice and water. Bring to a boil and reduce the heat to the lowest setting. You want to cook the rice very slowly until it becomes over-cooked and thick like a batter; this will take 3 to 4 hours.

Continued . . .

Stir the squid ink into the rice and spread onto a silicone mat or designated liner for a dehydrator in 1 very thin layer. Dehydrate at 63°C (145°F) for 6 to 8 hours or at 43°C (110°F) overnight until the crackers are fully crisp. You can also use your oven on the lowest setting with the door cracked open, for about 12 hours.

In a large pot, heat the canola oil to 200°C (400°F). The pot should be large enough that it is not more than half full.

Fry a few pieces of cracker at a time until they are puffy and crispy, just a few seconds per piece. Do not overcrowd the fryer, as each piece will double or triple in size. Transfer to paper towel to soak up excess oil.

CRAB & TUNA
SPHERES

Cut the crust off the bread. Dice into 1cm (½ in) square cubes.

Melt the butter in a sauté pan until it is foamy. Fry the bread until golden brown. Transfer to paper towel to soak up excess oil.

Using a sharp knife, slice the tuna loin into 6 even slices. Place each slice between two sheets of plastic wrap and gently pound it using a meat pounder until it is approximately 15cm (6 in) in diameter and 3mm (⅛ in) thick. Set aside in the fridge.

Peel and deseed the cucumber, and cut it into small dice. Peel the orange and cut into segments.

Using a mandoline, thinly slice the fennel bulb. Reserve in ice water for extra crispness.

In a mixing bowl, combine the croutons, diced cucumber, orange segments, and fennel with the jalapeno, crab meat, tomatoes, chives, lemon juice, olive oil, and salt to make a crab salad.

Pull the tuna out of the fridge 1 slice at a time. Discard the top layer of plastic wrap. Spoon ⅙ of the crab salad in the centre of each tuna slice, leaving 2.5–4cm (1–1½ in) of tuna around the outside. Use the bottom layer of the plastic wrap to fold the edges over and form the tuna into a ball shape, twisting the plastic wrap to secure it tight. Form all 6 spheres and refrigerate until you are ready to serve them.

PASSION FRUIT
SAUCE

Scoop the seeds out of the passion fruit and discard them. Purée the fruit in a blender, and strain through a fine-mesh sieve. Return to the blender, add the orange juice, lime juice, sugar, and sea buckthorn, and blend to combine. Add the oil a little at a time. Add the chili and shallot and blitz for another 10 seconds. Strain. Adjust the seasoning with salt.

SERVE

Place a spoonful of passion fruit sauce on the bottom of each plate. Remove the tuna spheres from the fridge. Unwrap them, using scissors to cut open the plastic wrap. Place a tuna sphere on top of the sauce, brush with olive oil, and season with sea salt. Garnish with a squid ink cracker. Optional additional garnishes, as pictured: fresh crab pieces, shaved fennel, and Basil Chips (page 319).

CRISPY BUTTERMILK FRIED CHICKEN & PICKLED RAMPS RANCH

Serves 6

This looks like a pretty straightforward fried buttermilk chicken—but we trialed, tested, and re-tested variations of this recipe for six whole months to get here. The best results are using boneless thighs brined in infused buttermilk for 48 hours and then dredged in a blend of equal parts flour and two starches. And everyone loves this dish: it's one of Nightingale's all-time bestsellers.

NOTE

The fermented hot sauce should be prepared five to seven days in advance, and lasts in the fridge for up to six months. You can substitute with a quality pre-bottled variety, like Frank's RedHot Original Cayenne Pepper Sauce.

INGREDIENTS

Fermented Hot Sauce

550g (6 cups) chopped fresh chilis (we use fresno and cayenne), stems removed

60g (6½ Tbsp) salt

360mL (1½ cups) distilled white vinegar

3 cloves garlic

225mL (¾ cup plus 3 Tbsp) canola oil

Buttermilk Marinade & Chicken

450mL (1¾ cups plus 1 Tbsp) buttermilk

8g (1 Tbsp) minced jalapeno

2 cloves garlic

½ lemon, zest

2.5g (¾ tsp) salt

1 sprig thyme, stem removed

1kg (2¼ lb) boneless, skinless chicken thighs, cut in 4cm (1½ in) pieces

Pickled Ramps Ranch

60mL (¼ cup) white wine vinegar

30mL (2 Tbsp) water

20g (scant 2 Tbsp) sugar

½ bunch ramps

250g (1 cup) sour cream

75mL (5 Tbsp) buttermilk

45g (⅓ cup) crumbled gorgonzola cheese

3g (1 tsp) salt

10g (¼ cup) dill, finely chopped

10g (¼ cup) parsley, chiffonade

½ clove garlic, finely chopped

½ lemon, juice

½ lemon, zest

4g (2 tsp) pepper

Dredging & Frying

150g (1 cup) flour

150g (¼ cup) cornstarch

150g (1¼ cups) tapioca starch

20g (3 Tbsp) garlic powder

20g (3 Tbsp) Aleppo or espelette pepper

20g (3 Tbsp) sweet smoked paprika

2L (8 cups) canola oil

Garnish

1 scallion, green parts only, finely sliced

Continued . . .

FERMENTED HOT SAUCE

In a blender, purée the chilis with 10g (2 tsp) of the salt to create a paste. Transfer to a glass mason jar and cover with a loose-fitting lid. Allow it to ferment, at room temperature, for 5 to 7 days.

When ready to use, spoon the paste into a fine-mesh sieve set over a mixing bowl. Press through with a wooden spoon so that the sauce drips into the bowl below.

Transfer the sauce to a blender and add the vinegar, garlic, and remaining salt. With the blender running, add the canola oil in a thin stream until entirely incorporated. Blend on high for 1 to 2 minutes. Allow to cool, then press plastic wrap directly onto the surface of the sauce to prevent a crust from forming.

BUTTERMILK MARINADE & CHICKEN

Mix the buttermilk, jalapeno, garlic, lemon zest, salt, and thyme together in a large bowl. Add the chicken and let marinate in the fridge for 24 to 48 hours to develop the flavour and tenderize the meat.

PICKLED RAMPS RANCH

Place the vinegar, water, and sugar in a pot and bring it up to a boil. Transfer to a heat-proof container and dunk in an ice bath immediately. Once cool, pour over the ramps. Cover and allow to pickle in the refrigerator for at least 4 hours.

Combine the sour cream, buttermilk, gorgonzola, and salt in a food processor or blender until smooth. Push the mixture through a fine-mesh sieve, using a ladle or rubber spatula for maximum extraction.

Finely chop the pickled ramps and fold into the buttermilk mixture along with the dill, parsley, garlic, lemon juice, lemon zest, and pepper. Stir to combine.

DREDGING & FRYING

Mix together the flour, cornstarch, tapioca starch, garlic powder, pepper, and paprika.

Remove the chicken from the marinade and let the excess marinade drip off. Toss the chicken in the flour mixture in batches to coat. Lay out on a baking tray before frying.

Heat the canola oil to 175°C (350°F) in a pot large enough that it is not more than half full.

Fry the chicken in batches until crispy and golden brown, about 5 minutes per thigh. Cut a piece open to check it is cooked through; continue to fry for a little longer if needed. Transfer to paper towel to soak up excess oil.

Plate and garnish with the fermented hot sauce, pickled ramps ranch, and sliced green onion.

FOIE GRAS, ARTICHOKE, TRUFFLE, MADEIRA JUS

Serves 6

I heard something about a dish like this when I was in the UK but never got to try it. So later I decided to make my own version at West. You have to start with large, beautiful artichokes. Cook them perfectly until just tender, not soft mush. Then fill them up with truffle-scented chicken mousse, a nugget of seared foie gras, more mousse, and finally some sliced black truffle. Then you steam them until the mousse is set and serve the artichokes with Madeira jus. Yes, it's rich, but it's also super-delicious.

NOTE

This recipe calls for black trumpet mushrooms, but you could use any other seasonal wild or cultivated mushrooms.

INGREDIENTS

Chicken Mousse

200g (7 oz) skinless, boneless chicken breast, cut in small chunks

I egg white

Salt

Pinch cayenne

150mL (⅔ cup) cream

75g (2½ oz) finely chopped prosciutto

25g (½ cup) chopped chives

Few drops good-quality white truffle oil

Artichokes

6 artichokes, turned (see page 210)

I stalk celery, cut in large pieces

½ onion, cut in large pieces

½ carrot, cut in large pieces

I sprig thyme

I bay leaf

50mL (3 Tbsp) white wine

50 mL (3 Tbsp) white wine vinegar

150g (5 oz) grade A foie gras

Salt and pepper

I small fresh black truffle

Good-quality black truffle oil, for drizzling

Garnish

5mL (I tsp) canola oil

15g (I Tbsp) butter

6 baby pearl onions, peeled

90g (2 cups) black trumpet mushrooms

I recipe Madeira Jus (page 318)

Sea salt

6 sprigs chervil (optional)

CHICKEN MOUSSE

Place the chicken, egg white, salt, and cayenne in a food processor. Turn it on and slowly add half the cream. Mix until smooth and combined.

Press the mixture through a fine mesh sieve into a large bowl and reserve over an ice bath. Gradually add the second half of cream, beating the mixture with a rubber spatula to incorporate some air and lighten the mousse. Gently fold in the prosciutto, chives, and truffle oil. Set aside in the fridge.

Continued . . .

ARTICHOKES

Place the artichoke hearts, celery, onion, carrots, and herbs in a large pot. Cover with the wine and vinegar and 2L (8 cups) of salted water. Bring to a boil, cover the surface of the mixture with a cartouche (disc of parchment paper), then reduce the heat to a slow simmer. Cook for approximately 20 minutes, until the artichokes are tender but not too soft. Turn off the heat and let cool in the liquid. Discard the celery, onion, carrots, and herbs.

Cut the foie gras into 2.5cm (1 in) squares and season with salt and pepper. Heat a pan over medium-high heat and very quickly sear the foie gras until it has colour on all sides.

Fill each artichoke with a generous tablespoon of mousse and place a square of foie gras in the centre. Cover the foie gras with more mousse to form a dome. Cover the surface of the artichoke with freshly shaved black truffle and add a few drops of black truffle oil.

Carefully cover each artichoke with a piece of plastic wrap, tucking it underneath to secure it tightly.

Fill a large pot with a few inches of water, and place the artichokes in a steam basket inside. Bring to a simmer over medium heat, cover, and steam for 8 minutes.

GARNISH
& SERVE

While the artichokes are steaming, prepare the onions and mushrooms. In a non-stick pan, heat the oil and butter over medium heat. Slowly cook and caramelize the pearl onions until they are golden. Add the mushrooms and cook until golden brown. Remove from the pan. Cut the onions in half and separate the layers.

Cut open the plastic wrap around the artichokes and unwrap them. Spoon each of 6 serving plates with some Madeira jus and top with a stuffed artichoke, then season with sea salt. Garnish with pearl onions, mushrooms, and a sprig of chervil.

MOSAIC OF VENISON, DUCK & QUAIL, PICKLED VEGETABLES

Serves 12

I still remember clearly the first time I saw a slice of this terrine being plated at the garde-manger at Le Manoir and exclaiming something unprintable under my breath. It was beautiful. It was a work of art, just mesmerizing to look at. All those gently cooked cuts of meat and fowl in different colours, with that torchon of foie gras running through the middle. This is an incredible terrine.

NOTE

Only use prime cuts of meat for this dish; the terrine requires tender meat. Be sure to let the terrine rest in the fridge for at least 24 hours before you slice it so that its flavours develop and meld properly. The pickled vegetables can be made up to a week in advance.

INGREDIENTS

Game Meat & Foie Gras Torchon

200g (7 oz) foie gras

200g (7 oz) venison loin

200g (7 oz) duck breast, skinned

200g (7 oz) quail breasts, skinned

55g (¼ cup) sugar

30g (3 Tbsp) salt

6g (2 tsp) curing salt

80mL (⅓ cup) Madeira

50mL (3 Tbsp) brandy

2 sprigs thyme

2 slices orange peel

Parfait Mix

100g (3½ oz) foie gras

100g (3½ oz) chicken livers

2 eggs

15mL (1 Tbsp) canola oil

3 shallots, finely sliced

2 cloves garlic

1 sprig thyme

1 bay leaf

50mL (3 Tbsp) brandy

50mL (3 Tbsp) port

50mL (3 Tbsp) Madeira

225g (1 cup) butter, melted

10g (1 Tbsp) curing salt

Finishing

100g (¾ cup) shelled pistachios

15mL (1 Tbsp) canola oil

200g (7 oz) chanterelle mushrooms

350g (12 oz) frozen lardo di Colonnata, about 20cm (8 in) long, trimmed of the rind

Pickled Vegetables

4 multicoloured baby carrots

5 baby zucchinis

100g (3½ oz) whole hon-shimeji mushrooms, trimmed

24 cauliflower florets

24 crosnes (or substitute with another small root vegetable, like sunchoke)

6 baby pearl onions

150mL (⅔ cup) white wine vinegar

100mL (7 Tbsp) water

50g (¼ cup) sugar

1 bay leaf

9g (1 Tbsp) peppercorns

3g (1 tsp) coriander seeds

3g (1 tsp) salt

2 slices beetroot (optional)

Toasted baguette or sourdough bread (optional)

Continued . . .

Pull the foie gras out of the fridge and let sit at room temperature until soft.

Remove all sinew from the game meat. Cut the venison and duck into 10–12cm (4–5 in) strips, 2cm (¾ in) wide. Leave the quail breasts whole. Place all in a shallow roasting pan.

Push the soft foie gras through a fine mesh sieve to remove any veins and sinews. Spread on a sheet pan, about 1cm thick (½ in).

Mix together the sugar, salt, and curing salt to make the cure mix. Sprinkle half the cure mix over the foie gras and the other half over the game meat. Then pour half the Madeira and brandy over the foie gras and the other half over the game meat. Divide the thyme and orange peel between the foie gras and the game meat. Cover both with plastic wrap pressed directly onto the surface. Refrigerate the meat for at least 8 hours or overnight. Refrigerate the fois gras for 80 minutes.

Take the foie gras out of the fridge, unwrap, and remove the orange peel and thyme. Rinse the foie gras thoroughly under cold running water.

Lay 2 layers of plastic wrap out on a clean surface wiped with a damp cloth so that the plastic wrap sticks to the surface. Place the foie gras mixture at the end of the plastic wrap near you and roll it up in a tight, sausage-like ballotine. Using a very fine metal skewer, poke several tiny holes in the foie gras while rolling, to prevent air pockets and bubbles from forming. The roll should be no more than 2.5cm (1 in) in diameter and 25cm (10 in) in length. Set in the freezer.

Place the foie gras, chicken livers, and eggs in a stainless-steel bowl. Cover with plastic wrap. Place the bowl in a warm spot near the stove and let sit until lukewarm. The mix should be just above body temperature.

Meanwhile, heat the canola oil in a heavy-bottomed pan over medium heat. Add the shallots, garlic, thyme, and bay leaf. Sweat the shallots until they are soft and translucent, about 5 minutes. Deglaze the pan with all the alcohol and reduce until the liquid has evaporated. Remove the herbs and transfer the shallot mixture to a blender.

Add the chicken liver, foie gras, and egg mixture to the blender. Turn on and slowly pour in the melted butter to emulsify the mixture. Add the curing salt, and mix again. Push through a fine-mesh sieve, and set aside in a bowl, covered, in the fridge. The parfait mix can be made a day ahead of time and stored in an airtight container with plastic wrap pressed to the surface to prevent oxidization and discolouration.

Preheat the oven to 175°C (350°F).

Spread the pistachios on a baking tray and toast in the oven until lightly coloured, about 6 minutes. Set aside.

In a large frying pan, heat the canola oil over medium heat. Sauté the chanterelles for 4 to 5 minutes. Set aside.

Remove the lardo from the freezer to thaw slightly. Using a meat slicer or a very sharp knife, slice as thinly as possible, ideally 1.5mm thick (1⁄16 in).

Place a 9.5 × 10 × 26cm (4 × 4 × 10 in) terrine mould on a work surface and line with 2 sheets of plastic wrap, 1 going each way (vertically and horizontally), leaving some overhanging the edge.

Working methodically, lower each sheet of lardo into the terrine mould and let it cover just over half the width of the base, before running it up the side. Place a sheet or two over each of the short sides of the mould too. You should use all of the sheets of lardo.

Take both the meat and the parfait mix out of the fridge. Remove the excess thyme and orange peel from the meat. Rinse the meat thoroughly under cold running water and pat dry.

Combine the meat, parfait mix, pistachios, and chanterelles. Carefully layer the mixture on top of the lardo, creating a pattern of different colours, sizes, and textures. Make sure to fill holes with either meat or parfait mix.

Once you have layered 4cm (1½ in) up from the bottom of the terrine mould with the meat mixture, remove the frozen torchon from the freezer and unwrap it from the plastic. Place the frozen, rolled foie gras torchon right in the middle of the terrine and press it down gently. If the roll is longer than the terrine mould, trim the end pieces slightly. Continue layering the meat until just above the edge of the terrine mould. Fold over the overhanging pieces of lardo and plastic wrap. Wrap the whole terrine with several layers of plastic wrap.

Preheat the oven to 150°C (300°F).

Place the terrine in a 10cm deep (4 in) roasting pan and pour enough boiling water into the pan to fill it to ⅔ full. Carefully transfer into the oven. Cook for 1 hour, or until a thermometer inserted into the middle reads 49°C (120°F).

Once the terrine has reached the desired temperature, remove it from the oven and submerge the terrine mould in an ice bath for 15 minutes.

Transfer to a flat roasting pan and set a cutting board (or similar) on top that fits just inside the terrine mould. Set a large 2kg can (4½ lb) on top. The idea is to compact the terrine gently with the weight so that its contents bind together.

After about 5 minutes, a couple of tablespoons of juices should have leached out of the sides of the terrine. If more than this, reduce the weight, and if no juices are showing, increase the weight. Keep an eye on the terrine for at least 30 minutes, to make sure you have achieved the right balance. Then leave in the fridge to press for 24 hours.

Remove the weight and board and lift the terrine out of the mould. Re-wrap the entire terrine in clean plastic wrap. Set aside in the fridge.

PICKLED VEGETABLES

Using a mandoline, shave the carrots and zucchinis into ribbons. Place the carrot ribbons, zucchini ribbons, mushrooms, cauliflower florets, crosnes, and pearl onions in 6 separate containers.

Combine the white wine vinegar, water, sugar, bay leaf, peppercorns, coriander seeds, and salt in a pot and bring to a boil. Strain the liquid and divide between each vegetable container, pouring in enough to submerge the vegetables. Let sit until cool. For a splash of colour, add a couple of slices of beet to the pearl onions container. Cover the containers until ready to serve. These can be stored in the fridge for up to 1 week.

SERVE

Dip a carving knife into hot water and carefully carve a slice of the terrine. Place on a plate and garnish with pickled vegetables all around. Serve with toasted bread.

Shaved Veal Tongue (page 42)

Grilled Ramps (page 250)

Arctic Char (page 178)

SHAVED VEAL TONGUE, TONNATO SAUCE, ANCHOVY BREADCRUMBS

Serves 6

(photo on page 40)

Veal tongue is a very underused product. It's got lots of rich flavour, which you have to combat with capers or something acidic like that. At Nightingale, we've found that tongue is the ultimate cut for an updated vitello tonnato. It's so much more flavourful than the traditional poached eye round. We make the tuna sauce with fresh albacore and scatter capers on top.

NOTE

Remember to start preparing the tongue well in advance: beyond the several days required for brining, you need to allow 24 hours to chill the braised tongue thoroughly enough that it can be cut thinly on the meat slicer.

INGREDIENTS

Veal Tongue Brine

500mL (2 cups) water

85g (⅔ cup) sea salt

50g (¼ cup) brown sugar

2 cloves garlic

1 sprig thyme

3g (1 tsp) coriander seeds

3g (1 tsp) mustard seeds

3g (1 tsp) fennel seeds

2 bay leaves

1 sprig rosemary

5g (2 tsp) curing salt

500g (2 cups) ice

1 veal tongue (about 400g/14 oz)

Veal Tongue Braise

1 carrot, roughly chopped

½ onion, roughly chopped

2 cloves garlic, crushed

Tonnato Sauce

175g (6 oz) albacore tuna, cut in 1cm
 (½ in) pieces

125mL (½ cup) Tuna Confit Oil
 (page 315)

1 egg

1 egg yolk

25g (2 Tbsp) Dijon mustard

50mL (3 Tbsp) lemon juice

4 cloves Garlic Confit (page 312)

3g (1 tsp) salt

30g (3 Tbsp) capers, for garnish

1 recipe Anchovy Breadcrumbs
 (page 309)

6 lemon wedges, for garnish

VEAL TONGUE

Bring all the brine ingredients except for the curing salt and ice to a rolling boil for 2 minutes. Mix in the curing salt. Pour the mixture over the ice in a large container. Refrigerate until cold.

Submerge the veal tongue in the brine and refrigerate for a further 24 to 48 hours.

Remove the tongue from the brine and transfer it to a large pot. Discard the brine. Add the braising ingredients to the pot and enough water to cover everything. Bring to a boil then reduce the heat and simmer until the tongue is tender, about 3 hours.

Remove the tongue from the pot and allow to cool slightly. While still warm, peel the skin from the tongue. Clean the underside of the tongue by removing all excess sinew and meat. Refrigerate overnight.

Use a meat slicer or a very sharp knife to shave the tongue very thinly.

TONNATO SAUCE

Combine the tuna and confit oil in a medium pot. Slowly heat over low heat until you start to see small bubbles appear around the tuna. Continue to poach until the tuna is just cooked, about 3 minutes. The tuna should flake apart, but not be overcooked. If it is not fully cooked, leave it in the oil off the heat to let the heat carry through a little more. Remove the tuna from the oil and cool. Also cool the oil, to room temperature.

Soft-boil the egg by placing it in a pot and covering it with water. Bring to a boil and let boil for 6 minutes, and then remove and submerge in ice water. Peel the egg.

Combine the tuna, soft-boiled egg, raw egg yolk, mustard, lemon juice, garlic, and salt in a food processor. Run it for 30 seconds to break up the ingredients. Slowly drizzle the tuna confit oil in a thin stream, scraping down the sides of the bowl as necessary. Add water (up to about 30ml/2 Tbsp), while blending, to adjust the consistency if it is too thick. Continue blending for approximately 3 minutes. The finished sauce should be smooth and homogeneous, like mayonnaise.

SERVE

Place the tongue slices on a platter, or divide them between individual plates, with a little of the tonnato sauce and some capers. Sprinkle with anchovy breadcrumbs. Serve with lemon wedges.

VANCOUVER: EARLY YEARS

I got my first summer restaurant job at a Vancouver fish and chip shop when I was 13. I washed dishes, peeled potatoes, and sometimes did assembly for the salad section. By the time I finished high school and started working in the kitchen at the Beach House, in Stanley Park, the people I worked for seemed to think I had a knack for it. They pushed me to do a culinary apprenticeship. That's what I was doing under Michel Jacob at Le Crocodile, when at age 18 I first knew for sure that I wanted my own restaurant. Nothing stuffy or conventional—instead it would be completely modern in style and atmosphere, and its food would be on an equal footing with the best you could find anywhere.

Understand that this was in the late 80s, when people in Vancouver were still given to selling the place short. They always talked as if great restaurants were things that belonged in big cities elsewhere, like in Europe, and would never happen here. "That's just the way it is," people said. I didn't like that attitude. Actually, I disliked it so much that I wanted to be the chef who would change things. The trouble was I really didn't know anything about great cooking yet. At least I'd been lucky enough to eat some. My first life-changing food experience was a taste of dry-aged tenderloin, served to me by my uncle, Clive, in his office at the Connaught Rooms, a swanky banquet facility in Covent Garden, London. He was their dapper head chef; I was a schoolboy on my summer vaca- tion—and I'll never forget the taste of that beef.

Later, when I was in high school in Vancouver, my stepdad, Brian, and my mum took me back to Europe regularly. From my teenage perspective, Brian was quite an expert on fine restaurants. He planned eating trips for us to France and Italy, where I was constantly amazed by the food we were served, even (and sometimes especially) when it was just pizza.

Once, on a trip to the UK, we drove all the way to Abergavenny, in Wales, just to eat at the Walnut Tree Inn. It's still there; today it serves British food and has a Michelin star. But back then we experienced the heyday of Franco Taruschio, the Italian chef who owned it for 30 years. Out there, in the middle of nowhere in the Welsh countryside, Taruschio was cooking classic, beautiful Italian fare of such quality that people would drive three hours from London just to try it. That made no sense to me; it seemed crazy—and I loved it.

Meanwhile, in Vancouver, I continued my apprenticeship, doing the circuit of what were then the city's best kitchens. After Le Crocodile, it was Il Giardino, then Settebello and Villa del Lupo. Somewhere along that journey, it occurred to me that everyone I worked for who knew how to cook was from Europe. Or if they were Canadian, they'd at least trained in Europe. That's the way it was in the early 90s.

There was also no social media yet. That's right: no Instagram for checking up on what the big-name chefs you'd heard about were up to in other places. Instead you went to bookstores and looked at cookbooks. Which is how on a day off I found myself leafing through Raymond Blanc's *Recipes from Le Manoir aux Quat' Saisons*. The pictures of the dishes and the recipes for the sauces left me breathless. Then I discovered Marco Pierre White's iconic first book, *White Heat*. This time it wasn't just the food—but the camaraderie and intensity radiating from those black-and-white photographs of the scenes in his kitchen. I just thought to myself, "Oh my God!" I had been feeling pretty good about having learned to make chicken with mustard sauce, to thicken stocks into sauces with beurre manié, and turn egg yolks and Parmesan into carbonara. And here suddenly was Le Manoir's crab and Dover sole soufflé with lemongrass and cream-accented vegetable nage, and Harveys' tagliatelle with oysters, caviar, cucumber, and beurre blanc. The cooking in those pages looked as if it was from another planet. And I wanted to be part of it.

So I started to plan my next move. While I was working at Tofino's Orca Lodge, where I'd joined the opening team, I got my resumé together and sent one off to both Raymond Blanc and Marco Pierre White. Then, hoping for the best, without even bothering to wait for a reply, I gathered my savings—plus a little extra from my parents and grandparents—and booked a flight to London. H

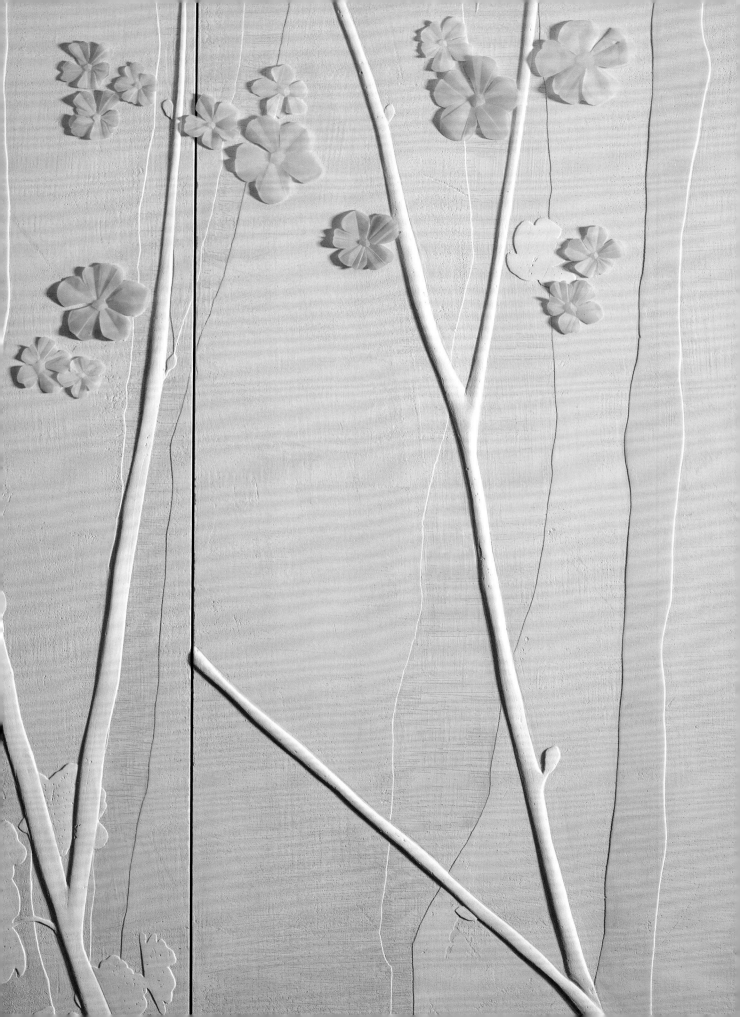

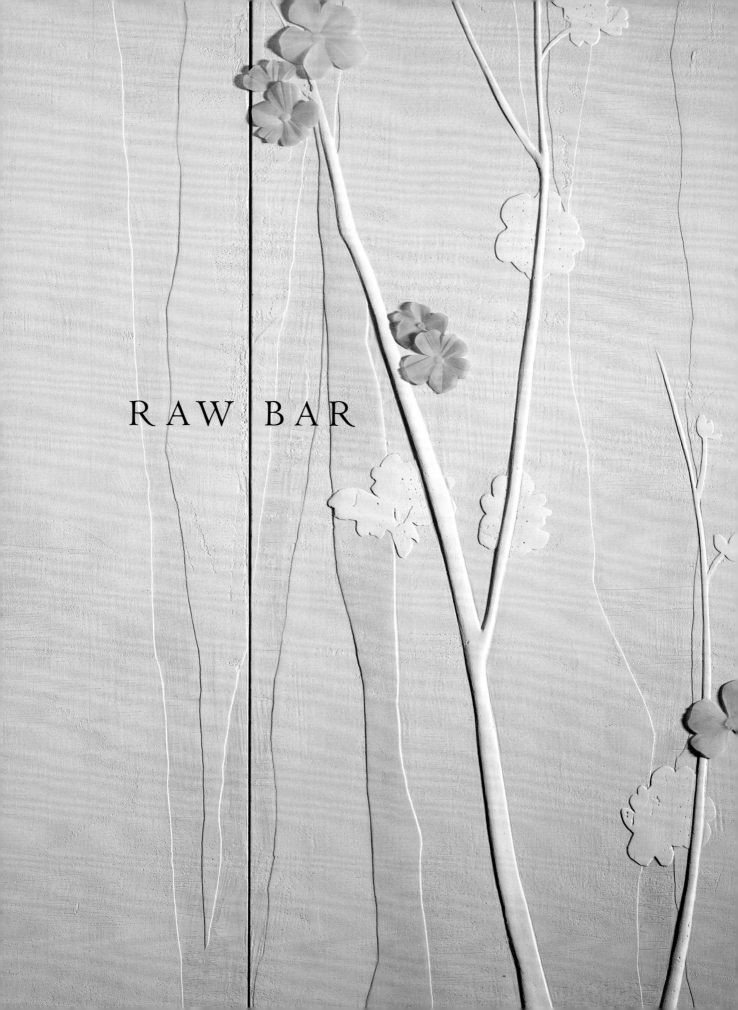

RAW BAR

ALBACORE TUNA, CHARRED ARTICHOKES, SALSA VERDE, CAPER BERRIES, CHARRED EGGPLANT PURÉE

Serves 6

We use albacore tuna from the Pacific for this dish at Hawksworth, and it's quite fatty and rich, so the loin is perfect tataki-style. Tuna tataki works really well with an olive tapenade, but in this recipe we make something similar with charred artichokes instead. The eggplant purée is like a more interesting stand-in for mayonnaise. Caper berries give an extra acidic counterpoint.

INGREDIENTS

Artichoke Oil

Oil from 1 jar of marinated artichokes (about 300mL/1¼ cups)

50g (1 cup) coarsely chopped parsley

25g (½ cup) coarsely chopped basil

25g (1 Tbsp) Garlic Confit (page 312)

Pinch chili flakes

Artichoke Salsa Verde

500g (about 12) marinated artichokes

60g (¼ cup) prepared horseradish

10g (1 Tbsp) salt

Eggplant Purée

1 eggplant

60mL (¼ cup) olive oil

30mL (2 Tbsp) sherry vinegar

3g (1 tsp) salt

Tuna

340g (12 oz) albacore tuna loin, belly attached

Salt

Pepper

Serve

80g (½ cup) caper berries, halved

Watercress sprigs, for garnish

Espelette pepper

Sea salt

ARTICHOKE OIL

Combine all the ingredients in a high-speed blender and blend, plunging constantly, until puréed. Stop and scrape down the sides of the bowl as necessary. The oil should turn green.

ARTICHOKE SALSA VERDE

Halve the artichokes and drain on paper towel for 15 minutes. Transfer to a grill pan set over high heat, and grill until slightly blackened on both sides. Transfer to a baking tray in a single layer and refrigerate.

Once cool, transfer to a food processor and purée with the horseradish and salt until mostly smooth but still a little chunky. Scrape down the sides of the bowl as necessary.

Combine the puréed artichokes with the artichoke oil. Adjust the seasoning if necessary.

Continued . . .

EGGPLANT
PURÉE

Char the eggplant over an open flame or barbecue until very charred on each side. Allow to cool slightly, then remove and discard the top stem. Transfer the eggplant to a blender, and purée until smooth.

Transfer to a stainless-steel bowl and mix with the olive oil, vinegar, and salt. Cover with plastic wrap pressed directly onto the surface and refrigerate as fast as possible.

TUNA

Season the tuna loin with salt and pepper and sear it very quickly in a non-stick pan over high heat, about 30 seconds each side. Transfer to a baking tray to cool down. Slice into 0.5cm thick (¼ in) slices.

SERVE

Plate the tuna (on a large platter or individual plates), and pipe a few dots of charred eggplant purée around it. Add a few spoonfuls of artichoke salsa verde and garnish with caper berries and watercress. Season with espelette pepper and sea salt.

YELLOWTAIL CRUDO, AVOCADO, PONZU

Serves 6

(photo on page 80)

Raw fish and avocado together taste so nice and buttery. I really like that umami flavour. Then you add citrusy soy—the ponzu—and it cuts right through the rich flavour without overpowering it. The combination of all these flavours is so clean.

NOTE

For this dish we usually use wild yellowtail from New Zealand, where they thrive in the waters around the North Island. But sometimes we substitute farmed yellowtail from Japan (hamachi) or Hawaii (kampachi). Use whichever yellowtail your fishmonger says is freshest. And if you can't find any good yellowtail, try albacore tuna. You can find bonito flakes and wakame in specialty Asian supermarkets.

INGREDIENTS

Ponzu

20g (2 Tbsp) finely chopped ginger

12g (1 cup) bonito flakes

4g (2 Tbsp) dried wakame seaweed

125mL (½ cup) soy sauce

25mL (scant 2 Tbsp) mirin

12mL (scant 1 Tbsp) vinegar

½ lemon wedge, zest and juice

½ lime wedge, zest and juice

½ orange wedge, zest and juice

Avocado Mix

2 avocados, pitted and peeled

15mL (1 Tbsp) lime juice

8g (⅛ bunch) finely chopped cilantro, stems removed

2.5g (¾ tsp) salt

½ lime, zest

Yellowtail

300g (10 oz) yellowtail, sliced 0.5cm (¼ in) thick (18–24 slices)

½ serrano chili, thinly sliced

PONZU

Combine the ginger with 500mL (2 cups) of water in a medium-sized pot and bring to a low simmer. Cook for 10 minutes.

Transfer to a large bowl and add the bonito flakes and wakame. Cover and steep for 45 minutes, then press through a fine-mesh sieve. Refrigerate until very cold. Stir in the remaining ingredients.

AVOCADO MIX

Combine all the ingredients in a large bowl and mash gently with a fork. If not using immediately, cover with plastic wrap pressed directly onto the surface.

SERVE

Spoon the avocado mix into 6 shallow bowls and cover with 3 to 4 slices of yellowtail each. Pour a little ponzu on top. Refrigerate any extra ponzu for up to 2 weeks. Garnish with serrano chili.

HAMACHI, LEMONGRASS & LIME LEAF SORBET

Serves 6

This coconut milk and lemongrass sorbet is such a refreshing complement to the hamachi and its spicy, fish sauce—accented dressing. You want to eat this dish when it's really nice and hot outside—that's when this combination really pops.

INGREDIENTS

Lemongrass & Lime Leaf Sorbet

250mL (1 cup) coconut water

60mL (¼ cup) coconut milk

60mL (¼ cup) lime juice

50g (¼ cup) sugar

1.5g (½ tsp) salt

1 stalk lemongrass

½ green jalapeno, deseeded

18 lime leaves

Coconut Lime Snow

300mL (1¼ cups) coconut milk

25mL (scant 2 Tbsp) lime juice

8g (½ Tbsp) palm sugar

5g (½ Tbsp) salt

1 thumb-sized knob ginger

¼ stalk lemongrass

6 lime leaves

Vietnamese Vinaigrette

125mL (½ cup) water

50g (¼ cup) palm sugar

2 lime leaves

½ Thai chili, deseeded

75mL (5 Tbsp) lime juice

50mL (3 Tbsp) fish sauce

½ shallot, minced

Hamachi

510g (18 oz) hamachi, blood line
    removed, skin off, in 1cm (½ in)
    dice, ice cold

3 red radishes, thinly sliced with a
    mandoline

½ sprig mint, stem removed, leaves torn

Micro cilantro, for garnish

LEMONGRASS
& LIME LEAF
SORBET

Combine the liquids with the sugar and salt. Purée the lemongrass, jalapeno, and lime leaves in a blender on high for 30 seconds. Add the liquids and blend for another minute. Strain, pressing gently through a fine-mesh sieve.

Spin the mixture in an ice cream machine according to the manufacturer's directions and freeze.

COCONUT
LIME SNOW

Combine the liquids with the sugar and salt. Blitz the ginger, lemongrass, and lime leaves in a blender on high for 30 seconds. Add the liquids and blend for another minute. Strain, pressing gently through a fine-mesh sieve.

Next there are two options: 1) Pour the liquid into a metal insert. Freeze with liquid nitrogen until rock hard, then blitz it in a Vitamix on high until the consistency of light powder. 2) Alternatively, make a granita: Pour the liquid into a baking dish (metal will be faster than glass or ceramic) so it comes about 1.5cm (½ in) up the side.

Continued . . .

Place on a flat surface in the freezer for 30 minutes. Remove and aggressively scrape with a fork from end to end, breaking up any clumps that are starting to form. Return to the freezer and repeat the scraping every 30 minutes until transformed into fluffy, icy flakes.

VIETNAMESE
VINAIGRETTE

Bring the water, sugar, lime leaves, and chili to a boil in a medium pot to dissolve the sugar. Blend, then strain. Add the lime juice, fish sauce, and shallot and set aside.

HAMACHI

Remove the hamachi from the fridge just before serving. Season with a little Vietnamese vinaigrette. Plate on 6 serving plates and top with radishes and coconut lime snow. Add a quenelle of sorbet to each and garnish with mint and micro cilantro.

HALIBUT CEVICHE, SHISO, ENDIVE, PASSION FRUIT

Serves 6 as a starter

(photo on page 59)

Ceviche is one of the best uses for halibut. It's not a fish people eat raw very often—but a light cure is a great way to show off its qualities. Be careful, though: you do not want to be making ceviche out of a piece of some big, 50-kilogram halibut. Ideally, you want to use a young, small one, lean and delicate. Those fish are easy to overcook and make dry, but with ceviche there's no moisture loss, so this technique will always give you a really beautiful flavour and texture.

INGREDIENTS

Puffed Quinoa

30g (3 Tbsp) raw white quinoa

500mL (2 cups) canola oil

Salt

Passion Fruit Marinade

4 passion fruits

20mL (1⅓ Tbsp) lime juice

1 small shallot, sliced

½ red Thai chili, stem and seeds removed

7g (½ Tbsp) sugar

Ceviche

720g (25 oz) fresh halibut fillet

1 large Belgian endive, sliced 0.5cm (¼ in) thick

½ small white onion, finely brunoised and rinsed under cold water

2 shiso leaves, chiffonade

2 radishes, thinly sliced

Thai chili slices, for garnish (optional)

PUFFED QUINOA

Cook the quinoa according to package instructions. Spread onto a silicone mat or designated liner for a dehydrator. Dehydrate at 55°C (130°F) for 4 to 6 hours (alternatively, use your oven on the lowest setting with the door cracked open, for about 12 hours.).

Heat the oil to 175°C (350°F) in a pot large enough that it is not more than half full. Sprinkle in the quinoa and cook until it puffs up, doubling in size (no more than 15 seconds). Remove with a spider or metal sieve. Transfer to paper towel to soak up excess oil and sprinkle with salt.

PASSION FRUIT MARINADE

Scoop the seeds out of the passion fruits and purée in a blender, then strain through a fine-mesh sieve. Return to the blender and add the lime juice, shallot, Thai chili, and sugar. Blend and strain again through a fine-mesh sieve.

CEVICHE

Slice the halibut fillet very thinly. If very wide, cut in half before slicing. Combine with the passion fruit marinade and refrigerate until ready to serve (you can let it marinate for up to a few hours ahead of time). The fish will cook slightly from the acidity of the lime and the passion fruit.

SERVE

Remove from the fridge and combine with the endive, white onion, and shiso. Divide between 6 serving plates, and sprinkle with crispy puffed quinoa and sliced radishes. If you like more heat, garnish with fresh chili slices.

Roasted Eggplant *(page 254)*

Citrus & Avocado Salad
(page 82)

Halibut Ceviche (page 57)

GRAVLAX

Serves 30
as a starter

Everyone is so comfortable putting salmon in a pan they forget about how perfectly suited it is to being cured. This gravlax is easy to make and is such a good appetizer to have ready to go when company is coming over. It's much better—and healthier—than just reaching for the cheese or charcuterie. We have such a wide variety of salmon on the west coast—from the higher-fat spring salmon to the leaner sockeye and coho—and all types work for this recipe.

NOTE

This recipe is easily scalable: you can use salmon fillets instead of a whole fish (one 1.8–2.3kg/4–5 lb fillet will be enough for 12 people, for example) and reduce the volume of the cure accordingly. The flavour of the gravlax can be enhanced further by adding some or all of the following to the curing mix: fresh fennel fronds, and/or caraway, coriander, and fennel seeds.

INGREDIENTS

145g (1 cup) salt

65g (⅓ cup) sugar

25g (½ cup) packed dill leaves

3 bay leaves

6 crushed black or pink peppercorns

3 sprigs tarragon

3 sprigs parsley

2 lemons, zest

1 whole 6–7kg (12–15 lb) skin-on salmon, filleted and pin bones removed

120g (½ cup) Dijon mustard

Create the cure: blend together all the ingredients except the salmon and the Dijon mustard in a food processor until coarse.

Spread half the cure on a baking tray lined with parchment paper. Place the salmon fillets, skin side down, on top and spread with a generous layer of Dijon mustard. Top with the remaining cure, thicker at the head part of the fish than the tail. Cover and refrigerate for 18 to 24 hours (depending on the thickness of your fillet).

Remove from the fridge and rinse the salmon well under cold water, then pat dry. Using a very sharp knife, slice the salmon on an angle into very thin (0.25cm/⅛ in) slices.

Serve with classic gravlax condiments such as rye toast, crème fraîche, red onion slices, lemon wedges, and capers.

SALMON & CUCUMBER ROLL, CURED ROE

Makes 2 dozen
canapés

Smoked salmon and cream cheese is a very rich combination, but when you roll it in a ribbon of thinly sliced cucumber, it gets balanced with crisp freshness, and you get a snack that is luxurious but also refreshing. Plus it's gluten-free—which has helped make it an incredibly popular item on our Hawksworth catering menu.

INGREDIENTS

200g (scant 1 cup) cream cheese, room temperature

120g (4 oz) smoked salmon, chopped

½ lemon, zest and juice

10g (¼ cup) chopped chives

3 English cucumbers, skin on

70g (⅓ cup) salmon roe

1 sprig dill

Mix the cream cheese, smoked salmon, lemon juice and zest, and chives together into a smooth spread.

Using a very sharp mandoline or vegetable peeler, slice the outer green part of the cucumber into 24 long, thin 18cm (7 in) rectangular strips. Discard the rest.

Spread 15mL (1 Tbsp) of the smoked salmon mixture onto each strip and roll up. Chill before serving.

Garnish with salmon roe and a few fronds of dill.

WAGYU BEEF TATAKI, MUSHROOM, CRISPY SUSHI RICE

Makes 2 dozen canapés

Rare, succulent beef, mushroom duxelles, and a crispy starch. This flavour profile sounds like beef Wellington—but the execution is Japanese, with the familiar flavours reconfigured in a newfangled nigiri. Crispy-fried sushi rice has such a great texture—this is a delicious and luxurious little treat.

INGREDIENTS

Beef Tataki
360–400g (12½–14 oz) wagyu beef sirloin cap
Salt
Pepper
15mL (1 Tbsp) canola oil

Mushroom Duxelles
15mL (1 Tbsp) canola oil
250g (5 cups) button mushrooms, roughly sliced
2 shallots, chopped
2 cloves garlic, chopped
1 sprig thyme, stem removed
100mL (7 Tbsp) white wine
Salt

Soy Glaze
8g (1 Tbsp) cornstarch
45mL (3 Tbsp) light soy sauce
15g (1 Tbsp) honey
7g (1 tsp) grated ginger

Sushi Rice
300g (1½ cups) white sushi rice
125mL (½ cup) sushi seasoned rice vinegar, cold
1.5L (6 cups) canola oil

Serve
Sea salt
Micro cilantro, for garnish
1 recipe Parsley Purée (page 315), for garnish

BEEF TATAKI

Season the beef with salt and pepper. Heat the oil to smoking point in a cast-iron or non-stick pan over high heat. Carefully sear the beef, about 1 minute per side. Allow to cool, then wrap in plastic wrap and freeze.

When fully frozen, allow to thaw slightly, then unwrap. Slice into very thin 2mm (⅛ in) slices using a meat slicer or very sharp knife. Keep refrigerated.

MUSHROOM DUXELLES

Heat the oil in a skillet over medium to high heat. Sear the mushrooms until golden brown, about 4 minutes, stirring occasionally. Add the shallots, garlic, and thyme and cook for 1 more minute.

Deglaze the pan with the white wine and reduce until all the liquid has evaporated. Transfer the mixture to a food processor and pulse until a finely chopped smooth paste forms. Season with salt.

Continued . . .

SOY GLAZE   Make a slurry with the cornstarch. Bring the soy sauce, honey, and ginger to a boil in a small pot over high heat. Stir in a touch of cornstarch, just a little at a time, until the mixture becomes a syrupy glaze.

SUSHI RICE   Rinse the rice under cold water until the water runs clear, about 5 minutes. Place the rice and 300mL (1¼ cups) fresh water in a heavy-bottomed pot and cover. Bring to a boil, then reduce the heat down to the very minimum, and let steam for 15 minutes. Remove from the heat and let sit for 10 minutes, still covered, then fluff the rice with a fork. (Alternatively, you can use a rice cooker.)

Mix the rice with the rice vinegar, then firmly press into a sheet pan lined with parchment paper, in a layer 1.5cm (½ in) thick. Refrigerate. When cool, cut into finger-sized strips, 6.5cm (2½ in) long by 1.5cm (½ in) wide.

Heat the oil to 175°C (350°F) in a pot large enough that it is not more than half full. Fry the rice strips in batches until crispy and golden brown, about 1 minute. Transfer to paper towel to soak up excess oil.

SERVE   Using a small offset spatula, spread some of the mushroom duxelles on top of each piece of fried sushi rice. Place a few slices of beef tataki on top and brush with a little soy glaze. Season with sea salt, garnish with micro cilantro or other microgreens, and add dots of parsley purée.

WAGYU BEEF CARPACCIO, PIQUILLO PEPPER, PARSLEY, PUFFED BEEF TENDON

Serves 6

I wanted a "beef two ways" concept that was both high end and low end. Wagyu is as high end and premium as beef gets, while most people think of tendon as very low—if they consider it at all. I really like tendon, though—I like it in pho—and puffed, it's even more delicious.

INGREDIENTS

Beef Tendon

250g (9 oz) beef tendons

1L (4 cups) Vegetable Nage (page 316)

Tomato Paper

1 recipe Roasted Tomato Vinaigrette (page 314)

60g (¼ cup) isomalt, ground in a spice grinder

130g (1 cup) maltodextrin

Tomato Powder

2 Roma tomatoes

Piquillo Gel

60g (½ cup) drained jarred or canned piquillo peppers

Pinch agar powder

Half pinch locust bean gum powder

5mL (1 tsp) mayonnaise

5mL (1 tsp) harissa concentrate

5mL (1 tsp) Banyuls vinegar

5mL (1 tsp) maple syrup

1.5g (½ tsp) salt

Wagyu Beef Carpaccio

600g (21 oz) sirloin cap wagyu beef

Serve

2L (8 cups) canola oil

Salt

Pepper

Olive oil, for brushing

Sea salt

½ small shallot, finely chopped

100g (3½ oz) Manchego cheese

1 recipe Parsley Purée (page 315)

Watercress, for garnish

Chives, finely chopped, for garnish

BEEF TENDON

Clean the beef tendons of any extraneous tissues or pieces of meat. Place in a pressure cooker and cover with the vegetable nage. (The pressure cooker should not be more than half full: this is an essential safety precaution.) Cook over medium heat at high pressure (105 kPa/15 psi) for 90 minutes from the point of the first hiss of pressure release. Remove from the heat and let stand for 15 minutes to allow the pressure to naturally dissipate; alternatively, run it under cold water.

Once cool, carefully transfer the tendons 1 at a time to a surface covered in plastic wrap, and lay them in a line. Roll the plastic wrap very tightly into a cylinder shape, tying the ends off. Place on a baking tray and freeze overnight.

Continued . . .

Spray food dehydrator trays with non-stick cooking spray. Unwrap the frozen tendons and slice them into extremely thin strips, almost translucent, using a meat slicer or very sharp knife. Be sure to work very quickly so that the tendons stay very cold. Lay the pieces flat on the prepared dehydrator trays.

Dehydrate the tendons at 49°C (120°F) for 6 to 8 hours, or until they snap between two fingers.

TOMATO PAPER

Whisk together the roasted tomato vinaigrette and isomalt, then transfer to a blender. With the blender running, add the maltodextrin in three additions. Pass the mixture through a fine-mesh sieve.

Tape a 30 x 30cm (12 x 12 in) square of acetate onto a dehydrator tray, and use an offset spatula to spread the tomato mixture into a very thin, almost translucent, layer on the acetate. Dehydrate at 49°C (120°F) for at least 24 hours, though 48 is preferable.

Peel the tomato paper off the acetate, and break it into abstract-shaped shards.

TOMATO POWDER

Prepare an ice bath. Bring a medium-sized pot of water to a rolling boil. Drop the Roma tomatoes in for just 30 seconds then dunk in the ice bath. Peel off the skin and discard or reuse everything else (flesh, seeds, etc.). Spread the skin onto a silicone mat or designated liner for a dehydrator. Dehydrate at 60°C (140°F) for several hours, until it snaps between two fingers. Blend into a powder in a blender or coffee grinder.

PIQUILLO GEL

Blend the peppers in a high-speed blender or small food processor until smooth, then transfer to a small saucepan and whisk in the agar and locust bean gum. Place the pan over low heat and simmer for about 1 minute to dissolve the powders. Transfer to a container and refrigerate until set solid.

Return to a high-speed blender and blend back into a liquid. Add the remaining ingredients and blend to combine. Refrigerate.

WAGYU BEEF CARPACCIO

Slice the beef very thinly with a meat slicer or very sharp knife and delicately place them on a wooden board or a plate. Cover and refrigerate.

SERVE

Heat the oil to 190°C (375°F) in a pot large enough that it is not more than half full. Fry the beef tendons in batches, very quickly, a few at a time. They will puff up almost immediately and double in size. Transfer to paper towel to soak up excess oil. Season with salt and pepper.

Brush the beef carpaccio with olive oil and season with sea salt. Top with the shallots, a few pieces of fried tendon, thin shavings of manchego, and tomato paper. Add dots of parsley purée and piquillo gel, and a sprinkle of tomato powder. Garnish with watercress and chives. Store extra tendons or tomato paper in an airtight container for up to 2 weeks.

UK: PART 1

I had no idea. Not a clue.

It was November 1992. Le Manoir had held two Michelin stars since it opened in 1984, and Raymond Blanc was still fighting hard for a third. Marco Pierre White had collected his second star for Harveys four years previous, making him the youngest chef to ever earn the honour (he was 28). His kitchen brigade there included future legends like Gordon Ramsay, Philip Howard, Éric Chavot, Stephen Terry, Tim Payne, and Tim Hughes. And I was thinking that I'd land at one restaurant or the other, and that either way it would just turn out to be mildly harder than working at Le Crocodile. In the end I got lucky. Marco had just gone into partnership with Michael Caine to open a casual restaurant at Chelsea Harbour. They called it the Canteen. It was big—huge back then— at nearly 200 seats, one of the first gastrodomes. Marco and his partners were scrambling to staff it. I arrived in London and pulled into my sad little hostel in Bayswater to find a message waiting there for me: "Someone named Marco rang for you. He wants you to come by the Canteen."

The next day I walked into the restaurant and promptly took a merciless ribbing from the chefs for showing up in a suit. There was no interview; they just asked if I could start the following day. I begged for two extra days to get settled, and then, when I showed up for work, was summarily informed, "Well, you're from Canada—you'll start on fish!" Based on what logic? Next thing I knew, some chef was yelling at me, "Hey—go get the *loup de mer!*" Or the bream or *rouget* or *turbot*. Turbo? I thought that was part of a car. I'd never heard of these fish and couldn't tell one from another. What happened to all the chinook and halibut?

The Canteen was insanely busy right out of the gate, and at the start I really had no idea what was going on. It was as if I had signed up for the army expecting to be made a clerk, and instead was told, "No—you're going to be a navy SEAL!" It was that difficult. A cook's work is extremely demanding physically. The hours were crazy. We worked from 7 a.m. to 1 a.m. There was hardly any time in the day left for sleeping—and even when I did, I was always waking up in a panic thinking I'd overslept and was going to be fired for showing up late.

The executioner would have been one of the two seasoned Harveys veterans— Stephen Terry and Tim Hughes—who then ran the Canteen kitchen. Tim in particular was a merciless taskmaster. You did not mess around in the kitchen when Tim was there. Stand still for a second, he'd yell at you.

My plan had originally been to stay in London for two years. After three months, I was thinking it would be better to just grab every recipe I could and get back home. I'd somehow landed in the Premier (Culinary) League. What I really needed was to start all over again, at the bottom. So instead of quitting, after four months at the Canteen, I wangled a job interview at Le Manoir in Oxfordshire, scheduled for my next day off.

So there I was, running late, fretting in the back seat of a minicab on the ride from the Oxford train station to Le Manoir, about 20 minutes away in Great Milton. We were getting close, when the driver began to drift into the right lane—into oncoming traffic— and I'm thinking, "Are we turning? I don't see a driveway, I don't see the Manoir . . ." We weren't turning. Not on purpose, anyway; my minicab driver had fallen asleep. We had a head-on collision. The noise was shocking, and I ended up headfirst in the front seat footwell, with blood and glass everywhere. I wanted to throttle the driver; instead, I was taken to hospital strapped to a gurney. From my hospital bed, I called the Canteen kitchen to tell them I couldn't make it in for work—and Tim Hughes got on the line, evidently thinking I was just another chancer phoning in sick after a night at the pub.

"I've had a car accident."

"Where?"

"Oxford."

"You've got one day off, and you're in Oxford? What the fuck are you doing in Oxford? *Whereabouts* in Oxford? You've been at the fucking Manoir, haven't you? You've been trying out for Blancie. Did you get the job?"

Not that time. But a month later I went back, and I did. H

SALADS

WATERMELON, CHERRY TOMATO & MACEDONIAN FETA SALAD

Serves 4 as a side

At Nightingale, we use watermelons from Foxglove Farm on Salt Spring Island. They're beautiful, but they're not seedless, so I've been known to make the chefs poke out the pips with toothpicks—and I guess they don't love me for that! We crumble a smooth and creamy Macedonian feta on top, and then add the purslane and a viscous 5-year-old balsamic vinegar. It's a perfect salad for peak summer.

INGREDIENTS

1 small (or ½ large) watermelon, rind removed, cut in 2cm (¾ in) cubes

8 multicoloured cherry tomatoes, halved

60mL (¼ cup) high-quality olive oil

45mL (3 Tbsp) 5-year-old aged balsamic vinegar

2 pinches sea salt

115g (¾ cup) Macedonian feta, crumbled

⅛ jalapeno, thinly sliced, for garnish

12 sprigs purslane, for garnish

12 sorrel leaves, for garnish (optional)

Squid Ink Cracker (page 27, optional)

Pepper

In a mixing bowl, combine the watermelon and tomatoes. Drizzle with half the olive oil and half the balsamic vinegar, and a pinch of sea salt. Gently toss to combine and refrigerate until cool.

Arrange the watermelon and tomatoes on a serving plate. Add the crumbled feta and garnish with jalapenos, purslane, and sorrel, if using. Finish with the remaining olive oil and balsamic vinegar, another pinch of sea salt, and some fresh cracked pepper. At the restaurant, we crumble a little Squid Ink Cracker on top for added colour and texture.

APPLE, BEET & BURRATA SALAD

Serves 6

It's good to change up your textures and deliver something unexpected when you can. When we opened Hawksworth, we used to make this with a Japanese slicing machine that shaved apples and beets into long ribbons in seconds flat. In the variation here, you still have apples and beets—just in slices and chunks—as well as a beet mousse.

INGREDIENTS

Pickled Beets

2–3 bunches assorted baby beets, tops removed

Pinch salt

250mL (1 cup) white wine vinegar

100g (½ cup) sugar

Beet Purée Base

1 large beet

250mL (1 cup) apple juice, plus more as needed

50mL (3 Tbsp) red wine vinegar

100g (⅓ cup) honey

¼ cinnamon stick

Salt

Beet Mousse

1½ sheets gelatin

120g (½ cup) crème fraîche

25mL (scant 2 Tbsp) whipping cream

Caramelized Honey Vinaigrette

50g (3 Tbsp) honey

65mL (4 Tbsp) white wine vinegar

65mL (4 Tbsp) olive oil

Pinch salt

Apple & Beet Salad

3 apples, thinly sliced with a mandoline

1 ball fresh burrata cheese

30mL (2 Tbsp) olive oil

Pepper

Sea salt

½ recipe Anchovy Breadcrumbs (page 309) (but leave out the anchovies)

2 sprigs dill, for garnish

PICKLED BEETS

Place the beets in different pots separated by colour. Cover with water, season with salt, and simmer over medium heat until tender when pierced with the tip of a knife. Peel while still hot by rubbing the skins with a cloth or paper towel. Place in dry bowls, still separated by colour.

In a fresh pot, heat the vinegar, 125mL (½ cup) of water, and the sugar over medium heat to dissolve the sugar. Pour over the beets and allow to cool, then refrigerate for at least 6 hours (and preferably 24) to fully pickle. Once pickled, the beets can be refrigerated for up to 1 week.

Continued . . .

BEET PURÉE BASE

Peel the beet and cut into 1cm (½ in) pieces. In a large pot, combine with the apple juice, red wine vinegar, honey, and cinnamon stick. Cook over low heat until tender when pierced with the tip of a knife. Transfer the beets to a blender. Keep simmering the liquid until it reduces to a sticky glaze. Pour the liquid into the blender, discarding the cinnamon stick.

Blend to a smooth purée, adding more apple juice as needed. Adjust the seasoning to taste.

BEET MOUSSE

While the beet purée is still hot, bloom the gelatin in a large bowl of ice water for a few minutes until softened. Remove the gelatin from the water, squeeze to drain any remaining water, and add to the hot purée, whisking well. Allow to cool to room temperature.

While the base cools, whip the crème fraîche and cream together until fluffy, then fold into the cooled beet base. Refrigerate to set.

CARAMELIZED HONEY VINAIGRETTE

Bring the honey to a simmer in a small pot over medium-high heat. Reduce the heat to low and simmer gently until the honey is a slightly darker amber colour, about 5 minutes.

Remove from the heat and carefully pour the white wine vinegar and 35mL (2 Tbsp) of water on top. It will bubble violently. When the bubbling subsides, whisk in the olive oil and salt. Allow to cool, then refrigerate.

APPLE & BEET SALAD

Cut the pickled beets into wedges and toss (still separated by colour) with some of the caramelized honey vinaigrette. Toss the apples in the vinaigrette separately, then roll them up.

Tear the burrata into equal-sized chunks and season with olive oil, pepper, and salt, then position on a serving plate or board. Place the beets and apples around the cheese and sprinkle with breadcrumbs. Add a quenelle of beet mousse and garnish with dill sprigs.

APPLE, CELERY & WALNUT SALAD, SZECHUAN VINAIGRETTE

Serves 6

We use beautiful fresh, crisp organic apples from the Okanagan. Cut them into bite-sized chunks, add walnuts, parsley, celery for a clean crunch, and a little tarragon, and then shave some good creamy cheddar on top. The Szechuan vinaigrette adds something unexpected. You don't need much to make a great fall salad.

NOTE

It's all about the apples. We use fantastic Aurora Golden Gala, but they're only available for two months. If you can't get them, you can use top-quality Fuji or Pink Lady apples.

INGREDIENTS

Szechuan Vinaigrette
75mL (5 Tbsp) lemon juice
50mL (3 Tbsp) olive oil
50mL (3 Tbsp) canola oil
20g (1 Tbsp) honey
3g (1 tsp) salt
Pinch Szechuan peppercorns, cracked

Salad
50g (½ cup) walnuts
3 Aurora Golden Gala apples
2 stalks celery, peeled
Handful parsley leaves
Handful tarragon leaves
50g (2 oz) aged cheddar, shaved

SZECHUAN VINAIGRETTE

Whisk all of the ingredients together until combined.

SALAD

Preheat the oven to 175°C (350°F).

Place the walnuts on a baking tray lined with parchment paper and toast until golden brown, about 8 minutes. Allow to cool.

Cut the apples into 2cm (¾ in) cubes, and the celery into 0.5cm (¼ in) slices, on the bias. In a large mixing bowl, combine the apples, celery, parsley, tarragon, and walnuts. Add the dressing and toss gently. Transfer to a serving bowl and sprinkle the aged cheddar on top.

Yellowtail Crudo (page 53)

Grilled Broccolini (page 242)

Apple, Celery & Walnut Salad (page 79)

CITRUS & AVOCADO SALAD

Serves 6

(photo on page 58)

This is a really good winter salad. It combines segments of pomelo, grapefruit, and orange with avocado—so it's acidic from all that citrus, but it has some avocado richness too. Plus, there's salty crunch from the deep-fried shallots. It's also vegan—and one of Nightingale's all-time bestsellers.

INGREDIENTS

100mL (7 Tbsp) lime juice

30g (2½ Tbsp) sugar

½ small shallot, finely chopped

1 lime leaf

Sea salt

3 large avocados

2 oranges

2 grapefruits

½ pomelo

Salt

¼ bunch cilantro, stems removed

4 sprigs Thai basil, stems removed

6 sprigs mint, stems removed, leaves torn

30g (¼ cup) crispy onions or shallots (available in most Asian supermarkets)

Blend the lime juice, sugar, shallot, lime leaf, and a pinch of salt on high for 90 seconds. Allow to stand and steep for 20 minutes. Press through a fine-mesh sieve.

Cut the avocados in half and remove the pit and peel. Slice each half into three wedges.

For the oranges, grapefruits, and pomelo, slice off the top and bottom of each fruit and cut away the peel and pith, then remove the segments of citrus flesh.

Place the citrus on the bottom of a serving platter, with the avocados on top. Season with salt. Mix the cilantro, Thai basil, and mint leaves together and sprinkle on top of the avocados. Spoon a generous amount of lime vinaigrette on top and garnish with crispy onions or shallots.

DELICATA SQUASH SALAD

Serves 6

(photo on page 256)

Delicata squash has a thin, edible skin and unusually sweet flesh. At Nightingale, we slice it, roast it skin-on, and give it an umami-rich roasted garlic dressing blended with raisins, anchovies, and capers. There's crumbled feta for added tang and creaminess and toasted sliced almonds for crunch. Then we finish it with pomegranate seeds to give it an acidic pop.

INGREDIENTS

Squash

1.5kg (3⅓ lb) delicata squash
   (3–4 squashes)

50g (2 Tbsp) honey

15mL (1 Tbsp) olive oil

2 sprigs sage

3 sprigs thyme

2 bay leaves

Salt

Dressing

50g (⅓ cup) golden raisins

50mL (3 Tbsp) cider vinegar

15g (1 Tbsp) Garlic Confit (page 312)

65mL (5 Tbsp) olive oil

50g (5 Tbsp) capers

10 anchovies

Salad

90g (1 cup) sliced almonds

200g (2 cups) Macedonian feta

90g (⅔ cup) pomegranate seeds

Aleppo or espelette pepper

SQUASH

Preheat the oven to 200°C (400°F).

   Cut the squashes in half lengthwise and discard the seeds. Cut into 2cm (¾ in) slices. Toss with the honey, olive oil, sage, thyme, bay leaves, and salt, then lay out in 1 layer on a baking tray lined with parchment paper. Roast until tender and golden at the edges, about 15 minutes. Remove from the oven and discard the herbs.

DRESSING

Soak the raisins in the cider vinegar for 30 minutes.

   Pulse the garlic confit, olive oil, capers, and anchovies in a food processor until coarsely chopped. Add the raisins and vinegar. Pulse again until coarse.

SALAD

Preheat the oven to 175°C (350°F).

   Lay the sliced almonds on a baking tray lined with parchment paper and toast until golden brown, 8 to 10 minutes.

   Place the roasted squash on a serving platter or individual plates. Crumble the feta on top and generously drizzle with dressing. Garnish with the toasted almonds, pomegranate seeds, and a light sprinkle of Aleppo or espelette pepper.

KALE & QUINOA SALAD

Serves 6

This salad from Bel Café is based on the ultimate trendy, healthy combination of kale and quinoa. Add some crunch with cucumber and almonds, the sweetness of ripe cherry tomatoes, some creamy richness from crumbled fresh goat cheese, and a great dressing, and now you have a healthy salad with very broad appeal.

INGREDIENTS

Lemon & Oregano Vinaigrette

½ shallot, coarsely chopped

2 cloves garlic

120mL (½ cup) lemon juice

40g (2 Tbsp) honey

10g (2 tsp) Dijon mustard

250mL (1 cup) canola oil

125mL (½ cup) olive oil

2 sprigs oregano, stems removed, chopped

2 pinches salt

2 pinches red chili flakes

Kale & Quinoa Salad

90g (½ cup) quinoa

40g (⅓ cup) sliced almonds

6 bunches curly kale, in bite-sized pieces

1 cucumber, peeled, quartered, deseeded, and diced

225g (1½ cups) cherry tomatoes, halved

24 Castelvetrano green olives, pitted and cut in half

180g (6 oz) crumbled fresh goat cheese

LEMON & OREGANO VINAIGRETTE

Blend the shallot and garlic with the lemon juice, honey, and mustard in a blender until smooth. Slowly drizzle in the canola oil and olive oil in a slow thin stream. Add the oregano, salt, and chilis and pulse to combine.

KALE & QUINOA SALAD

Preheat the oven to 175°C (350°F).

Cook the quinoa according to the package instructions.

Lay the sliced almonds on a baking tray lined with parchment paper and toast in the oven until golden brown, 8 to 10 minutes.

Gently massage the kale with half the salad dressing to coat each leaf. Add the quinoa and half the cucumbers, tomatoes, almonds, and olives. Toss with the kale, adding more dressing if required.

Place on a serving tray or in individual bowls and top with the rest of the tomatoes, cucumbers, almonds, and olives, and the crumbled goat cheese.

DANDELION SALAD

This is fundamentally a Caesar salad, but more exciting, with more appealing textures and a mild bitterness to counter the creamy, garlicky dressing. For it all to work properly though, you have to use choice ingredients: small, delicate dandelion greens picked in early spring, and those beautiful white anchovies from Catalonia's Costa de l'Anxova, the Anchovy Coast.

INGREDIENTS

Pickled Onions

90mL (6 Tbsp) white wine vinegar

60mL (4 Tbsp) water

30g (2½ Tbsp) sugar

½ red onion, thinly sliced

2 anchovies

30mL (2 Tbsp) olive oil

60mL (¼ cup) lemon juice

Salt

Pepper

Creamy Garlic Dressing

20 cloves garlic

100mL (7 Tbsp) cream

4 egg yolks

50g (½ cup) grated Parmesan

30mL (2 Tbsp) red wine vinegar

20g (½ Tbsp) Dijon mustard

Salad & Garnish

500g (about 6 cups) freshly picked dandelion greens, washed and trimmed

½ recipe Anchovy Breadcrumbs (page 309)

12 high-quality white anchovies

7.5g (1½ tsp) freshly grated horseradish

PICKLED ONIONS

Bring the white wine vinegar, water, and sugar to a boil in a pot. Remove from the heat and pour over the sliced red onions. Allow to pickle for an hour.

CREAMY GARLIC DRESSING

Place the garlic cloves in a medium pot, cover with cold water, and bring to a boil. As soon as the water boils, drain the garlic and place it back in the pot. Immediately refill with fresh cold water. Repeat this process 7 more times to diminish the bitterness of the garlic.

In a food processor, combine the blanched garlic with the cream, egg yolks, cheese, vinegar, mustard, and anchovies, and blend until emulsified, about 30 seconds. With the food processor running, slowly drizzle in the olive oil in a thin stream. Season with the lemon juice, salt, and pepper, to taste. Refrigerate in an airtight container for up to 2 weeks.

SALAD

Toss the dandelion greens with some of the creamy garlic dressing and place on a serving platter. Garnish with breadcrumbs, pickled onions, white anchovies, and horseradish.

TUNA, ARUGULA & AVOCADO SALAD

Serves 6

(photo on page 213)

All the fatty bellies from the albacore tuna that we serve at Nightingale get used up in this salad. We give them a quick cure in jalapeno and citrus—seasoned salt, slow bake them until they're just cooked through, then flake them over charred avocado, arugula, and fava beans. There's toasted sunflower seeds for crunch and yuzu dressing to bring it all together.

INGREDIENTS

Yuzu Dressing
100mL (7 Tbsp) yuzu juice
50mL (3 Tbsp) good-quality canola oil
50mL (3 Tbsp) lemon juice
30mL (2 Tbsp) mirin
8g (2 tsp) Dijon mustard
5g (1 tsp) sugar
Salt
1 thin slice ginger

Tuna Belly
30g (3 Tbsp) salt
15g (1 Tbsp) sugar
3 sprigs cilantro, coarsely chopped
⅓ jalapeno, deseeded and coarsely chopped

½ lemon, zest
½ lime, zest
350g (12 oz) albacore tuna belly

Sunflower Seeds
15mL (1 Tbsp) olive oil
50g (⅓ cup) sunflower seeds
Pinch smoked sweet paprika
Pinch salt

Salad
150g (⅔ cup) fava beans, shelled
3 avocados
120g (6 cups) arugula
½ small red onion, finely sliced

YUZU DRESSING

Blitz all the ingredients in a blender on high for 1 minute. Press through a fine-mesh sieve.

TUNA BELLY

Blend the salt, sugar, cilantro, jalapeno, lemon zest, and lime zest in a food processor for 60 seconds, until the salt turns green and everything has broken down. Rub the green salt on all sides of the tuna and allow to sit on a baking tray lined with parchment paper for 20 minutes. Rinse under cold water to remove all the salt.

Preheat the oven to 120°C (250°F).

Place the tuna on a baking tray lined with parchment paper and cook until flaky and tender, about 5 minutes. Be careful not to overcook.

SUNFLOWER SEEDS

Heat the olive oil in a skillet over medium heat. Add the sunflower seeds and toast until golden brown, stirring occasionally. Transfer to paper towel to soak up excess oil. Toss the seeds with the smoked paprika and season with salt.

Continued . . .

Bring a large pot of water to a boil. Blanch the fava beans until just cooked, about 1 minute, then dunk in ice water. Once cool, peel off the skins.

Cut the avocados in half and remove the pit and peel.

Heat up a grill pan on the stovetop over high heat. Place the avocados, flat side down, and grill until charred, then turn 90 degrees and grill until charred again. This creates a crosshatch grill pattern.

Gently toss the arugula, red onions, and fava beans together with some of the yuzu dressing and transfer to a serving platter. Add the grilled avocado and fill the centre of each avocado half with more yuzu dressing. Top with some of the flaky tuna belly and sprinkle with toasted sunflower seeds.

SPICY CHICKEN & GREEN PAPAYA SALAD

Serves 6

Crispy lemongrass chicken, crunchy vegetables, bean sprouts, green papaya, rice noodles, crunchy cashews, and a tangy, spicy dressing. This is a healthy salad with lots of texture and flavour. When we put it on the menu at Bel Café, it was so popular that the cooks couldn't keep up with the knife work, so they started spiralizing the carrots and daikon instead.

NOTE

The chicken thighs will develop a lot more flavour if they are marinated the day before, and up to 24 hours before grilling.

INGREDIENTS

Chicken

30mL (2 Tbsp) canola oil

20g (1 Tbsp) thinly sliced ginger

5 cloves garlic, thinly sliced

½ stalk lemongrass, thinly sliced

10g (2 tsp) palm sugar

70mL (5 Tbsp) soy sauce

125mL (½ cup) hoisin

50mL (3 Tbsp) sesame oil

30mL (2 Tbsp) Sriracha-style chili sauce

20g (1 Tbsp) tamarind paste

6 boneless, skinless chicken thighs

Vinaigrette

50g (¼ cup) palm sugar

2 lime leaves

½ fresh jalapeno or red Thai chili, deseeded

15mL (1 Tbsp) fish sauce

250mL (1 cup) lime juice

1 shallot, finely chopped

Salt

Spicy Papaya Salad

200g (7oz) vermicelli noodles

Salt

1 carrot

½ small daikon radish

¼ green papaya, peeled, deseeded, and julienned

100g (1⅓ cups) bean sprouts

½ bunch cilantro, stems removed

75g (½ cup) toasted cashews, crushed

½ red jalapeno, deseeded and thinly sliced

CHICKEN

Heat the canola oil in a sauté pan over medium heat, then add the ginger, garlic, and lemongrass and cook for about 3 minutes. Add the palm sugar and soy sauce and continue to cook until the sugar has dissolved.

Transfer to a blender and add the sesame oil, chili sauce, and tamarind paste. Blend on high until smooth, then strain through a fine-mesh sieve into a large bowl. Toss the chicken thighs in the marinade then refrigerate overnight (and up to 24 hours).

Preheat the oven to 175°C (350°F).

Remove the chicken from the marinade and scrape off any excess.

Continued . . .

Using a grill pan or barbecue on high heat, char the chicken to create grill marks on both sides. Transfer to a baking tray lined with parchment paper and roast in the oven for 7 minutes. Remove from the oven and set aside to cool before slicing into 1cm (½ in) strips.

DRESSING   Bring the palm sugar, lime leaves, chili, and 60mL (¼ cup) of water to a boil to dissolve the sugar. Transfer to a blender and blend for 1 minute until combined, then strain through a fine-mesh sieve. Add the fish sauce, lime juice, and shallot, and season with salt. Refrigerate to cool.

SALAD   Place the noodles in a large heatproof bowl and sprinkle with salt. Pour boiling water overtop to cover them completely, and allow to stand according to the package instructions, about 6 minutes, stirring from time to time. Drain, rinse with cold water, then drain again. This stops the cooking process and prevents the noodles from sticking together.

Cut the carrot and daikon radish into fine julienne strips or create ribbons using a spiralizer. Combine with the green papaya, bean sprouts, and noodles, and gently toss with some of the vinaigrette. Divide between 6 bowls and top with slices of chicken. Garnish with cilantro, cashews, and jalapeno slices.

CRISPY DUCK SALAD

Serves 6

When I was working in London, I heard of a salad like this on the menu at Le Caprice, in St. James's. It got started with chefs eating out in Chinatown, coming back to the restaurant with some whole barbecued ducks, breaking them down, and deep-frying the meat crispy. So later at West, we did our own version with the crispy duck tossed in a sweet and tangy dressing made with ketchup, soy sauce, and honey, with a spicy, crunchy salad of watercress, carrot, and daikon.

NOTE

If you don't want to roast a duck for this salad, do as those London chefs did and pick up a barbecued duck in Chinatown.

INGREDIENTS

Roasted Duck

½ Peking duck

6g (1 Tbsp) five spice powder

Sea salt

½ orange, peel on, sliced

1 knob ginger (about 7.5cm/3 in), peeled and sliced

2 cloves garlic, sliced

2 star anise pods

Soy & Ginger Vinaigrette

125mL (½ cup) grapeseed oil

50mL (3 Tbsp) sesame oil

75mL (5 Tbsp) soy sauce

20g (2 Tbsp) finely grated ginger

1 lime, juice

Duck Dressing

200mL (¾ cup) ketchup

20g (1 Tbsp) honey

25mL (scant 2 Tbsp) soy sauce

10mL (2 tsp) sesame oil

3g (1 tsp) black sesame seeds

½ orange, juice

Crispy Duck Salad

500mL (2 cups) canola oil

1 carrot

½ small daikon radish

1 small beet

120g (6 cups) watercress

18g (⅛ cup) crispy onions or shallots (available at Asian supermarkets)

Black and white sesame seeds, toasted, for garnish

ROASTED DUCK

Preheat the oven to 120°C (250°F). Season the duck with the five spice powder and salt.
Place the orange slices, ginger, garlic, and star anise in a roasting pan, with the duck on top. Roast for 1½ to 2 hours, until the skin is golden brown and crispy. Remove from the oven and allow to rest on a wire rack until cool enough to handle. Carve the duck: cut the breast into 0.75cm thick (⅓ in) slices, and pull the leg meat into bite-sized pieces. Set aside.

SOY & GINGER VINAIGRETTE

Whisk together all of the ingredients.

Continued . . .

Whisk together all of the ingredients.

Heat the canola oil to 175°C (350°F) in a pot large enough that it is not more than half full. Fry the sliced duck in batches until crispy, about 1 to 1½ minutes. Transfer to a large bowl, add the duck dressing, and toss to coat.

Peel the carrot, daikon, and beet, and cut into fine julienne strips or ribbons using a spiralizer. Mix with the watercress and toss with some of the soy and ginger vinaigrette. Divide between 6 serving plates. Top with crispy fried duck and garnish with crispy onions and sesame seeds.

UK: PART 2

Imagine that you're 22 years old, never attended cooking school, and have completed only a rudimentary apprenticeship in Canada and one baptism by fire, at a freshly opened beast of a restaurant. There, at the Canteen, you hung on by your fingernails. Now, though, you've made it to Le Manoir, and a year in, as a cook you're beginning to hit your stride. It's not easy, but you're learning something every day.

Chef puts you on hot starters. You've got eight dishes to master in the regular repertoire—plus a daily special. When you start in the morning, you find out that the special is a sunchoke mousse with asparagus sauce. There are 100 people coming for lunch—and you have to be prepared for 20 of them ordering this *gâteau de topinambours au coulis d'asperges*. The morning begins with scraping dirt off ten kilograms of knobby, gnarly sunchokes, then scrubbing them, peeling them, and cooking them down with shallots, thyme, and stock. Purée the mix, cook it down some more, and you're ready to make the *gâteaux*. Technically these are *royales*—a custard. So you have to fold egg yolks and cream into the thick sunchoke purée, butter ramekins, fill them with the mixture, cover each one with a fitted disc of parchment paper, and finally transfer them all to a bain-marie to cook and set.

Meanwhile Chef has just yelled, "The vegetable order is here!" and you've got to run and help put that away in the walk-in, and you've lost 45 minutes. Now you have to rotate the stocks, get your sunchoke *gâteaux* ready to plate, make their asparagus sauce—and get set up for your other eight dishes. Remember: there are 100 people coming for lunch. Understand that if you are not in that kitchen by 6 a.m. at the latest you are so f-u-c-k-e-d. And that even if you're there by 5 a.m., you might still be.

The attrition rate at Le Manoir was high. It took me two and a half, maybe three years to earn respect for my cooking and work ethic there. And Raymond? Let's just say Chef Blanc was very interesting to work for. A force of nature; one of a kind. Raymond was far too disorganized and distracted to run his own kitchen through service (thankfully, he almost never tried), but when he focused on a single dish, the results were often incredible. There was some culinary genius there.

When Blanc asked me, after four years there, to be the opening chef at his new brasserie in Oxford proper, I had to say yes. What we opened as Le Petit Blanc is now called Brasserie Blanc, and has spawned another 19 locations across the UK. But it got off to a very rough start. At opening I worked five straight days with no sleep. Nothing worked—and I mean nothing. Like, when Blanc had designed the kitchen he forgot there was a staircase in front of the meat locker, so its door wouldn't open (we had to cut it in half and crawl in on our hands and knees). And in the midst of all that, Blanc decided that in addition to lunch and dinner we should open for breakfast. But we didn't have a permit, and the neighbours were all over us. I got my fill of abuse. After four and a half years for Blanc, I thought I'd earned a little more respect. I was done.

Marco had by then sold Harveys and opened the Restaurant Marco Pierre White at the Hyde Park Hotel. He had plenty of new positions to fill in his expanding turf. Like at Mirabelle, in Mayfair, and at L'Escargot, the old film set hangout in Soho, which he had just taken over in a new partnership with Jimmy Lahoud. He offered me a job there, as head chef upstairs for the private events dining room. I grabbed it, and when I could, complemented the gig with shifts as a *stagiaire* at the Restaurant.

Marco was a very strange boss. Machiavellian. It was incredible what he could get other people to do for him in the hopes of earning his approval and respect. He was an exceptional chef. A master technician. Every time that he borrowed another chef's concept for a dish and modified it, everything he changed made his version a conspicuous improvement on the original. Every time. His talent was incredible. But the head games. Whenever I did a shift at the Restaurant, the other chefs would warn me to not even look at Marco during service. Look him in the eye, then you're a target—and you're finished.

It was insanity, but I was usually safe in my small kitchen upstairs at L'Escargot, doing special meals for their private event spaces, the Picasso Room and the Barrel Room. And that's where I met Annabel, my future wife. She was the hostess. Then she managed those private events, from the menus to the service. We were young, just 26. Soho then was like it always is: mad and bustling. And we were always working. There wasn't time for much else.

But for our first date, I took her to Windows, at the Hilton on Hyde Park corner where Marc Meneau had come in from L'Espérance to be guest chef for a night. Meneau was a legend, and all the London chefs were there for his dinner: Heston Blumenthal, Gordon Ramsay. We had a great meal. Then I guess Annabel thought, "Uh-oh, here come all the moves," but I was so exhausted, and doing my best not to screw anything up. So I just put her in a cab after and said, "See you tomorrow." It was about a week later that she moved in. H

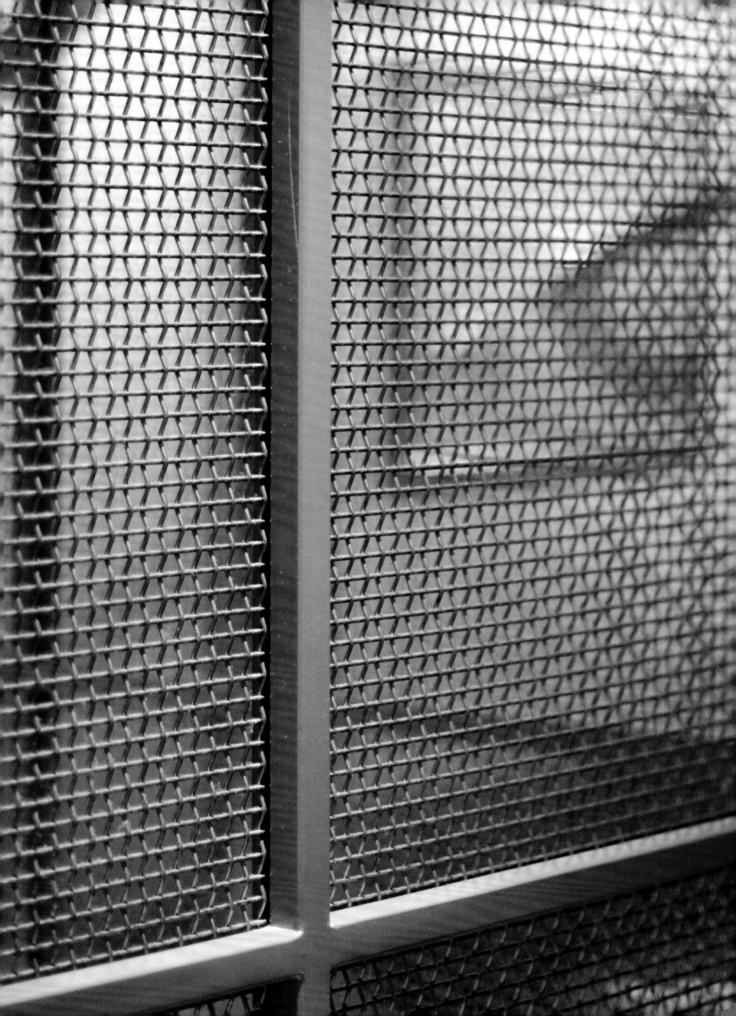

SOUPS

CUCUMBER & GRAPE SOUP, SMOKED STURGEON SKEWERS

Serves 6

A chilled cucumber soup with a little creaminess is great in summertime. It's so nice and fresh, this one especially because of the added sweetness of the grapes. The trick is to make sure it's not *too* sweet. You need to combat the sweetness of the grape with some good acidity; in this case lemon juice works well.

INGREDIENTS

6 English cucumbers, deseeded, cut in 6mm (¼ in) dice (reserve 12 pieces for garnish)

4 scallions, white and pale-green parts only, coarsely sliced

4 sprigs dill

500g (3½ cups) green grapes, coarsely chopped

½ lemon, juice

9g (1 Tbsp) salt

Pepper

250mL (1 cup) Greek yogurt

45mL (3 Tbsp) olive oil

6 red grapes, halved

100g (6 slices) smoked sturgeon, halved

Combine the cucumbers, scallions, dill, green grapes, lemon juice, salt, and a few cracks of pepper in a large bowl. Refrigerate for at least 30 minutes, and up to a few hours, mixing halfway through.

Transfer to a blender. Add the yogurt and olive oil and purée until well combined. Strain through a fine mesh sieve. Refrigerate again.

Slide 2 red grape halves, 2 pieces of cucumber and 2 slices of smoked sturgeon onto each of 6 small metal or bamboo skewers.

Whisk the soup before serving. Divide into small bowls or cups and garnish with the skewers. Refrigerate for up to 2 days.

TOMATO GAZPACHO, DUNGENESS CRAB & AVOCADO TIAN

Serves 6

This is based on the gazpacho I made at the Square. It's very special to me because I wooed Annabel with this soup. She'd be on break at L'Escargot and walk up to Mayfair from Soho. I'd cut out of the back door of the Square with a cup of her favourite summer soup. And we'd meet right there in Berkeley Square, where she'd sip my gazpacho while we caught up. Then we'd each head back to work.

INGREDIENTS

Red Wine Vinegar Gastrique

25g (2 Tbsp) sugar

25mL (scant 2 Tbsp) water

50mL (3 Tbsp) red wine vinegar

Gazpacho

6 very ripe Roma or vine tomatoes

½ red bell pepper, deseeded

½ cucumber, peeled and deseeded

¼ red onion

150g (1 cup) cherry tomatoes, halved

2 cloves garlic, crushed

¼ bunch cilantro, coarsely chopped

¼ small jalapeno, coarsely chopped

500mL (2 cups) tomato juice

75mL (5 Tbsp) olive oil

Salt

Hot sauce

Dungeness Crab & Avocado Tian

½ red bell pepper, deseeded

1 recipe Tomato Concassé (page 312)

2 avocados

1 lemon, juice

Salt

2 Dungeness crabs (450g/1 lb each) (cooked according to the method on page 23) or 300g (10½ oz) picked Dungeness crab meat

20g (½ cup) chopped chives

50g (3 Tbsp) Japanese mayonnaise (this is sweeter than regular, but regular is fine)

Serve

Olive oil, for drizzling

6 sprigs chervil

RED WINE VINEGAR GASTRIQUE

Heat the sugar and water in a small saucepan with high sides over medium-low heat until the water has fully evaporated and the sugar becomes caramel with a noticeably golden to dark shade of brown, about 5 minutes. Very carefully add the red wine vinegar—it will bubble up—swirling the pan a few times, until the reduction has thickened to the consistency of thin maple syrup, 3 to 5 minutes.

Continued . . .

GAZPACHO
Cut the tomatoes, red pepper, cucumber, and onion into 2.5cm (1 in) cubes. Place in a large bowl or container and add the cherry tomatoes, garlic, cilantro, jalapeno, tomato juice, olive oil, and gastrique. Season with salt and toss to combine. Refrigerate overnight to fully develop the flavour of the soup.

Purée in a blender until smooth and strain through a fine-mesh sieve. Season to taste and add hot sauce if you like a little heat. Refrigerate.

DUNGENESS CRAB & AVOCADO TIAN
Using an open flame, or barbecue, char the outside of the red pepper until the skin starts to blister and turn black. Place in a stainless-steel bowl and cover with plastic wrap. Let sit for 5 to 10 minutes, to allow the pepper to steam. This will make it easier to peel the skin off. Remove and discard the peel from the pepper, running it under cold water to help as needed. Dice the pepper and combine with the tomato concassé.

Slice the avocados in half lengthwise, and remove the pits. Scoop out the flesh and combine with the lemon juice and salt. Using a fork, gently mash the avocados to the texture of a chunky guacamole.

Mix the crab meat with the chives and mayonnaise. Season to taste.

Create the tians: Place six 5cm (2 in) ring moulds in the centre of 6 serving bowls. Divide the avocado between the moulds and pack tightly. Top with the crab, then the red pepper and tomato mix.

SERVE
Remove the ring moulds and pour the gazpacho around the tian. Drizzle with a good-quality olive oil, and garnish each bowl with a sprig of chervil.

ROASTED TOMATO SOUP

Serves 6

For the opening of Bel Café we wanted to do some menu items that absolutely everybody would like: from travellers staying in the hotel to locals working at a desk nearby. Something that's light and fresh, rich but vegetarian—vegan even. It had to be tomato soup. This is just a simple purée, but it works. It's been on the café menu since day one.

INGREDIENTS

20 Roma tomatoes, halved

Olive oil, for drizzling

30g (2½ Tbsp) sugar

Salt

30mL (2 Tbsp) vegetable oil

1 small onion, diced

3 cloves garlic, sliced

1 stalk celery, diced

1 carrot, diced

½ fennel bulb, diced

½ Thai chili, deseeded

30g (2 Tbsp) tomato paste

30mL (2 Tbsp) balsamic vinegar

¼ bunch basil

¼ bunch parsley

Pepper

Preheat the oven to 200°C (400°F).

Season the tomatoes with a drizzle of olive oil, the sugar, and a generous sprinkling of salt. Roast on a baking tray lined with parchment paper until the skins burst open and a little colour has developed, about 15 minutes.

Heat the vegetable oil in a large pot over medium heat, and sweat the onion and garlic until translucent, about 5 minutes. Add the celery, carrot, fennel, and chili and increase the heat. Sauté until the vegetables have a bit of colour, about 5 minutes.

Add the tomato paste and continue to cook, stirring continuously, until the paste has caramelized, about 5 minutes. Season with salt. Add the roasted tomatoes. Add just enough water to cover and an extra pinch of sugar and salt. Bring to a boil then lower the heat and simmer until all the vegetables are very soft, about 30 minutes.

Add the balsamic vinegar and herbs and let steep for 5 minutes. Blend in batches in a high-speed blender until smooth. Season with salt.

Enjoy with a drizzle of good-quality olive oil and cracked black pepper.

SUNCHOKE VELOUTÉ, BLACK TRUFFLE & MUSHROOM CROSTINI

Serves 6 We used to cook a lot of sunchokes at Le Manoir, where we would often turn them into gâteaux de topinambours, a custard or royale. They are very knobby. Dirt always clings to them. So they're a nuisance to scrub and peel—but they're worth it. Their flavour is so rich, with an earthy sweetness. Sunchokes and truffles go hand in hand. So do truffles and wild mushrooms. All three together make an irresistible combination.

NOTE *This soup also works well with cauliflower in place of the sunchokes. If preferred, you can use truffle oil in place of the fresh truffles—look for a quality oil infused with genuine truffle and not the more common artificial flavouring. For a vegetarian version of the soup, use vegetable stock instead of chicken stock.*

INGREDIENTS

Velouté

1kg (2¼ lb) sunchokes

Lemon, for acidifying water

30mL (2 Tbsp) vegetable oil

1 small onion, diced

1 leek, white part only, sliced into rings

2 cloves garlic, sliced

Salt

30g (2 Tbsp) butter

750mL (3 cups) chicken stock

500mL (2 cups) milk

250mL (1 cup) cream

Freshly grated black truffle, or a drizzle good-quality white truffle oil, for garnish

Sunchoke Chips

2 sunchokes

500mL (2 cups) canola oil

Salt

Crostini

6 long, thin slices baguette

15mL (1 Tbsp) olive oil

Sea salt

10mL (2 tsp) vegetable oil

50g (1 cup) black trumpet mushrooms, halved

50g (1 cup) yellowfoot mushrooms

50g (1 cup) morel mushrooms, sliced in rings

½ small shallot, finely chopped

1 small clove garlic, finely chopped

15g (1 Tbsp) butter

Juice ¼ lemon

Microgreens, for garnish

VELOUTÉ Wash and peel the sunchokes (if they are very clean and young they may only need to be brushed) then slice very thinly using a knife or mandoline (about 3mm/⅛ in thick). Place in a bowl of water with a squeeze of lemon to keep them from browning.

Continued . . .

Heat the vegetable oil in a heavy-bottomed pot, over medium heat. Add the onion, leek, and garlic and season with salt. Sweat until translucent but no colour has formed, about 3 minutes. Add the butter and continue to cook over low heat, 5 to 7 minutes.

Add the chicken stock and milk and bring to a boil. Add the sunchokes, reduce the heat, and simmer until they are tender but not mushy, about 20 minutes. Add the cream and bring back to a boil.

Blend in batches on high speed using just enough of the cooking liquid to maintain a soup consistency. Strain through a fine-mesh sieve.

SUNCHOKE CHIPS

Wash and brush the sunchokes. Using a mandoline, slice them paper thin.

Heat the oil to 150°C (300°F) in a pot large enough that it is not more than half full. Fry the sunchoke slices until they are golden brown. Transfer to paper towel to soak up excess oil. Sprinkle with salt.

CROSTINI

Preheat the oven to 190°C (375°F).

Lay the baguette slices on a baking tray. Brush with olive oil and season with salt, then toast in the oven until golden brown—this happens fast so keep an eye on them.

Heat the vegetable oil in a large skillet over high heat. Sauté all the mushrooms until shrunken and just golden at the edges, about 3 minutes. Add the shallots, garlic, and butter and heat until foamy, stirring from time to time. Stir in the lemon juice. Transfer to paper towel to soak up excess oil.

Divide the mushrooms between the crostini and season with salt. Garnish with sunchoke chips and microgreens.

SERVE

Bring the soup to a boil, whisking quickly. Serve garnished with freshly grated black truffle or a drizzle of white truffle oil, and the black truffle and mushroom crostini alongside.

ENGLISH PEA SOUP, LOBSTER, CRÈME FRAÎCHE

Serves 4
(photo on page ii)

English peas are so sweet, especially when you peel them: the difference is night and day. Although this is really just a basic pea soup, you chill the vegetables and stock before you blend them, which means the soup is bright green and tastes fresher. You need to keep your temperature low to maintain that. Adding lobster just works: peas and lobster go hand in hand.

NOTE

Peeling the outer skin from each individual pea is a great way to salvage older peas: it rids them of their woody notes. If you can't find quality fresh English peas, use frozen ones. If you don't like cooking live lobster, buy one that's pre-cooked, or substitute Dungeness crab. Even unadorned, without crustacean, this is a lovely pea soup. Substitute vegetable stock for the chicken stock if you want a vegetarian version.

INGREDIENTS

Lobster
1 lobster (about 900g/2 lb)

English Pea Soup
400g (2¾ cups) freshly peeled English
    peas
100g (3⅓ cups) spinach
50g (2½ cups) mint
45mL (3 Tbsp) olive oil
2 small shallots, sliced
1 clove garlic, sliced
1L (4 cups) chicken stock
Salt

Serve
Yuzu juice, to taste
20g (4 tsp) crème fraîche
Pepper
Chives, for garnish
½ recipe Anchovy Breadcrumbs
    (page 309), minus the anchovy
4 sprigs pea shoots, for garnish

LOBSTER

Bring a large pot of heavily salted water to a rapid boil. Add the live lobster (it should be fully submerged) then turn down the heat and simmer for 5 minutes. Remove and dunk in an ice bath until chilled. When cool, crack open the lobster and remove the meat from the shell. Cut into spoon-sized pieces and refrigerate.

Continued . . .

ENGLISH PEA SOUP

Bring a large pot of heavily salted water to a boil. Add the peas, spinach, and mint and blanch for 60 seconds, then strain. Submerge the strainer in an ice bath to shock the peas, spinach, and mint—this helps maintain the green colour and stops the cooking process. Set aside a handful of peas for garnish.

In a separate pot, heat the olive oil over medium heat. Sauté the shallots and garlic until translucent. Add the stock and simmer for 10 minutes. Remove from the heat and chill the stock completely.

Remove the peas, spinach, and mint from the ice water and squeeze out any residual water.

Once the stock is cool, blend with the peas, spinach, and mint in a blender until smooth. Strain with a fine-mesh sieve. Add water as needed to adjust the consistency. Season with salt.

SERVE

Preheat the oven to 150°C (300°F). Place the lobster on a baking sheet lined with parchment paper and heat through for a few minutes.

Slowly reheat the soup until it comes to a bare simmer and adjust the seasoning at the last second with yuzu juice, to taste.

Season the crème fraîche with pepper.

Artfully arrange the lobster in 4 soup bowls with fresh chives, breadcrumbs, pea shoots, and the reserved blanched peas. Top with a quenelle of crème fraîche. Pour the soup around the lobster; you can do this tableside to wow your guests.

BLUE HUBBARD SQUASH SOUP

Serves 6

We get young blue Hubbard squash from Zaklan Heritage Farm and they are very sweet, like pumpkin, and make such a creamy, texturally amazing, delicious soup. Your key to success here is a really powerful blender, like a Vitamix, and to never worry about overcooking your squash—because that only improves things.

INGREDIENTS

2kg (2 medium) Hubbard squash

Olive oil

Salt

110g (scant ½ cup) butter

1 onion, diced

125g (1¼ cups) roughly diced fennel bulb

3 cloves garlic, coarsely chopped

25g (3 Tbsp) salt

750mL (3 cups) water

500mL (2 cups) heavy cream

500mL (2 cups) milk

55g (⅓ cup) pumpkin seeds, toasted, for garnish

Preheat the oven to 150°C (300°F).

Cut the squash in half and discard the seeds. Drizzle the squash with olive oil and season with salt. Lay on a baking tray lined with parchment paper and roast until tender, at least 35 minutes. Remove from the oven and scoop the squash pulp out of the skin.

Make a brown butter by melting the butter in a heavy-bottomed pot over medium heat—use a pot with a light-coloured bottom so you can keep track of the colour. Swirl the pot occasionally and whisk the butter to be sure it is cooking evenly. As the butter melts, it will begin to foam, and the colour will progress from lemony-yellow to golden-tan to, finally, toasty brown. Once you smell a nutty aroma, take the pot off the heat and transfer into a heatproof bowl to cool.

In a large, heavy-bottomed pot, sweat the onions, fennel, and garlic in the brown butter until soft. Add the water, cream, and milk and bring to a boil. Add the squash pulp and stir to combine. Remove from the heat.

Transfer the mixture to a blender and purée in batches until smooth, using just enough of the cooking liquid to maintain a soup consistency. Strain through a fine-mesh sieve.

Serve with a drizzle of olive oil and a sprinkle of toasted pumpkin seeds.

PROVENÇALE FISH SOUP, GRILLED FOCACCIA, ROASTED RED PEPPER & SAFFRON ROUILLE

Serves 6

Marco had a fish soup like this on the menu when I started at Canteen. I had one taste and I was like . . . f-u-c-k. It was a revelation to me. In London, we could order fish soup mix from the fish supplier, and they'd deliver bags of super-fresh red mullet and all the other little fish that were perfect for a Provençal-style fish soup. This is my version from my time at West, using local rockfish and flatfish bones for the base, finished with more BC fish and shellfish, like halibut, Manila clams, and spot prawns, all cooked à la minute.

NOTE

Always make sure to choose very fresh clams and "purge" them to get rid of all possible sand: flush them in ice-cold salted water (35g/2 Tbsp salt per 1L/4 cups), changing the solution two or three times during the process.

This focaccia recipe makes a whole sheet pan. Store in an airtight container for up to four days or wrapped in the freezer for up to one month.

INGREDIENTS

Focaccia

1.45kg (11 cups) bread flour

28g (3 Tbsp) salt

15g (1 Tbsp) sugar

1L (4 cups) water

110mL (7 Tbsp) olive oil, plus more for drizzling

80g (½ cup plus 2 Tbsp) fresh yeast or 40g (¼ cup) active dry yeast

Sea salt

Rosemary, chopped, for garnish

Fish Base

2kg (4½ lb) bones from white fish such as ling cod, halibut, or rockfish

250mL (1 cup) Pernod

250mL (1 cup) white wine

100mL (scant 7 Tbsp) olive oil

65g (¼ cup) tomato paste

1 carrot, cut in large cubes

1 onion, cut in large cubes

2 stalks celery, cut in large cubes

6 Roma tomatoes, cut in large cubes

½ fennel bulb, sliced

4 cloves garlic, sliced

½ jalapeno, sliced

1 sprig thyme

3 bay leaves

3g (1 tsp) coriander seeds

3g (1 tsp) fennel seeds

3g (1 tsp) peppercorns

3g (1 tsp) ground star anise

Pinch saffron

Pinch cayenne

Fish Soup

100mL (scant 7 Tbsp) canola oil

45g (3 Tbsp) butter

30g (2 Tbsp) tomato paste

2L (8 cups) Fish Stock (page 316 or store-bought) or water

Continued . . .

Saffron Rouille

½ red bell pepper

6 basil leaves

2 cloves garlic, roughly chopped

1 egg yolk

15g (1 Tbsp) Dijon mustard

10mL (scant Tbsp) white wine vinegar

Pinch saffron

75mL (5 Tbsp) canola oil

75mL (5 Tbsp) olive oil

Pinch xanthan gum

Salt

Tabasco or other hot sauce

Fish and Shellfish

25mL (scant 2 Tbsp) canola oil

6 halibut portions, 60g (2 oz) each

Salt

Pepper

5g (1 tsp) butter

12 large spot prawns, heads on

450g (1 lb) (20–25) mussels (we get ours from Salt Spring Island)

450g (1 lb) (20–30) Manila clams (see note above)

Serve

Olive oil, for drizzling

FOCACCIA Place the flour, salt, and sugar in the bowl of a stand mixer and mix to combine. In a separate bowl, mix the water, olive oil, and yeast using an immersion blender.

Pour the wet ingredients into the dry ingredients. Using the dough hook attachment, mix the dough. Start on low speed until combined, then increase to medium for about 8 minutes until smooth and elastic. You should be able to stretch a windowpane in the dough: To test, cut off a small piece and hold it between your thumb and first two fingers. Gently spread your fingers and thumbs apart to stretch the dough until thin and translucent (a windowpane). If you can stretch without breaking the dough, the gluten is well developed and the dough ready to rise. If not, mix for another 2 minutes and try the windowpane test again.

Once ready, remove the dough from the bowl and wrap with plastic wrap. Let rise for 30 minutes at room temperature, or until doubled in size. Coat a 32 × 44.5cm (12½ × 17½ in) baking tray with non-stick cooking spray. Line the tray with parchment paper, and spray again with cooking spray. Carefully spread the dough evenly out on the tray, trying to not deflate it too much, and poke dents in the top with your fingers. Drizzle with olive oil and sprinkle with sea salt and chopped rosemary.

Preheat the oven to 175°C (350°F).

Bake for 30 minutes. Reduce the heat to 165°C (325°F) and bake until golden brown all over, another 30 to 45 minutes. Transfer to a wire rack to cool.

FISH BASE Using a meat cleaver, cut the fish bones into 5–7.5cm (2–3 in) pieces. Combine all the ingredients in a large container and marinate in the fridge overnight.

The next day, drain the fish bones and vegetables, reserving the liquid, then separate the fish bones from the vegetables.

FISH SOUP   In a rondeau (or sauté pan or Dutch oven) with high sides over high heat, heat half of the canola oil with the butter until foamy. Sear the fish bones without stirring too much so that the bones get caramelized and cook until light brown. Set aside.

Using the same rondeau, heat the remaining oil and sweat the vegetables until soft and light in colour. Add the fish bones back, and the tomato paste, and stir to combine.

Deglaze the pot with the reserved liquids. Simmer until the liquid has reduced to a thin glaze and almost evaporated. Add the fish stock, just enough to barely cover the bones. Reduce the heat to a slow simmer and cook for 1 hour.

Work in batches using a high-speed blender or Vitamix to purée half the soup solids with half the liquids for 1 minute. Strain through a fine-mesh sieve. Separately strain the other half of the liquid and set aside. Discard the remaining solids.

Combine the purée and the strained liquid and cook over low heat until reduced to a thick soup. Strain through a fine-mesh sieve. Season to taste.

SAFFRON ROUILLE   Using an open flame, or barbecue, char the outside of the red pepper until the skin starts to blister and turn black. Place in a stainless-steel bowl and cover with plastic wrap. Let sit for 5 to 10 minutes, to allow the pepper to steam. This will make it easier to peel the skin off. Remove and discard the peel from the pepper, running under cold water to help as needed. Cut the pepper in half and discard the seeds and pith. Pat it dry with paper towel until completely dry, then cut into large chunks.

Use a food processor or immersion blender to blend the pepper, basil, garlic, egg yolk, Dijon mustard, vinegar, and saffron until smooth. With the machine running, pour in the oils in a slow thin stream to emulsify like a mayonnaise. Add the xanthan gum, and blend for another 30 seconds. Pass through a fine-mesh sieve and season to taste with salt and Tabasco.

FISH AND SHELLFISH   Heat the canola oil in a large non-stick pan over medium heat. Season the halibut with salt and pepper and sear for 3 minutes. Flip, add the butter, and cook for an additional 1 minute. Transfer to paper towel to absorb excess oil.

Bring the fish soup to a boil and drop in the prawns, mussels, and clams. Cook until the shellfish are fully open, 2 to 5 minutes, and discard any that remain closed.

SERVE   Slice the focaccia and grill 6 slices in a grill pan or on a barbecue over high heat until char marks appear, about 1 minute per side.

Divide the soup, fish and shellfish between 6 shallow serving bowls, and drizzle with a good-quality olive oil. Serve with grilled focaccia, smeared with saffron rouille.

MANILA CLAM CHOWDER, SMOKED SABLEFISH

Serves 6

Sablefish is very fatty and rich. Smoke it and it becomes extremely rich. So you don't want to eat more than a couple of small pieces. In the winter at West, we'd make a beautiful chowder with cherrystone clams. When you add a couple of small pieces of that smoked sablefish, it puts the chowder right over the edge.

INGREDIENTS

Chowder Base

25mL (scant 2 Tbsp) canola oil

300g (6 cups) button mushrooms, roughly sliced

5 small shallots, roughly sliced

2 cloves garlic, sliced

1 sprig thyme

500mL (2 cups) white wine

500mL (2 cups) Noilly Prat (dry vermouth)

2L (8 cups) Fish Stock (page 316 or store-bought)

500mL (2 cups) cream

1 lemon, juice

Salt

Clam Chowder

120g (1 cup) peeled and diced Yukon Gold potatoes

120g (1 cup) diced carrots

60g (½ cup) shelled and peeled fava beans

100g (⅔ cup) corn kernels

100g (½ cup) bacon lardons, chopped into 2 × 0.5cm (¾ × ¼ in) pieces

20 Manila clams (see Note on page 112)

400g (14 oz) smoked sablefish, in 30g (1 oz) portions

15g (¼ cup) sea asparagus

1 recipe Tomato Concassé (page 312)

Serve

15g (⅓ cup) chopped chives

Olive oil, for drizzling

CHOWDER BASE

Heat the oil in a rondeau pan (or sauté pan or Dutch oven) over medium heat, and sweat the mushrooms, shallots, garlic, and thyme until translucent with very little to no colour, 4 to 5 minutes.

Add the wine and vermouth and reduce until all the liquid has evaporated. Add the fish stock and reduce again by half. Add the cream, bring to a boil, then lower the heat to a medium simmer. Allow to reduce for 20 more minutes. Strain through a fine-mesh sieve. Add the lemon juice and season to taste with salt.

CLAM CHOWDER

Bring 2 small pots of salted water to a boil. Cook the potatoes in 1 pot just until tender, 3 to 5 minutes. Cook the carrots in the other just until tender, about 5 minutes. Drain. Blanch the fava beans and corn kernels for 1 minute then dunk in an ice bath.

In a medium sauté pan over medium heat, fry the bacon lardons until crispy, stirring occasionally, about 3 minutes. Transfer to paper towel to soak up excess oil.

Bring the chowder base to a boil in a rondeau (or sauté pan or Dutch oven). Add the clams and sablefish but do not overcrowd; cook in 2 batches if necessary. Simmer over medium heat for 3 minutes. Discard any clams that remain closed.

Add the potatoes, carrots, sea asparagus, fava beans, corn, and bacon, and slowly simmer for another minute, then add the tomato concassé.

SERVE   Divide the chowder between 6 bowls and garnish with chives and a drizzle of olive oil.

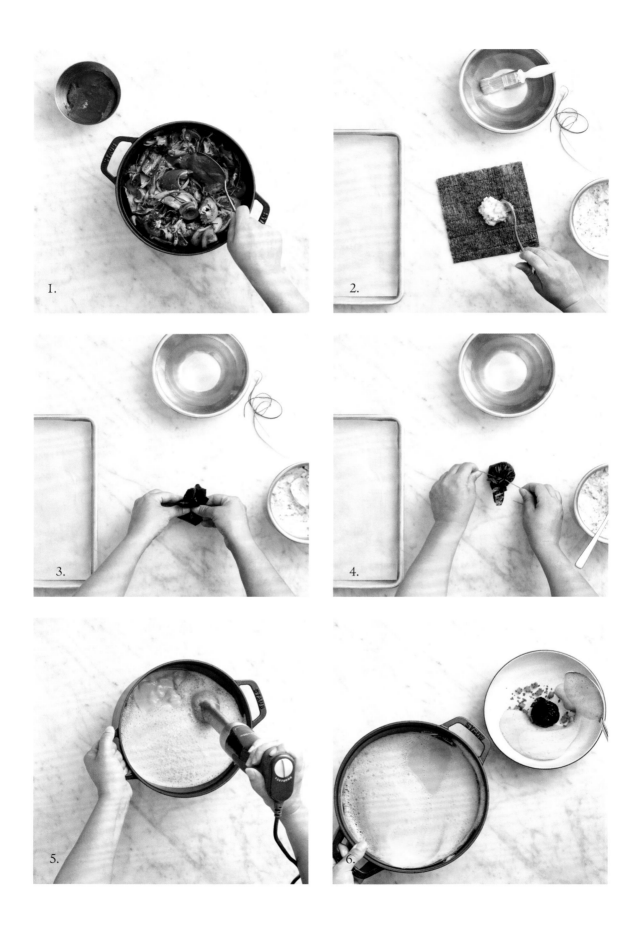

LOBSTER BISQUE, NORI BEGGAR'S PURSE

Serves 6

Crisp nori-wrapped beggar's purses filled with scallop mousse, scallop, and chunks of lobster add an extra element of taste and texture to this classic soup. The bisque itself is straightforward. Keep the flavours bright by cooking it quickly and efficiently and not letting it stew—just like with all fish and shellfish soups.

NOTE

For this recipe, you are going to cut up the lobster before cooking. It's not necessary, but if you want, you can kill the lobster first by driving a knife into the centre of its head and pushing down to split the head open.

Both the bisque and scallop mousse can be made a day ahead and stored in the fridge. If you decide to make it all the same day, make the bisque first, as the nori beggar's purses can't sit for very long or they get soggy.

INGREDIENTS

Lobsters

2 lobsters (450g/1 lb each)

Scallop Mousse

140g (5 oz) (about 4 large)
    U-15 scallops, cut in large chunks

1 egg white

Pinch salt

Pinch cayenne

75mL (5 Tbsp) cream

Lobster Bisque

30mL (2 Tbsp) canola oil

60g (¼ cup) butter

1 small onion, sliced

2 carrots, sliced

3 stalks celery, sliced

½ bulb fennel, sliced

3 cloves garlic

1 leek, white part only, sliced

1 bunch fresh tarragon

1 orange, peel only

4g (1 tsp) peppercorns

2g (½ tsp) fennel seeds

2 pods star anise

2 bay leaves

Pinch cayenne

480g (2 cups) canned San Marzano
    tomatoes

225g (¾ cup) tomato paste

150mL (⅔ cup) dry vermouth

150mL (⅔ cup) white wine

100mL (7 Tbsp) brandy such as
    Armagnac

1½L (6 cups) Fish Stock (page 316)

1¼L (5 cups) water

250mL (1 cup) cream

Lemon juice, to taste

Salt, to taste

Dash brandy, to taste

Nori Beggar's Purse

60g (2 oz) (about 2) large
    U-15 scallops, in small dice

10g (¼ cup) chopped chives

1 lemon, zest

½ lemon, juice

6 chives

6 sheets nori seaweed, in 16.5cm
    (6½ in) squares

2L (8 cups) canola oil

Serve

Chives, for garnish

1 recipe Tomato Concassé (page 312),
    for garnish

Continued . . .

LOBSTERS

Grab the tail and the upper carapace of the lobster firmly in your hands. Twist off the tail and set aside. Then twist off the claws below the first knuckles and set aside.

Remove the gills from the lobster heads and discard. Using a rolling pin or a mallet, crush the shells from the heads and bodies into about 2.5cm (1 in) pieces and set aside.

Bring a large pot of heavily salted water to a boil, submerge the lobster tails and claws, and immediately remove from the heat. Allow to sit for 10 minutes. Remove the lobster from the pot and allow to cool. Remove the meat from the shells and cut into small dice. Set aside.

SCALLOP
MOUSSE

Pulse the scallops in a food processor until smooth. Add the egg white, salt, and cayenne and mix briefly. Add the cream and blend until smooth and silky, about 20 seconds. Transfer to a stainless-steel bowl and cool immediately over an ice bath.

LOBSTER
BISQUE

Heat the canola oil in a heavy-bottomed pot to smoking point. Carefully add the broken lobster shells and sear over high heat for 4 to 5 minutes, stirring occasionally with a wooden spoon to scrape up any lobster meat residue on the bottom. Remove the shells and set aside.

Using the same pot, lower the heat to medium and add the butter. When melted and foaming, add the onion, carrots, celery, fennel bulb, garlic, leek, tarragon, orange peel, peppercorns, fennel seeds, star anise, bay leaves, and cayenne, and sauté until the onions are translucent, about 5 minutes.

Add the tomatoes and tomato paste (1). Cook for 1 minute, coating the vegetables with the tomato paste, then add the shells back to the pot.

Deglaze the pot with the vermouth, white wine, and brandy, and reduce until all the liquids have evaporated.

Add the Fish Stock and water. Bring the mixture to a boil, then reduce the heat to low. Simmer slowly for an hour, skimming off any scum that appears on the surface.

Transfer ⅓ of the solids (including the shells) and some of the liquid to a Vitamix or high-speed blender and carefully blend on high speed—hold the blender container with both hands and cover the lid with a dry towel. Pass through a fine-mesh sieve. Pass the rest of the liquid, without blending, through the same fine-mesh sieve, pressing the shells and vegetables with a ladle for maximum extraction.

Return the liquid to the stove and simmer over low heat. Allow to reduce for 30 more minutes, skimming as needed. Pass through a fine-mesh sieve one more time.

Stir in the cream, lemon juice, salt, and another dash of brandy to taste.

NORI
BEGGAR'S
PURSE

While the bisque is reducing, gently fold half the diced lobster, and the diced scallops, chopped chives, lemon zest, and lemon juice into the scallop mousse. Keep the bowl on the ice bath to keep cool.

Quickly dip the whole chives into boiling water to soften them.

Using a pastry brush, very lightly wet the nori sheets with water, so just pliable.

Place 40g (¼ cup) of the scallop and lobster filling in the centre of each nori square (2) and fold the edges up to form a beggar's purse (3). Tie together with a piece of softened chive (4). Set aside on a baking tray lined with parchment paper.

Heat the canola oil to 175°C (350°F) in a pot large enough that it is not more than half full. Drop the nori beggar's purses into the oil 3 at a time and cook for 2 minutes. Transfer to paper towel to absorb excess oil. Season with salt.

SERVE   Preheat the oven to 150°C (300°F). Lay the remaining lobster pieces on a baking tray lined with parchment paper and warm them in the oven for a couple of minutes.

Meanwhile, slowly bring the bisque to a boil. Once boiling, use an immersion blender to gently foam the bisque (5).

Place a beggar's purse in the middle of each of 6 serving bowls. Divide the warm lobster pieces between the bowls. Garnish with chopped chives and a little tomato concassé. Ladle the bisque carefully into each bowl (6).

UK: PART 3

I had an idea of the type of chef I wanted to be when I reached 40, and I still had a lot to learn to get there. For as long as I could stay and work in the UK, I wanted to be a sponge and learn as much as I could from anyone who had something to teach me. I heard Phil Howard was looking for chefs for his Mayfair restaurant the Square. So I took a job there as a junior sous-chef. I wanted to start near the bottom again. Every time I walked into a new kitchen, I'd look around and say to myself, "Okay, who is the best in here? Who's laying it down? Who is super-organized and clean and has his mise-en-place always done and is getting no aggravation from the chef? Who is that, and what makes them so good?" And then I would try and emulate what they did, how they ran, what made them so skilled and organized.

I had the pleasure of working with Phil directly for four months. He was such a gent, a real breath of fresh air. Smart, personable, well-spoken, and—maybe most important after what I'd been through—a really nice person. Above all else, he was a very unorthodox and original chef. He didn't follow tradition if he didn't have to. Phil liked to do things his way, and I found that refreshing. There was a lamb dish he used to make, a classic. He took a saddle, boned it, then put the meat down flat on its fatty back. Then he'd take off the belly flaps—the trim—and one of the tenderloins, turn that into a lamb mousse to fill in the gap where the bone used to join the two loins, and set one of the tenderloins down the middle. He'd drape a parsley crust on top of the perfect arch—and we'd roast it whole and slice each saddle into inch-thick portions. Each portion showed three textures of lamb dressed up with a perfect array of Mediterranean flavours: dried tomatoes, artichokes, and shallot purée. Great flavours, great technique; Phil really was an inspiration.

Next, I wanted to work for Bruno Loubet, the great French chef who—fresh from the success of L'Odeon in London—had collaborated with the restaurateur Oliver Peyton on the massively successful Atlantic Bar and Grill. The two were now launching something new in Knightsbridge called Isola, a Manhattan-inspired 250-seat Italian extravaganza spread over two floors of architectural dazzle. Looking back, there were warning signs. Some were skeptical that a chef from Bordeaux was the right choice for hard-core Italian. The cultural messaging was further muddled on the floor, where the 50 great Italian waiters that Peyton had in mind could not be found in London, so we had settled instead for waitstaff who *looked* sort of Italian.

We got hammered right out of the gate. Picture it. The place was running two restaurant concepts. The more upscale Isola proper was upstairs. And I was downstairs, in the more casual Osteria d'Isola. It was all so haphazard, it was ridiculous. One restaurant, two menus, 64 different wines by the glass, and 50 waiters with no grasp of Italian. We went through four restaurant managers in our first two weeks. I was working 16-hour days seven days a week. In the run-up to Christmas, I had worked for two months straight. Finally, we reached Christmas Eve, our last shift of the year before going on a desperately needed break. After lunch service was done, someone suggested we head out the back door and down the laneway to the neighbouring pub for a quick one before the final service. I was thinking this was not a good idea. But off we went. I ordered a Beck's, had a swig, and looked down the bar to see that my sous-chef already had two empty pint glasses in front of him and was getting into the whiskey. For sure, he had lost his mind. We'd had no sleep for so long. What was he thinking?

Dinner service came up quickly, and it was raging in the Osteria. Now, we had this beautiful branzino dish on the menu that was a lot of work: you boned the fish but kept it intact, stuffed it with a *panzanella* salad, tied it back together again, and roasted it whole in the wood-burning oven. Of course it was popular, and soon that night we had seven of them on order at the same time. I was trying to run the pass. My sous was wobbling around in front of the wood-burning oven, and I was thinking, "How about those sea bass? What is going on over there?" When I looked over again, more closely, I saw that he was trying to chop basil with the blunt edge of a spatula in place of a knife. Next, as I watched, he slowly slumped forward onto the counter and passed out. I rushed over to have a look inside the oven. The seven branzinos that should have been on tables by then were all there. And they were on fire. Like, in flames. No other branzino were prepped and ready to go. You do not recover from that. It's just over. I grabbed him by the scruff of the neck and threw him out.

And I quit. At this point I required some normality. I needed rest. I wanted to reset and refresh. I needed to go home. H

PASTA & PIZZA

MUSHROOM & TRUFFLE RISOTTO

Serves 6

With risotto, you first have to find the right rice to work with. At the restaurant we use Acquerello, the very best aged Italian Carnaroli rice. You start with onion and olive oil, and you sweat, not sauté—you want no colour. Then you add the rice and wine, and start working that starch until you get it all nice and creamy. The key to it all—what Marco had going at the Canteen—is to finish with acidulated butter, basically a beurre blanc with heavy acid. Then, your secret weapon is some lightly whipped cream, which you stir in at the very end. It puts this dish over the edge.

NOTE

Arborio: *The most widely available risotto rice, the grain is typically wider and longer than Carnaroli. It's not as starchy, and it absorbs liquid a little less well. It is available in most supermarkets.*

Carnaroli: *Variously hailed as the "king" or the "caviar" of Italian rices, Carnaroli is the preferred risotto rice in most regions of Italy. It's said to produce the creamiest risotto, yet it's also more resistant to overcooking than Arborio. It is available in specialty shops and some supermarkets.*

INGREDIENTS

Acidulated Butter

¼ small white onion, roughly sliced

80mL (⅓ cup) white wine

40mL (scant 3 Tbsp) white wine vinegar

1 sprig thyme

1 bay leaf

100g (7 Tbsp) butter, cold, diced

Risotto

60mL (4 Tbsp) olive oil

60g (¼ cup) butter

125g (2½ cups) chanterelle mushrooms, whole or halved depending on the size

125g (2½ cups) morel mushrooms, sliced in rings

75g (1½ cups) oyster mushrooms, cut in big pieces

1 package (150g) white shimeji mushrooms, stems removed

1.5–2L (6–8 cups) Chicken Stock (page 317 or store-bought)

1 medium onion, finely chopped

250g (1¼ cups) Carnaroli or Arborio rice (see Note above)

Pinch salt

125mL (½ cup) dry white wine

200g (2 cups) grated Parmesan

30mL (2 Tbsp) cream, lightly whipped

¼ lemon, juice

15g (⅓ cup) chopped chives

1 small fresh black truffle, very finely julienned, or a drizzle of good-quality white truffle oil

ACIDULATED BUTTER

Bring all the ingredients except the butter to a boil in a small pot over high heat. Reduce the heat, and simmer until most of the liquid has evaporated. You should be left with about 30mL (2 Tbsp) of liquid.

Continued . . .

Remove from the heat and vigorously whisk in the butter until fully incorporated, making sure the butter stays emulsified. Purée in a blender until smooth. Strain through a fine-mesh sieve and let cool (in the refrigerator or on the counter) until set.

RISOTTO   Heat 30mL (2 Tbsp) of the oil and 30g (2 Tbsp) of the butter in a large skillet or a cast-iron pan over medium to high heat. When the butter has melted and starts to foam, add all of the mushrooms (1). Depending on your pan, you may have to cook in batches. Cook and stir the mushrooms until lightly browned, about 5 minutes, adding a little more oil and/or butter if needed. Reduce the heat to medium and cook for an additional 3 minutes. Set aside.

Heat the stock to a simmer in a medium pot then lower the heat so it just stays hot.

Heat the remaining oil and butter in a large, heavy-bottomed pot over medium heat. When the butter has melted, add the onion and sweat for 2 minutes, until slightly translucent. Add the rice, and a pinch of salt, and stir with a wooden spoon so that the grains are coated with the oil and melted butter. This allows the rice to get a slightly nutty aroma. Deglaze the pot with the white wine and reduce until all the liquid has evaporated.

Add a ladle of the hot chicken stock to the rice (2) and stir until the liquid is fully absorbed (3). When the rice appears almost dry, add another ladleful of stock and repeat the process (4). It's important to stir constantly—especially while the stock gets absorbed, to prevent scorching—and to add the next ladleful as soon as the rice is almost dry.

Continue adding the stock, a ladle at a time, until the grains are tender but still firm to the bite, without being crunchy, about 20 minutes. If you run out of stock, you can finish the cooking with hot water, a ladle at a time.

Add the mushrooms (5), and stir in half the grated Parmesan (6), 75g (3 Tbsp) of the acidulated butter, and all of the lightly whipped cream, lemon juice, and chives. Season with salt if required.

Place a generous ladleful of risotto in each serving bowl. Garnish with the remaining grated Parmesan, and the truffle or a drizzle of good-quality white truffle oil.

1.

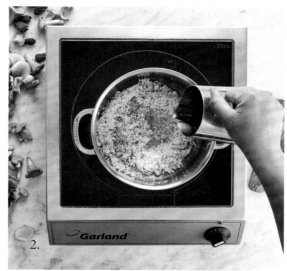

2.

3.

4.

5.

6.

ENGLISH PEA & BURRATA TORTELLINI, ARUGULA PESTO

Serves 6

(photo on page 213)

When you're making this dish, remember: frozen peas are your friend (they save you a lot of time, and you'll need it). For this recipe, you purée the peas with burrata, fior di latte, and ricotta. Then you make your pasta, roll it out, cut it into discs, and shape your tortellini. It's a fun way to entertain the family for a few hours.

NOTE

Be sure to get started on your tortellini well ahead. These tortellini freeze well and can be cooked from frozen.

INGREDIENTS

Tortellini Filling

575g (4 cups) English peas

60g (¼ cup) butter

1 small onion, diced

45g (½ cup) sliced scallions

4 cloves garlic, chopped

15g (1½ Tbsp) salt

25g (½ cup) chopped parsley leaves

125g (½ cup) ricotta cheese

¼ ball fresh burrata

½ lemon, zest

125g (¼ ball) fior di latte, shredded

Arugula Pesto

125mL (½ cup) olive oil

120g (6 cups) arugula

60g (3 cups) basil leaves

60g (½ cup) pine nuts, toasted

60g (½ cup plus 1 Tbsp) grated pecorino cheese

Tortellini

1 recipe Pasta Dough (page 309)

Cornmeal or flour, for dusting

Lemon Butter

110g (½ cup) butter

25mL (scant 2 Tbsp) water

1 lemon, juice

Serve

300g (2 cups) English peas, blanched

Pea shoots, for garnish

TORTELLINI FILLING

Bring a large pot of heavily salted water to a boil. Blanch the peas until bright green, about 1 minute. Dunk in an ice bath and transfer to a baking tray lined with paper towel to dry.

Melt the butter in a large skillet over medium heat. Cook the onion, scallions, garlic, and salt until softened but not caramelized, 10 to 15 minutes. Add the parsley at the very end and stir thoroughly to wilt. Transfer everything to a baking tray and refrigerate until very cold.

In a food processor, blend the ricotta, burrata, and lemon zest together until homogeneous. Scrape down the sides as necessary. Transfer to a bowl.

Mix the peas and the onion mixture together until incorporated. Transfer to a food processor and blend until it reaches a coarse texture. Transfer to a stainless-steel bowl. Add the shredded fior di latte and the ricotta mixture. Use a wooden spoon or spatula to stir and combine everything thoroughly. Transfer to piping bags.

ARUGULA PESTO

Combine all the ingredients in a food processor and purée until combined but still slightly chunky. Do this quickly so that it does not heat up. Keep at room temperature until ready to serve.

TORTELLINI

Cut the pasta sheets into rounds using a 7.5cm (3 in) round cutter, as close together as possible; you should get 40 to 50 rounds.

Pipe about 15mL (1 Tbsp) of filling in the middle of each round. Do not overfill or they will not seal properly and burst while cooking. Dip your finger in a bowl of water and run it around the edge of the round to moisten. Fold 1 side of the round over the filling to form a half moon, then pull the corners together to form a rounded bonnet shape. Press tightly to seal. Set aside on a baking sheet well-dusted with flour or cornmeal and cover with a loose piece of plastic wrap. Repeat with the remaining rounds of dough, rerolling the scraps as needed to cut out more pasta rounds.

Bring a large pot of heavily salted water to a boil. Lower the tortellini into the water in batches with a slotted spoon. Stir occasionally to prevent them sticking to the pot or each other. Cook until they have all bobbed to the surface, about 4 minutes. Taste one to check for doneness.

LEMON BUTTER

While the tortellini are cooking, prepare the lemon butter. In a large skillet, melt the butter with the water and whisk in the lemon juice to emulsify.

SERVE

Bring a large pot of heavily salted water to a boil. Blanch the peas until bright green, about 1 minute. Dunk in an ice bath.

Remove the tortellini from the water, and shake off as much excess water as possible. Transfer directly to the pan with the lemon butter and gently toss to coat. Add the peas and heat for 1 minute.

Spoon several dollops of arugula pesto onto a serving platter or 6 individual plates. Add the tortellini and peas on top, with more pesto as desired. Garnish with pea shoots.

CAVATELLI, FIDDLEHEADS, MORELS, PEAS & ASPARAGUS

Serves 6

Asparagus, mushrooms, and peas are a classic spring flavour combination. Their bright, sugary notes make a nice change from all the winter heaviness that came before.

INGREDIENTS

Cavatelli

500g (3⅔ cups) semolina

9g (1 Tbsp) salt

250mL (1 cup) water

Vegetables

6 medium green asparagus, cut in 2.5cm (1 in) pieces on the bias

200g (2 cups) fiddleheads

25mL (scant 2 Tbsp) canola oil

300g (6 cups) fresh morel mushrooms, in 5mm thick (¼ in) discs

30g (2 Tbsp) butter

1 shallot, finely chopped

2 cloves garlic, finely chopped

1 sprig thyme, stem removed

100g (⅔ cup) fresh English peas

200mL (¾ cup) Chicken Velouté (page 318)

Pinch salt

Serve

Pea shoots, for garnish

Parmesan shavings, for garnish (optional)

CAVATELLI

Place the semolina in the bowl of a stand mixer fitted with the hook attachment.

Bring the salt and the water to a rolling boil in a pot over high heat. Immediately transfer to the stand mixer and start the mixer on low speed. Mix for 10 minutes, checking the bowl occasionally to scrape down the sides if needed. Remove the dough and wrap with plastic wrap. Let rest at room temperature for 30 minutes minimum.

If you have a cavatelli machine, cut the dough into long strips and then feed them through the machine. Otherwise, form the dough into long logs about 6mm to 1.5cm (¼–½ in) in diameter. Cut each log into 6mm (¼ in) slices. If you have a gnocchi board, push each piece of dough away from you, down the board, using your thumb. The dough should curl over the board and look like a little canoe. Alternatively, smear the dough against a lightly floured work surface using your thumb to create a similar result.

Bring a large pot of heavily salted water to a rolling boil. Blanch the cavatelli for 6 minutes. Remove using a spider or slotted spoon and set aside.

VEGETABLES & SERVE

Bring a medium pot of water to a boil. Blanch the asparagus for 30 seconds, then blanch the fiddleheads for 30 seconds.

Heat the oil in a large skillet and cook the morels over high heat for 2 minutes. Add the butter, shallot, garlic, and thyme. Reduce the heat to medium. Add the cavatelli, asparagus, fiddleheads, and peas. Add the chicken velouté and continue cooking for 2 to 4 minutes, until the liquid reduces down to nicely coat the pasta. Season with salt. Split the pasta between 6 serving dishes. Garnish with pea shoots and Parmesan shavings, if using.

POTATO GNOCCHI, ROASTED TOMATO SAUCE, BURRATA, BASIL

Serves 6

When I was a teenager working at the Beach House restaurant in Stanley Park, I bought a book called *Italian Cooking*. It had no pictures. But it had a recipe for gnocchi with tomato sauce that was one of the very first things I ever made successfully at home. I made the sauce, rolled the gnocchi, boiled them, added some olive oil, and I thought, "This isn't just edible, it's delicious!" I still have that book.

NOTE

This recipe keeps the skin on the potatoes, as we do for a more rustic feel for our gnocchi at Nightingale.

INGREDIENTS

Gnocchi

2–3 medium Yukon Gold potatoes, unpeeled (you need 500g/17 oz cooked potato)

1 egg yolk

8g (1 Tbsp) salt

130g (scant 1 cup) flour

Olive oil, for drizzling

Sauce & Garnish

1 recipe Roasted Tomato Sauce (page 310)

25mL (scant 2 Tbsp) canola oil

15g (1 Tbsp) butter

1 ball fresh burrata, torn into 2.5cm (1 in) chunks

12 basil leaves

Pinch chili flakes

Olive oil

GNOCCHI

Preheat the oven to 175°C (350°F).

Stab the potatoes in a few places with a fork to allow the steam to escape when cooking. Place on a wire rack set on top of a baking tray and cook for 1 hour, then rotate the baking tray and also flip the potatoes. Cook until tender, up to another hour.

Once cooked, slice the potatoes in half and put them through a meat grinder. Weigh out 500g (17 oz) of potato flesh, then thoroughly incorporate the egg yolk and salt into this flesh. Cut the flour into the potatoes using a plastic bench scraper; do not overmix. Once the flour has been incorporated, form the dough into a ball.

Divide the dough into quarters. On a lightly floured work surface, roll each quarter into a long, thin tube. Cut each tube into 2.5cm (1 in) lengths. Transfer to a baking tray well-dusted with flour and refrigerate for 15 to 20 minutes.

Bring a pot of heavily salted water to a simmer but not a rolling boil, as this will damage your gnocchi. Gently place the gnocchi in the pot in batches and simmer until cooked through. They are ready once they float to the top.

Transfer to a baking tray lined with parchment paper and drizzle with olive oil. Allow to dry slightly before the next step.

**SAUCE &
GARNISH**

Heat the tomato sauce in a pot over medium heat.

Heat the canola oil in a large non-stick frying pan over medium to high heat. Drop in the cooked gnocchi in batches and sear for 2 minutes, turning them around to get even browning. Add the butter and continue cooking until the gnocchi are golden brown.

Spoon the tomato sauce onto the bottom of a serving platter or divide between individual plates. Place the gnocchi on top. Garnish with burrata and freshly torn basil leaves. Sprinkle with chili flakes and drizzle with good-quality olive oil.

CLAM SPAGHETTI

Serves 6

For this Nightingale dish, we always use fresh spaghetti and BC Manila clams poached in fragrant clam stock. And we use fresh jalapeno, not chili flakes, because I like the way the heat hits you farther back in the throat. We finish it with lots of lemon juice and butter and keep it loose. Spaghetti, clams, white wine, and clam nectar all go so incredibly well together. No other dish has stayed on the menu as long as this one.

NOTE

Making fresh pasta is easy and fun. But if you don't want to, buy the best-quality dried pasta available; we like Rustichella d'Abruzzo.

INGREDIENTS

Clam Stock

Olive oil, for sautéing

1 small fennel bulb, thinly sliced

1 small onion, thinly sliced

12 cloves garlic, chopped

500mL (2 cups) white wine

30mL (2 Tbsp) canola oil

1 small can (295mL/10 oz) clam juice

3 bay leaves

Clam Spaghetti

1 recipe Pasta Dough (page 309) or 400g (14 oz) good-quality dry spaghetti

50mL (3 Tbsp) olive oil

4 cloves garlic, finely chopped

1lb (about 30) Manila or littleneck clams (see Note on page 112)

110g (½ cup) butter

Pinch dried red chili flakes

¼ bunch parsley, chiffonade

1 lemon, juice

3 scallions, finely sliced

½ small jalapeno, halved and finely diced

Salt

CLAM STOCK

Heat the olive oil in a large pot over medium heat. Sweat the fennel, onions, and garlic, stirring frequently, until softened, 8 to 12 minutes. Add the white wine and reduce the liquid by half. Add the clam juice and bay leaves. Bring to a boil, then reduce the heat and simmer for 20 minutes. Strain the stock and discard the solids. Set aside.

CLAM SPAGHETTI

Using the spaghetti attachment on your pasta machine, a spaghetti roller, or a very sharp knife, cut the fresh pasta sheets into long thin strips of spaghetti.

Bring a large pot of heavily salted water to a rapid boil. Cook the fresh pasta until al dente, about 3 minutes. For dry pasta, cook according to package instructions.

Heat the olive oil in a large skillet with a lid over medium heat. Add the garlic and sweat for 1 minute. Add the clams and some of the clam stock (you may not require all of it, depending how saucy you like your pasta), and cover immediately. Keep covered until the clams are fully open, 3 to 4 minutes; discard any that remain closed. Add the cooked spaghetti, butter, and chili flakes and cook for a few more minutes. Adjust with more clam stock if needed. Add the parsley, lemon juice, scallions, and jalapeno and toss well to combine. Season with salt as needed and serve.

SPOT PRAWN RAVIOLI, BASIL & CORIANDER SAUCE VIERGE

Serves 6 as an appetizer

I learned how to make sauce vierge at Canteen in the early 90s, and it's still one of my favourite sauces for shellfish. Shallots, a little garlic, some olive oil, and then you hit that with fresh lemon juice, coriander seeds, tomato concassé, and basil. It's so bright and delicious. Spot prawns are in season for only a short time every year here in BC, and they're in high demand. Quite rightly so; they're better than lobster.

INGREDIENTS

Sauce Vierge

100mL (7 Tbsp) olive oil

2 large shallots, finely chopped

3g (1 tsp) toasted and roughly crushed coriander seeds

2 cloves garlic, finely chopped

1 recipe Tomato Concassé (page 312)

6 basil leaves, chiffonade

25g (½ cup) chopped chives

½ lemon, juice

Salt

Prawn Ravioli

18 large spot prawns, heads removed

18 large basil leaves

½ recipe Pasta Dough (page 309)

Cornmeal or flour, for dusting

Serve

Handful basil leaves or 1 recipe Basil Chips (page 319), for garnish

SAUCE VIERGE

Combine the olive oil, shallots, coriander, and garlic in a small pot. Heat over very, very low heat to just gently warm up the shallots, garlic, and spices, 15 to 20 minutes. Remove from the heat and set aside. When ready to serve, reheat over low heat, and add the tomato concassé, basil, chives, and lemon juice. Season with salt.

PRAWN RAVIOLI

Bring a pot of water to a boil and dip the prawns in for just a few seconds. The flesh of the prawns tends to stick to the shell when they are really fresh; this quick blanching helps you to peel the prawns without damaging the flesh. Peel the prawns and pat dry. Wrap each with a single leaf of basil and set aside.

On a lightly floured work surface, use a 7.5–10cm (3–4 in) round cutter (depending on the size of your prawns) to cut the pasta sheet into 18 rounds, spacing as close together as possible. Keep the rounds under a slightly damp towel or layered between plastic wrap.

Place 1 prawn on each disc of dough. Dip your finger in a bowl of water and run it around one half of the edge of the round to moisten. Fold the dough over to form a half moon and press it down to remove air bubbles and seal the ravioli. Set aside on a baking tray dusted with cornmeal or flour, and cover with the damp towel.

Bring a large pot of heavily salted water to a boil. Lower the ravioli into the water a few at a time with a spider or slotted spoon. Stir occasionally to prevent the ravioli from sticking to the pot or each other. Cook until all the ravioli have bobbed to the surface, about 3 minutes.

SERVE   Split the ravioli between serving bowls and spoon the sauce vierge on top. Garnish with fresh or crispy basil leaves.

RAVIOLI OF QUAIL, MUSHROOMS, FAVA BEANS, QUAIL LEG CONFIT

Serves 6

These ravioli are teardrop shaped because the pasta is wrapped around a full individual quail breast topped with truffled *mousse de volaille*. The pasta and quail and mousse all cook perfectly in the exact same amount of time, and then you douse them with foamed quail jus. It's rich, but it's *so* delicious.

INGREDIENTS

Quail Leg Confit

3 quail (200g/7 oz each)

30g (2 Tbsp) coarse salt

6 parsley leaves

1 bay leaf

1 sprig thyme, stem removed

Pinch Szechuan peppercorns, crushed

Pinch coriander seeds, crushed

1 star anise pod

Pinch ground cinnamon

Pinch peppercorns

1 clove garlic, smashed

250g (1 cup) duck fat

Mousse

100g (3½ oz) boneless, skinless chicken breast

½ egg white

Pinch salt

75mL (7 Tbsp) cream

10mL (2 tsp) canola oil

100g (1 cup) sliced mixed wild and/or cultivated mushrooms

15g (⅓ cup) chopped chives

Ravioli

½ recipe Pasta Dough (page 309)

Cornmeal or flour, for dusting

Fava Beans & Morels

70g (¾ cup) shelled fava beans

10mL (2 tsp) canola oil

100g (2 cups) small morels

15g (1 Tbsp) butter

Salt

Cook & Garnish

1 recipe Madeira Jus (page 318), made using quail bones

125mL (½ cup) Chicken Velouté (page 318)

Microgreens, for garnish

QUAIL LEG CONFIT

Remove the quail breasts and legs off the crown, keeping the skin on the legs and removing it from the breasts. Set aside the breasts.

Using a coffee grinder or food processor, blitz the salt with all the herbs, spices, and garlic until coarse to create a cure. Rub the cure all over the quail legs, and refrigerate for 6 to 8 hours. When ready to use, rinse off the cure.

Preheat the oven to 107°C (225°F).

Melt the duck fat in a small pot over low heat. Place the legs in a small roasting pan, making sure they do not overlap, and pour over the melted fat. Cover the legs with a piece of parchment paper and cook until you can easily wiggle the knee joint, 2½ to 3 hours.

Continued . . .

Let the quail legs cool in the fat until you can handle them, then transfer to a baking tray lined with parchment paper, skin side down. Place another piece of parchment paper on top and then another baking tray. Add a small weight on top of the baking tray, so that the legs are gently pressed down and slightly flattened. Refrigerate until ready to use.

MOUSSE

Place the chicken, egg white, and salt in a food processor and blend until smooth. With the machine running, slowly add half the cream.

Press the mixture through a fine mesh sieve into a large bowl and reserve over an ice bath.

Place the oil in a frying pan over medium heat. Sauté the mushrooms until golden brown and tender. Allow to cool and then chop finely.

Gradually mix the remaining cream into the chicken mixture, beating with a rubber spatula to incorporate some air. Fold in the chives and cooked mushrooms.

RAVIOLI

Prepare the quail breast by spreading each breast with an even layer of chicken mousse, covering the whole surface. Set aside.

Use a wheeled pasta cutter or a sharp knife to cut out 12 squares of pasta dough, each 13cm (5 in) on a side. Moisten the tip of a pastry brush with water and brush the surface of 1 pasta square. Place a quail breast in the centre and cover with another square of pasta. Gently press the pasta dough against the meat with a cupped hand and seal the sheets tightly, avoiding air bubbles. Cut off the excess pasta from around the filling, leaving a 1cm (⅜ in) edge. Place on a baking tray dusted with a thin layer of cornmeal. Set aside.

FAVA BEANS &
MORELS

Bring a small pot of salted water to a boil. Drop the fava beans in and cook for 30 seconds. Drain and dunk in an ice bath. Once cool, peel and you will be left with a bright green bean.

Heat 5mL (1 tsp) of the oil in a non-stick pan over low heat. Remove the quail legs from the baking tray and place in the pan, skin side down. Slowly cook until golden brown and crispy. Flip the legs and cook for an additional 3 minutes. Transfer to paper towel to soak up excess oil and then to a baking tray lined with parchment paper. Keep warm in the oven at very low temperature.

Wipe the fat off the pan and use the same pan to heat the rest of the oil. Add the morels and cook for 3 minutes, stirring from time to time. Add the butter and a pinch of salt and continue cooking until golden brown, an additional 2 minutes. Set the morels aside on the same tray as the quail legs.

COOK &
GARNISH

Bring a large pot of heavily salted water to a boil. Gently add the ravioli and cook until they firm up slightly and float, 5 to 6 minutes. Remove using a slotted spoon and transfer to a tray lined with paper towel. Drop the fava beans into the same water to reheat for 30 seconds. Meanwhile in separate small pots, heat the Madeira jus and chicken velouté. Blend the velouté lightly with an immersion blender so it is frothy.

Place 1 ravioli and 1 crispy confit leg on each serving plate. Spoon a few morels and fava beans around them, drizzle with warm Madeira jus, and top with frothy chicken velouté. Garnish with microgreens.

SQUASH AGNOLOTTI, BROWN BUTTER, CRISPY SAGE

Serves 6

The squash filling in this pasta is bound with crushed amaretti and mostarda. It's very traditional and beyond delicious. The first time I had it was at the Walnut Tree Inn, in Abergavenny, Wales, when Stephen Terry was cooking. The recipe came from his business partner there, Francesco Mattioli—actually from Francesco's grandmother, who was from Positano. Later, Stephen cooked this at West when he came over to be a guest chef, and I just kept it on the menu afterward.

NOTE

Mostarda is a northern Italian condiment made of candied fruit and a mustard-flavoured syrup. You can find both it and amaretti biscuits for this recipe in specialty Italian shops.

INGREDIENTS

Squash Filling

1 small butternut or kabocha squash

5 amaretti biscuits

150g (1½ cups) grated Parmesan

25g (2 Tbsp) mostarda

Pinch sugar

Pinch English mustard powder

½ lemon, zest and juice

Pinch freshly grated nutmeg

2 pinches salt

Agnolotti

1 recipe Pasta Dough (page 309)

Cornmeal or flour, for dusting

Sauce & Garnish

110g (½ cup) butter

12 sage leaves

½ lemon, juice

Freshly grated Parmesan, for garnish (optional)

SQUASH FILLING

Preheat the oven to 175°C (350°F).

Cut the squash in half and scoop out the guts. Place the squash, flat side down, on a baking sheet lined with parchment paper and roast for 45 minutes to an hour until soft to the touch.

Remove from the oven and scoop out the flesh, making sure not to scoop any skin. Place the flesh in a fine-mesh sieve, preferably lined with cheesecloth, to drain any excess liquid; the drier your squash, the better. Allow to cool completely, even overnight.

Transfer to a food processor and blend with the amaretti biscuits, Parmesan, mostarda, sugar, mustard powder, lemon zest, lemon juice, nutmeg, and salt until smooth. Transfer to a piping bag with a 1.5cm (½ in) opening.

AGNOLOTTI

Lay the first pasta sheet on a lightly floured work surface with the long side facing you (1). Pipe a straight line of filling along the bottom of the pasta sheet, leaving enough pasta on each side (about 2cm/¾ in) to be able to fold it over the filling (2).

Continued . . .

Moisten the tip of a pastry brush and run it along the dough to help the edges stick together (3). Fold the bottom of the pasta over the filling. Press firmly to seal tightly, and remove any pockets of air.

Use the tips of your fingers to pinch the tube of pasta into equal-sized sections (4), creating a seal between pockets of filling. Leave about 2cm (¾ in) between each, or they may come unsealed when separated.

Use a wheeled pasta cutter or a sharp knife to remove the extra pasta and then quickly cut apart the sections (5) to create your agnolotti. Place the agnolotti on a baking sheet dusted with flour or cornmeal. Don't let them touch each other, or they may stick together (6).

Repeat with the remaining pasta, and then all of the pasta sheets, until all of the filling has been used.

NOTE

You can freeze the agnolotti on a baking tray at this point. Once frozen, transfer to an airtight freezer bag or container and store for up to 2 months. You can then cook the agnolotti directly from frozen.

SERVE

Bring a large pot of heavily salted water to a boil.

Place the butter in a pan set over medium heat, whisking from time to time. When the butter starts to foam and turn brown, add the sage leaves and fry until crispy. Continue cooking until the butter browns deeply and is very fragrant. Swirl in the lemon juice. Set aside.

Gently place the agnolotti into the pot of boiling water and cook in batches until they float and firm up slightly, 3 to 4 minutes. Scoop out with a slotted spoon, or drain in a colander, and gently shake out as much water as possible. Add to the pan with the brown butter and gently toss to coat.

Divide the agnolotti between 6 plates or bowls and drizzle with any remaining brown butter sauce. Sprinkle with freshly grated Parmesan and serve.

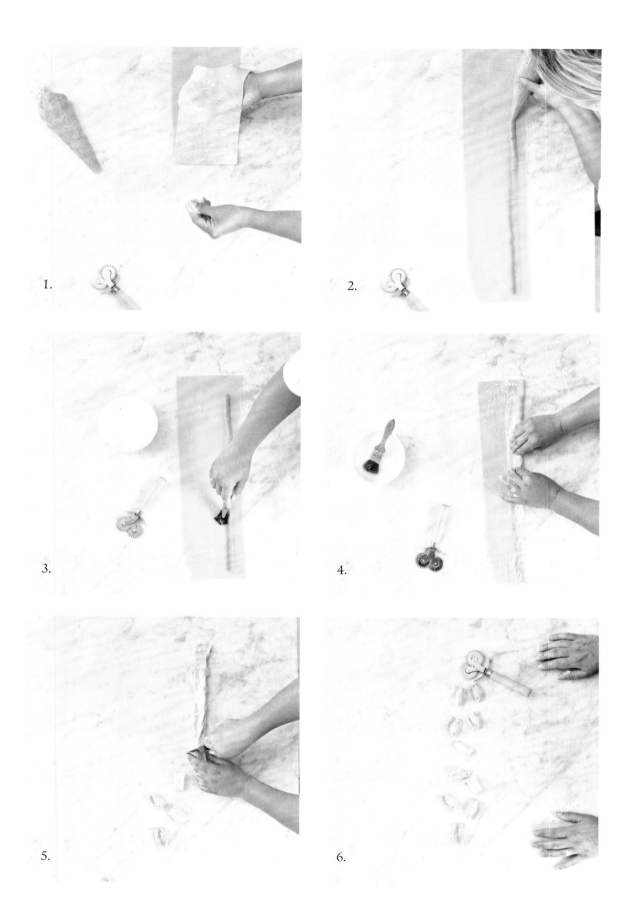

1.

2.

3.

4.

5.

6.

SALUMI PIZZA

Makes three 30cm
(12in) pizzas;
serves 6

In the lead-up to opening Nightingale, I had a few ideal pizzas in mind. Mostly they were from Los Angeles, where Bestia does a Neapolitan-style pizza that's shockingly good. Gjelina's pizza is less traditional, but the first time I tried it, I thought it was the pizza I'd always dreamed of—just perfect, in every way. So I went back home, bought a pizza oven to put in my backyard, and spent months fooling around with different recipes. I was on the right path. Then we hired one of those nomadic expert *pizzaioli* from the home country. He spent six months with us, and he nailed it.

This pizza—with a sauce of San Marzano tomatoes slow-simmered to sweetness with garlic and onion, plus the contrast of thin-sliced spicy salumi and burrata added for richness—is our best-selling red-sauced pizza.

INGREDIENTS

1 recipe Pizza Dough (page 308), room temperature

Semolina, for dusting

1 recipe Pizza Tomato Sauce (page 310)

1 ball fresh burrata, torn into 2.5cm (1 in) pieces

180g (1½ cups) thinly sliced cured Italian dry sausage, such as soppressata or spianata

Salt

15mL (1 Tbsp) olive oil

Preheat the oven to 230°C (450°F). If your oven will go higher, use the higher setting—the hotter the better.

Create 1 pizza at a time. On a lightly floured surface, gradually flatten and carefully stretch 1 of the dough balls into a circular shape about 30cm (12 in) in diameter. Dust a pizza stone or baking tray with semolina flour, and transfer the dough to the stone or baking tray.

Place ⅓ of the tomato sauce, burrata, and cured sausage on each pizza. Season with salt and drizzle with olive oil. Bake until charred with a few black spots, 6 to 12 minutes. Check the bottom of the pizza for doneness: you're looking for a slight charring.

Repeat for the other 2 pizzas.

RAMP, FARM EGG & TALEGGIO PIZZA

Makes three 30cm (12 in) pizzas; serves 6

Char-grilled ramps are a perfect complement to the mild tang of Taleggio and the richness of baked egg. This is a great springtime pizza, and I love making it in the pizza oven in my backyard—don't let ramp season go by without trying it.

INGREDIENTS

White Sauce

75g (5 Tbsp) cream cheese, room temperature

75g (5 Tbsp) ricotta, room temperature

75g (5 Tbsp) sour cream

15mL (1 Tbsp) milk

Pinch ground nutmeg

Pinch pepper

Pinch salt

Ramps

1 bunch ramps

Olive oil, for drizzling

Pizza

1 recipe Pizza Dough (page 308), room temperature

Semolina, for dusting

90g (1 cup) grated pecorino

210g (7½ oz) Taleggio, sliced

3 farm eggs (organic, as high quality as you can find)

Salt

Olive oil, for drizzling

Basil leaves, torn

Pepper

WHITE SAUCE

Combine all the ingredients using a firm whisk. There should be no large chunks, and the mixture should be totally smooth.

RAMPS

Clean the ramps and cut in half to separate the leaves from the bulbs. If the bulbs are quite large, slice down the middle to butterfly open. Coat with a drizzle of olive oil.

Heat a grill pan or barbecue on high heat. Grill the bulbs for 1 minute on each side, then grill the leaves for just 10 seconds.

Cut the bulbs into 2.5cm long (1 in) pieces. Leave the leaves intact.

PIZZA

Preheat the oven to 230°C (450°F). If your oven will go higher, use the higher setting—the hotter the better.

Create 1 pizza at a time. On a lightly floured surface, gradually flatten and carefully stretch 1 of the dough balls into a circular shape about 30cm (12 in) in diameter. Dust a pizza stone or baking tray with semolina flour, and transfer the dough to the stone or baking tray.

Spread ⅓ of the white sauce on top. Sprinkle with ⅓ of the pecorino and place ⅓ of the ramps and sliced Taleggio on top of each. Crack 1 egg right in the middle. Season with salt and drizzle with olive oil. Bake until charred with a few black spots, 6 to 12 minutes. Check the bottom of the pizza for doneness: you're looking for a slight charring. Garnish with basil, pepper, and another drizzle of olive oil.

Repeat for the other 2 pizzas.

OUEST AND WEST

British Columbia was calling. I wanted space—and to go fishing and skiing and see the great outdoors again. And just like that, here was Brian Hopkins on the line from Vancouver, calling on behalf of the restaurateur Jack Evrensel, who was planning something big and new. He described the project to me, but I just knew it wasn't the right next move for me. I needed to play my hand just right. But before I realized, I'd been off work for a month and was getting desperate. Which is when Jack Evrensel himself called, with a new plan.

He was still months away from opening the first restaurant we had discussed (which became Blue Water Café), but in the meantime a restaurant on Granville Street called Johnny's had gone under, and he had decided to pick up the lease for that too. The room was 75 seats, max. Jack wasn't known for great fine dining yet and he had decided that this would be the place to change that for good. He wanted it to be a jewel, a genuinely great restaurant. Not just "great for Vancouver," but for any place, by anyone's standards, just like I'd always wanted to open in my hometown.

Over the next six weeks, I proposed to Annabel, had a full English wedding, and we moved to Vancouver. It was a big gamble, for both of us.

Jack and I got started right away. Talking about where we should go with our fine dining food program was fine, but sometimes I just wanted to show him something on the plate instead. So I'd say, "Can I just cook something for you?" The first time I did, Jack said, "Sure—but nothing with feathers."

"What?"

"I don't eat anything with feathers."

Seriously. No chicken, no duck, no squab, no quail. If it's got feathers, Jack won't eat it.

"Sweetbreads?"

"No. No offal."

So there we are, trying to set up the best restaurant Vancouver has ever seen, and I'm working through menu ideas, and the owner only wants to eat beef tenderloin, fish, and vegetables. But we forged on, and soon enough the pieces started to come together.

Naming the restaurant was easy—we thought. At the end of the 90s, fine dining everywhere still had a strong French accent. Ferran Adrià's molecular gastronomy had not yet caught on outside Spain, and the New Nordic cuisine didn't exist. The contemporary British cooking that had just earned the world's attention was built with French techniques and French flavours. In the UK, we'd advanced local cooking by applying French methods to great British ingredients, from their wonderful fish and lamb to the incredible dairy and farm produce. Back home I wanted to do the same with West Coast products, wild, foraged, and farmed. And there was one word that summed up that French–West Coast equation perfectly: *Ouest*.

The easy part was that everyone wanted to come and work for me—because I'd worked for Marco and I'd worked for Raymond. All these young cooks were like, "Great! I can just go work for this guy and I won't have to bother going to the UK!" The hard part was that Vancouver cooks hadn't seen anything like what I wanted to do. To come clean, every cook in my entire opening brigade was in tears at least once over the first week. It's an intense business. It's a stressful situation—and I'm not always proud of what that intensity does to me. But frankly the kitchen at Ouest wasn't anything super-aggressive. I just ran it like a normal kitchen back in the UK. If it was tough going at the start, it was only because I wanted those young chefs to raise their game.

Once we got that machine rolling, we had a really solid team. I'm still proud of what it was and what they went on to do. We opened with Paul Moran, who's now executive chef at 1909 Kitchen in Tofino, Nicole Gomes, who won Top Chef Canada All-Stars, Stéphanie Noël, who's back with me running our Air Canada recipe development program, and Nathan Guggenheimer, Dale Mackay's partner in the Grassroots Restaurant Group in Saskatoon. Later in that first year we had a young David Zilber, now head of fermentation at Noma in Copenhagen. The amount of talent that went through that kitchen at Ouest and on to other good things was very, very large.

The opening menu was cutting-edge haute cuisine, and ultra-seasonal. We launched in December, so the dishes were conceived for cold weather, and with the holidays on, were intended to be indulgent and festive too. One of my favourite dishes from our opening repertoire was the pot-au-feu with squab. Pot-au-feu is a French farmhouse cold-weather classic: a basic braise of a few tough cuts of beef, a marrow bone—and sometimes a little stewing hen—with root vegetables and water, slow-cooked together in one pot. But swap its basic broth out for a perfect clear consommé and the old hen for a delicate squab, roasted à point on the crown, add turned baby vegetables and delicate parsley dumplings, and you lift that peasant fare into the realm of haute cuisine. That was a great dish.

A lot of what we were doing was new to Vancouver. That level of cuisine combined with our fine-tuned seasonality was something different then. So was the service, with choreographed servers placing plates in front of customers under cloches that they then lifted simultaneously. It was impressive, but maybe it was a little much. Vancouver is not London. Vancouverites did not embrace that formality, and they were far more health conscious in their appetites, especially at lunch. And something else: a lot of

West Coasters were unfamiliar with what Ouest meant, or how to pronounce it. So a few months in we relaunched as West, with a handful of design tweaks cueing a more casual restaurant and menu. We still did tasting menus at lunch if anyone wanted one, but we also sold fish and chips.

For the next seven years, the story of the food at West became ever lighter. There was less and less butter in the mix. It leaned less French and more West Coast, with Asian influences mingling with the classical Western European techniques. As time went on, I spent more time on the floor, learning more about local customers and their tastes. The restaurant's evolution marched lock-step with my own: I had never wanted a restaurant where people would come once to put a check mark in their culinary souvenir program, and off they'd go, never to return. My goal was that people would come regularly. I gave West everything, and my efforts and everyone else's were well rewarded. We were busy. There were lots of accolades: *Vancouver Magazine* named us restaurant of the year four times in our first seven years. But I had told Jack from the very beginning that whatever we might achieve together, I still wanted to have my own restaurant one day. Seven years on, my need to set out on my own was stronger than ever.

I'll be blunt: once you achieve your goals as a chef, and you get to a certain age and want a family, you start looking hard for ways to not have a coronary over a hot stove when you're 60. At some point no matter how good your paycheque, it's not enough of a reward; you need to be in the driver's seat. My dream had always been to own my own restaurant, and the time had come to make that happen. H

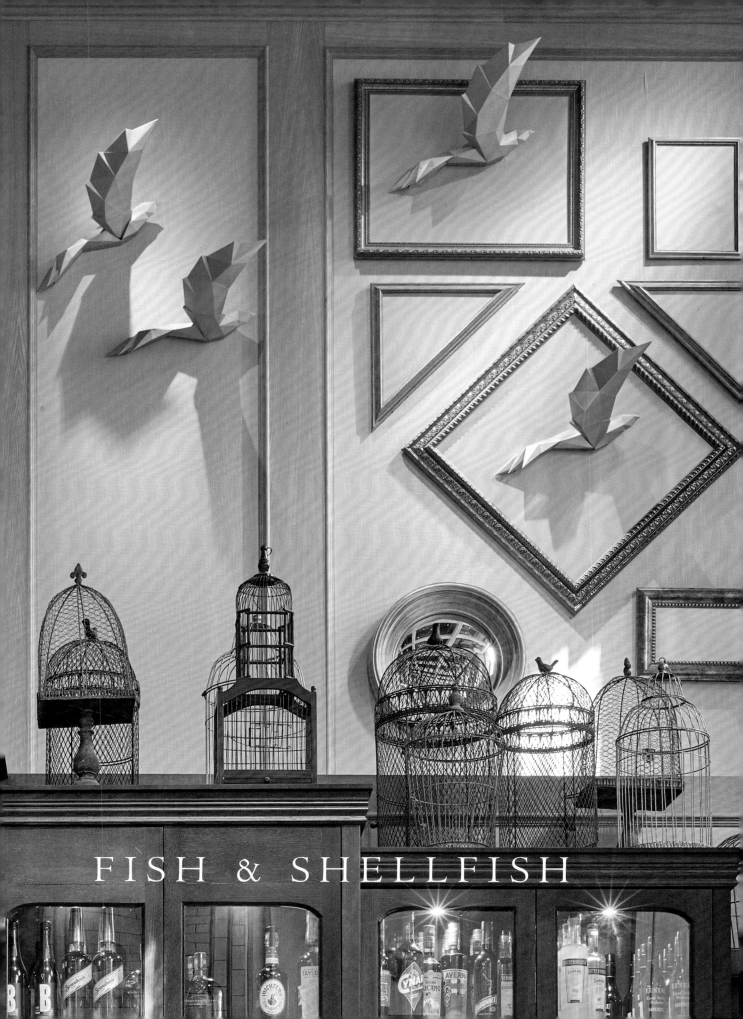

FISH & SHELLFISH

CHORIZO-CRUSTED LING COD WITH TOMATO, SQUASH & MANILA CLAM RAGOUT

Serves 6

Ling cod has lean, flaky, mild-flavoured flesh that goes really well with the heady spiciness of chorizo. We slice the cured sausage into thin discs and then stick them down on the filleted fish like scales. Then we serve it with a ragout of clams, tomato, and squash that's rich but balanced with natural acidity.

NOTE

Place the chorizo on top of the cod one day ahead of time so it sticks to the surface better. The tomatoes also need to be dehydrated one day ahead of time.

INGREDIENTS

Crusted Ling Cod

1 piece (300g/10½ oz) Spanish wine chorizo

6 portions (140g/5 oz each) ling cod, skin off

1 egg white, lightly whisked

Butternut Squash

1 medium butternut squash, skin on, cut in half

50g (3 Tbsp) butter, cubed

Tomato, Squash & Clam Ragout

15mL (1 Tbsp) olive oil

50g (⅓ cup) finely chopped shallots

1L (4 cups) Chicken Stock (page 317 or store-bought)

15g (1 Tbsp) butter

200g (4 cups) button chanterelles

18–24 Manila clams

1 recipe Semi-Dried Tomatoes (page 311)

15g (¾ cup) parsley, chiffonade

15g (⅓ cup) chopped chives

Serve

25mL (scant 2 Tbsp) olive oil

Salt

Handful micro sorrel, for garnish

LING COD CRUST

Using a meat slicer or very sharp knife, slice the chorizo into 2mm thick (⅛ in) slices.

Using a pastry brush, brush the top surface of the fish with the egg white. Place the slices of chorizo on top in an overlapping pattern, superimposed like fish scales. Wrap each portion individually and tightly in plastic wrap. Set in the fridge overnight.

BUTTERNUT SQUASH

Preheat the oven to 190°C (375°F).

Scoop the seeds and pulp out of each squash half and discard. Place one of the squash halves, cut side down, on a baking tray lined with parchment paper and roast until fork-tender, 30 to 40 minutes. Remove from the oven, scoop out the flesh, and purée it with the butter in a blender or food processor until smooth. Set aside until serving.

Continued . . .

Peel the second half of the squash, and cut ¾ of it into a fine brunoise. Set aside for the ragout.

With the remaining squash, use a vegetable peeler to make 1cm wide (⅜ in) ribbons for the garnish. Set aside for serving.

TOMATO, SQUASH & CLAM RAGUT

Heat the olive oil in a large pot over medium heat. Sweat the shallots until translucent, about 3 minutes. Add the stock and simmer until the liquid has reduced by half. Set aside.

In a large frying pan, melt the butter. Sauté the chanterelles until golden brown and tender, and beginning to release juices, about 5 minutes. Add the squash brunoise and sweat on medium heat for 1 minute.

Return the shallot stock to the heat. Turn up to high, add the clams, cover, and cook until all the clams are fully open; discard any that remain closed. This shouldn't take more than 2 minutes. Stir in the chanterelles and squash brunoise, and the semi-dried tomatoes, parsley, and chives. Set aside.

SERVE

Preheat the oven to 165°C (325°F).

Heat 15mL (1 Tbsp) of the olive oil in a large ovenproof non-stick skillet over medium-high heat until shimmering. Season the sides of the fish not coated with chorizo with salt.

Carefully place the fish in the skillet, chorizo scales facing down. Cook for 3 minutes, flip, and then transfer the skillet to the oven until the fish is cooked through, about 4 additional minutes.

Season the squash ribbons with salt and the remaining olive oil. Let sit for a few minutes to soften slightly.

Warm the squash purée in a small pot over low heat. Transfer to a piping bag.

Dot the squash purée around each of 6 serving plates. Place a generous spoonful of clam ragout on 1 side of each, with a piece of fish on the other. Garnish with the squash ribbons and micro sorrel.

AROMATIC SABLEFISH RICE BOWL

Serves 4

At lunchtime in Vancouver, most businesspeople want something healthy and fresh that they can eat fairly quickly. At Hawksworth, they also expect refinement and a lot of flavour. So we came up with this Asian-forward meal-in-one, with marinated sablefish and brown rice, kimchi-style carrots, cabbage, and bean sprouts, and a spicy Asian vinaigrette. It hit all the right notes—and resonated well. At the restaurant we also add a tempura-battered egg yolk to tip it over the edge.

INGREDIENTS

Sablefish & Brine

75g (⅓ cup) brown sugar

125mL (½ cup) water

215mL (¾ cup plus 1 Tbsp) low-sodium soy sauce

125mL (½ cup) sake

1 Thai chili, seeds removed, coarsely chopped

½ bunch cilantro, torn

10g (1 in knob) ginger, peeled and coarsely chopped

2 cloves garlic, coarsely chopped

½ orange, zest

4 portions (125g/4½ oz each) sablefish

Rice

185g (1 cup) brown rice

250mL (1 cup) water

250mL (1 cup) rice wine vinegar

85mL (6 Tbsp) mirin

85g (scant ½ cup) sugar

¼ large sheet dried kombu seaweed

Pickled Red Cabbage

75ml (5 Tbsp) rice wine vinegar

50ml (3 Tbsp) water

25g (2 Tbsp) sugar

120g (1¼ cups) julienne red cabbage

Kimchi Carrot

120g (⅔ cup) julienne carrot

30ml (2 Tbsp) kimchi sauce

Charred Scallion & Ginger Vinaigrette

25g (¼ cup) minced scallions

45g (5 Tbsp) brunoise ginger

¼ red onion, brunoise

100mL (7 Tbsp) canola oil

65mL (¼ cup) dark soy sauce

30g (2½ Tbsp) brown sugar

1½ limes, juice

10mL (2 tsp) fish sauce

8mL (½ Tbsp) hoisin sauce

8mL (½ Tbsp) Sriracha-style chili sauce

2½mL (½ tsp) sesame oil

30mL (2 Tbsp) rice wine vinegar

Pinch salt

Rice Bowl

1½ avocados, peeled and sliced into 0.5cm (¼ in) wedges

120g (1⅓ cups) bean sprouts

120g (2 cups) snap peas, thinly sliced

60g (⅔ cup) pea shoots or daikon sprouts

½ bunch cilantro, stems removed

¼ bunch scallions, chopped

Continued . . .

SABLEFISH & BRINE   Mix the sugar into the water to dissolve. Add all the remaining ingredients except the sablefish and mix to combine. Add the fish, cover, and set in the refrigerator overnight.

RICE   Bring the rice and water to a boil in a medium pot over medium heat. Reduce the heat to low and cover. Simmer until the rice is tender and most of the liquid has been absorbed, 40 to 50 minutes. Alternatively you can use a rice cooker. Let stand for 5 minutes, then fluff with a fork.

While the rice is cooking, combine the rice wine vinegar, mirin, sugar, and kombu seaweed in a small pot and bring to a boil. Reduce the heat and simmer for 15 minutes. Strain out the seaweed. Add the liquid to the rice and fluff with a fork. Keep warm.

PICKLED RED CABBAGE   Bring the vinegar, water, and sugar to a boil. Pour over the cabbage and let sit for 30 minutes until completely cooled down. Drain before serving.

KIMCHI CARROT   Mix the carrots with the kimchi sauce and allow to sit for 30 minutes.

CHARRED SCALLION & GINGER VINAIGRETTE   Combine the scallions, ginger, and red onion in a large pot with deep sides.

Heat the oil in a small pot until it is very hot and beginning to smoke. Very carefully pour the hot oil over the vegetables. Whisk in the soy sauce, sugar, lime juice, fish sauce, hoisin sauce, chili sauce, sesame oil, vinegar, and salt and allow to cool to room temperature.

RICE BOWL   Preheat the oven to 200°C (400°F). Turn the broiler to high.

Remove the sablefish from the brine and place on a baking tray lined with parchment paper. Broil until a caramelized golden brown, then finish in the oven until cooked through, about 3 minutes.

Spoon 100g (½ cup) of brown rice onto each of 4 serving bowls and place all the different vegetables around the rice. Drizzle 30mL (2 Tbsp) of the vinaigrette over each serving and top with a piece of warm sablefish. Garnish with pea shoots, cilantro, and scallions. Serve immediately.

SALT-CRUSTED WILD SALMON WITH KELP

Serves 12

When Stéphanie Noël was a chef at the Outpost, a West Coast Fishing Club salmon lodge, she started doing this dish for group dinners with a whole small chinook salmon. It's a classic salt-baked fish—but with an extra layer of flavour delivered by the kelp that you arrange between the fish and its salt crust. At the Outpost, they served the fish with all kinds of different sauces, but my favourite was always when served on a bed of delicate young vegetables flooded with vegetable nage—as we used to do with seared chinook when Stéphanie worked with me back at West.

NOTE

This recipe is intended for a large group. Cracking the crust at the table and unveiling the fish is sure to entertain your guests. To let the fish be the star of the show, it should be served very simply with seasonal vegetables.

INGREDIENTS

Broth

45mL (3 Tbsp) olive oil

½ yellow onion, diced

½ fennel bulb, cored and sliced

1 small carrot, sliced

1 stalk celery, sliced

1 shallot, sliced

Salt

3g (1 tsp) coriander seeds, toasted

3g (1 tsp) fennel seeds, toasted

250mL (1 cup) dry white wine

100mL (7 Tbsp) white wine vinegar

1L (4 cups) Fish Stock (page 316)

3 sprigs thyme

1 bay leaf

3 sprigs tarragon

1 sprig rosemary

1 handful dried bonito flakes

1 piece dried kombu seaweed

30mL (2 Tbsp) white soy sauce (shiro)

Lemon juice

Salmon

5kg (11 lb) coarse salt (we use Gros sel de Guerande)

5 egg whites

1 bunch fresh bull kelp, in 65–75cm long (25–30 in) strips, like lasagna sheets

1 spring salmon (4.5kg/10 lb), head on, skin on, gutted, and tail trimmed (ask your fishmonger for help, if necessary)

Chives, chopped, for garnish

Flat-leaf parsley, chopped, for garnish

BROTH   Heat the olive oil in a large pot over medium heat. Add the onion, fennel bulb, carrot, celery, and shallot and season with salt. Sweat the vegetables until they are soft, 12 to 15 minutes.

Add the coriander and fennel seeds, wine, and vinegar and simmer until the liquid is reduced by half, about 10 minutes. Add the fish stock and thyme, bay leaf, tarragon, and rosemary. Simmer for 15 minutes. Turn the heat off. Add the bonito flakes and dried kombu and steep for 15 minutes.

Strain through a fine-mesh sieve and discard the solids. Add the white soy sauce. Check the seasoning and add a touch of lemon juice to balance the acidity if necessary. Set aside in the pot.

SALMON   Preheat the oven to 260°C (500°F).

In a large mixing bowl, combine the salt and egg whites and mix thoroughly with your hands to make a paste. Add a little water a bit at a time until it resembles moist sand.

Spread about ⅓ of the salt mixture on a rimmed baking tray lined with parchment paper to create a 2.5cm thick (1 in) layer of salt in the shape of the fish, but slightly larger.

Lay strips of the kelp down on top of the salt, overlapping each other by about 2.5cm (1 in). Place the fish on top and fold the kelp back over the fish. Trim the excess kelp with scissors. Top with the remaining salt mixture, pressing down to cover the entire fish. This layer of salt should again be 2.5cm (1 in) all over.

Bake for 35 to 45 minutes, until the centre of the fish is warm. Allow it to rest for at least 15 to 20 minutes. The resting time is crucial, as the heat inside the crust will carry over and finish cooking the fish.

While the fish is resting, reheat the broth to piping hot.

Using a serrated knife, break the salt crust and remove it in sections. Unwrap the kelp and peel the skin off the fish. Cut off 1 side of the fish in 6 equal pieces, and then transfer the pieces to a plate. Remove and discard the spine from the whole fish, then cut and transfer a further 6 pieces of fish from the other side, and add to the plate.

SERVE   Serve each portion of fish in a large shallow bowl with your choice of seasonal vegetables. Garnish with freshly chopped chives and parsley, and then pour the boiling hot broth on top, tableside.

SOCKEYE SALMON, SCALLOP & NORI

Serves 8

Raymond Blanc came up with the original version of this dish when I was at Le Manoir. We'd do it with big wild seabass—they were three pounds at least. You split and boned them from the shoulders down and left the belly intact, then lined the cavity with nori, filled it with scallop mousse, put the fish back together again, wrapped it, and let it set. The next day you'd cut it into portion-sized medallions, sear it, and bake it on a bed of intense aromatics. After it was cooked through, you served it with two sauces and a colourful array of vegetable chips scattered on top. There was nothing like that happening in North America—nothing. What a dish. This is my West Coast version.

INGREDIENTS

Lemon Butter

60g (¼ cup) butter, softened

1 lemon, juice and zest

Pinch salt

Stuffed Salmon

1 sockeye salmon (3.6kg/8 lb) head removed, skin on but scaled, gutted, and deboned from the back, leaving the belly still intact (ask your fishmonger, if necessary)

4 sheets nori

200g (7 oz) scallops, cut in 1.5cm (½ in) cubes

200g (7 oz) spot or sidestripe prawns, peeled and heads removed

Vegetable Chips

1 small carrot

1 small parsnip, peeled

⅓ zucchini

1 fingerling potato

1L (4 cups) canola oil

Cornstarch, for coating

26 parsley leaves

Salt

Fennel Purée

1 fennel bulb, cored and chopped into medium dice

½ onion, coarsely chopped

3 cloves garlic, coarsely chopped

250mL (1 cup) cream (or enough to cover the vegetables in the pot)

Salt

Beurre Blanc

75mL (5 Tbsp) dry white wine

75mL (5 Tbsp) white wine vinegar

1 small shallot, finely chopped

50mL (3 Tbsp) cream

200g (¾ cup plus 2 Tbsp) butter, cubed and chilled

Pinch salt

½ sprig rosemary, very finely chopped

Continued . . .

Aromatics	*Roast & Serve*
2 lemons, halved	15mL (1 Tbsp) vegetable oil
200mL (¾ cup) olive oil	Sea salt
20g (¼ cup) dried ginger pieces	Lemon juice
2–3 dried licorice sticks	100mL (7 Tbsp) red wine jus (see
9g (1 Tbsp) peppercorns	Madeira Jus recipe on page 318,
9g (1 Tbsp) pink peppercorns	and substitute red wine for Madeira)
9g (1 Tbsp) coriander seeds	
1 strip lemon peel	
1 strip orange peel	
½ head garlic, unpeeled	
Fennel tops from 1 head of fennel	

LEMON BUTTER

Mix together the butter with the lemon juice and zest, and salt.

STUFFED SALMON

Place the fish on a double layer of plastic wrap. Spread the lemon butter over the inside of the salmon and lay the nori on top. You may have to trim the nori sheets if bigger than the fish. Place the scallops and prawns inside. Roll the fish up in the plastic and form into a ballotine (large sausage) shape. Tie with string and let sit in the fridge overnight.

VEGETABLE CHIPS

Using a vegetable peeler, cut long thin strips of carrot and parsnip, from top to bottom. Keep separate. Using a mandoline, very thinly slice the zucchini and fingerling potato into rounds. Cover the potatoes with water.

Heat the oil to 150°C (300°F) in a pot large enough that it is not more than half full.

Drain the potatoes and place on a baking tray lined with paper towel to absorb as much water as possible.

Separately toss the carrots, parsnips, zucchinis, and potatoes with enough cornstarch to coat each piece. Place in a sieve, one vegetable at a time, and shake well to remove any excess cornstarch.

Carefully drop the vegetables, one kind at a time, into the hot oil and fry until light brown and crispy. Remove using a spider or a slotted spoon and transfer to paper towel to soak up excess oil. Do the same with the parsley leaves. Season with salt immediately.

FENNEL PURÉE

Combine the fennel, onion, garlic, and cream in a medium-sized saucepan over medium heat. You want the cream to come just to the top of the vegetables. Bring to a light boil, then reduce the heat to low and simmer for 15 minutes, stirring periodically.

Once the vegetables are cooked through, drain and reserve the excess cream. Place the drained vegetables in a high-speed blender and season with salt. Purée until smooth, adding the reserved cream as necessary. Adjust seasoning to taste.

Bring the wine, vinegar, and shallots to a boil in a saucepan over medium heat. Cook until the liquid has reduced to a syrup, 3 to 5 minutes. You should have 30–45mL (2–3 Tbsp) left in the pot.

Add the cream and bring to a boil. Remove from the heat and add a few cubes of butter, whisking constantly. As the butter melts and incorporates, slowly add more, whisking constantly (the sauce should maintain the consistency of hollandaise). Return to the heat momentarily if needed, but never let it boil.

Season with salt and pass through a fine-mesh sieve, pressing on the solids with a rubber spatula. Discard the solids. Gently stir the rosemary into the cream. Keep warm until serving.

AROMATICS

Heat up a grill pan or barbecue on high. Char the lemons until blackened on all sides. Transfer to a roasting pan and add all the aromatics.

ROAST
SALMON &
SERVE

Preheat the oven to 175°C (350°F).

Remove the salmon from the fridge, and unwrap. Cut into 4cm thick (1½ in) medallions. Let rest at room temperature for 15 minutes.

Heat the vegetable oil in a non-stick pan over medium heat, and sear the salmon medallions for 1½ minutes on each side.

Transfer to the roasting pan, and place on top of the aromatics. Roast for 5 to 7 minutes until the fish is cooked through. Remove from the oven, discard the aromatics, and sprinkle the salmon with sea salt and lemon juice.

Spoon some of the fennel purée onto each of 8 serving plates. Place a salmon medallion on top of the purée. Drizzle with red wine jus and beurre blanc. Garnish with vegetable and parsley chips.

BARBECUED SALMON COLLARS

Serves 6

Salmon collars should never be wasted. They are delicious—fatty, and incredibly rich. Collars are the tastiest part of the fish! The Japanese understand this, and their treatment works really well.

NOTE

The marinade for this recipe can be stored in an airtight container in the fridge for up to two weeks.

INGREDIENTS

250mL (1 cup) mirin or maple syrup

250mL (1 cup) sake

250mL (1 cup) soy sauce

4 slices orange or honey tangerine

5cm (2 in) knob ginger, roughly sliced

12–18 salmon collars (ask your fishmonger, if necessary)

Combine all of the ingredients except the salmon collars to create a marinade. Pour over the salmon collars and marinate in the fridge for 6 hours.

Remove the collars from the marinade, and grill over a charcoal fire (ideally in a grill basket) until lightly charred on 1 side, 4 to 5 minutes. Alternatively, place them on a baking tray and grill under the broiler on high heat, or bake in the oven at 175°C (350°F) on a baking tray lined with parchment paper. Flip, and brush the second side with a little leftover marinade before returning to the grill for another 4 to 5 minutes. Keep checking the salmon collars to be sure they don't burn.

GRILLED SPOT PRAWNS

Serves 6

Spot prawns need to be eaten whole. Do not eat just the tail. You must use the whole thing. There is so much flavour in the head. When they're in season here in BC—and commercially, that's only six weeks out of the year—they are fantastic grilled quickly over charcoal in a basket. To eat them, pull them apart, dip the tails in garlic butter with chili and herbs, and suck the heads.

INGREDIENTS

24–30 (1.3kg/3 lb) large spot prawns
1 recipe Garlic Butter (page 312)

Grill Basket Options

3 slices lemon
2 stalks lemongrass

If using a grill basket, place the prawns in the basket with the lemon slices and lemongrass in 1 even layer without overlapping. If you do not have a grill basket, place the prawns directly on the barbecue.

Grill the prawns for 3 to 4 minutes on each side, depending on their size. Transfer to a serving dish and spoon the butter over top, and/or use it as a dip.

ARCTIC CHAR, FARRO & ALMOND DRESSING

Serves 6
(photo on page 41)

Char is a really good fish, but, like salmon, it's got high oil content. Serve it with a good acidulated sauce to dial back the richness. In this recipe the fish is pan-seared and dressed with a squeeze of lemon. Its accompaniments follow the vegetable-forward Nightingale formula, with lots of flavours and textures in a healthy base of grains and squash, then some crispy deep-fried artichokes for another layer of more decadent flavour.

INGREDIENTS

Lemon Vinaigrette

80mL (⅓ cup) lemon juice

6 cloves Garlic Confit (page 312)

12g (2 tsp) honey

Pinch salt

Pinch pepper

80mL (⅓ cup) canola oil

Almond Dressing

90g (1 cup) sliced almonds

75mL (5 Tbsp) water

Pinch salt

Pickled Red Onions

75mL (5 Tbsp) white wine vinegar

50mL (3 Tbsp) water

25g (2 Tbsp) sugar

1g (⅓ tsp) salt

1 bay leaf

Pinch pepper

Pinch coriander seeds, toasted

½ red onion, sliced in 2.5cm thick (1 in) rings

Farro Salad

70g (½ cup) peeled butternut squash, cut in small dice

1 sprig thyme, stem removed

Salt

Olive oil, for drizzling

40g (⅓ cup) trimmed and finely sliced green beans

250g (1⅓ cups) farro

80g (⅔ cup) diced radishes

70g (¾ cup) Brussels sprout leaves

½ lemon, juice

Garnishes

12 fiddleheads, trimmed

500mL (2 cups) canola oil

6 good-quality canned artichokes, drained and quartered

Salt

2 lemons, sliced into 2.5cm (1 in) slices

10g (2 tsp) butter

Artic Char

25mL (scant 2 Tbsp) canola oil

6 skinless arctic char portions (155g/5½ oz each)

15g (1 Tbsp) butter

Salt

Lemon juice

LEMON
VINAIGRETTE

Combine the lemon juice, garlic confit, honey, salt, and pepper in a bowl. Slowly incorporate the oil, pouring it into the bowl while whisking until completely emulsified.

ALMOND
DRESSING

Preheat the oven to 200°C (400°F).

Place the sliced almonds on a baking tray lined with parchment paper. Toast until golden brown, 3 to 4 minutes. Allow to cool. Set aside 60g (½ cup) of the almonds.

Combine the remaining 30g (¼ cup) of toasted almonds with the lemon vinaigrette, water, and salt in a blender and blend on high speed for 90 seconds.

PICKLED RED
ONIONS

Bring the vinegar, water, sugar, salt, bay leaf, pepper, and coriander seeds to a boil. Poor over the onion rings while hot. Let sit until completely cooled down.

Heat a grill pan or barbecue over high heat. Grill the onions for 1 minute a side, until all surfaces are charred. Allow to cool and then dice.

FARRO SALAD

Preheat the oven to 200°C (400°F).

Rinse the farro in a fine-mesh sieve under cold water. Drain. Transfer to a medium pot with a lid and cook according to package instructions. Allow to cool.

Place the diced squash in a mixing bowl and season with thyme and salt. Drizzle with olive oil and toss to combine. Lay the squash on a baking tray lined with parchment paper. Roast in the oven until golden and tender, 4 to 6 minutes, tossing halfway through for even colour on all sides.

Bring a medium pot of salted water to a boil. Blanch the green beans, about 2 minutes, then dunk in an ice bath.

Mix the cooked farro with the pickled red onions, roasted squash, radishes, blanched green beans, Brussels sprout leaves, 30g (¼ cup) reserved toasted almonds, and the almond dressing. Season with salt, more olive oil if needed, and the lemon juice. Set aside.

PREPARE THE
GARNISHES

Bring a medium pot of salted water to a boil. Blanch the fiddleheads for 2 to 3 minutes, then dunk immediately in an ice bath.

Heat the oil to 175°C (350°F) in a pot large enough that it is not more than half full.

Drain the artichokes on paper towel to absorb any excess liquid, then fry in batches for a few minutes until golden brown. Transfer to paper towel to soak up excess oil. Season with salt.

Heat a grill pan or barbecue on high heat. Grill the lemon slices until charred on 1 side.

Heat a small frying pan on medium heat. Add the butter and sauté the fiddleheads for 2 minutes. Season with salt.

ARCTIC CHAR

Heat the oil in a large non-stick pan over high heat. Sear the arctic char for 2 minutes. Flip, add the butter, and cook for an additional 2 minutes. Season with salt and a squeeze of lemon.

Place the farro salad in a serving dish. Place the arctic char on top and garnish with fried artichokes, charred lemon, fiddleheads, and toasted almonds.

GRILLED STURGEON, SAUCE BAGNA CAUDA, CHARRED LEEKS

Serves 6

(photo on page 183)

We get great-quality fresh sturgeon in BC from organic caviar farms like Northern Divine on the Sunshine Coast. Sturgeon is intensely meaty and doesn't really taste like fish—more like swimming chicken. It's firm like monkfish, but way beyond. It's great for grilling and stands up well to robust flavours like bagna cauda.

INGREDIENTS

Sturgeon

125mL (½ cup) canola oil

20mL (1⅓ Tbsp) olive oil

3 cloves garlic, crushed

1 bay leaf

1 sprig thyme

Few leaves sage

25mL (scant 2 Tbsp) red wine vinegar

6 sturgeon portions (170g/6 oz each), skin off

Roasted Garlic & Anchovy Purée

Cloves from half head of Garlic Confit (page 312)

2 anchovy fillets

5mL (1 tsp) white wine vinegar

10mL (2 tsp) water

Pinch salt

Bagna Cauda

30g (2 Tbsp) butter

1 small shallot, thinly sliced

20mL (1⅓ Tbsp) red wine vinegar

500mL (2 cups) Chicken Stock (page 317 or store-bought)

15mL (1 Tbsp) olive oil

¼ lemon, zest

Pinch xanthan gum

Salt

Charred Leeks

2 leeks, white part only, cut in 1.5cm (½ in) rings

3 sprigs tarragon

2 bay leaves, sliced

Pinch salt

65mL (¼ cup) olive oil, plus more for garnish

1 recipe Chicken Stock (page 317)

2g (1 tsp) fennel pollen, plus more for garnish

¼ lemon, zest

STURGEON

Heat the canola oil and olive oil in a small pot over medium heat. Add the garlic and herbs, and reduce the heat to low. Cook until soft, about 5 minutes.

Allow to cool to room temperature, then blend in a high-speed blender until combined. Add the vinegar and blend again for 1 minute.

Marinate the sturgeon in this marinade for at least 24 hours and up to 3 days.

| ROASTED GARLIC & ANCHOVY PURÉE | Mash together all the ingredients with a rubber spatula or fork. |

ROASTED GARLIC & ANCHOVY PURÉE

Mash together all the ingredients with a rubber spatula or fork.

BAGNA CAUDA

Melt the butter in a medium pot over medium heat and sweat the shallot until soft. Add the roasted garlic and anchovy purée, vinegar, and chicken stock and bring to a boil. Simmer until the liquid has reduced by half.

Place all the ingredients except for the xanthan gum and salt in a high-speed blender. Add the xanthan gum slowly while the machine is running, making sure there are no visible lumps in the mixture. Season with salt. Pass through a fine-mesh sieve and cool with plastic wrap in direct contact with the surface.

CHARRED LEEKS

Combine the leeks, tarragon, bay leaves, and salt with 30mL (2 Tbsp) of the olive oil in a medium pan. Add just enough chicken stock to cover the leeks. Cover with a cartouche (circle of parchment paper) and simmer over low heat until tender, 12 to 15 minutes.

When ready to serve, heat a large sauté pan over high heat. Sear the leek rings until uniformly charred on 1 side, about 2 minutes. Remove from the heat and separate the layers of the rings. Mix the leek rings with the remaining olive oil, fennel pollen, and lemon zest.

SERVE

Preheat the oven to 150°C (300°F).

Heat up a grill pan or barbecue on high. Remove the sturgeon from the marinade and scrape off any excess. Lay the fish on the grill for 1 minute. Turn 90 degrees to create a crosshatch pattern and cook for another minute. Transfer to a baking tray lined with parchment paper.

Bake in the oven for 5 minutes, until the fish is just cooked through.

Spoon the bagna cauda sauce onto the centre of a serving plate, and place the fish on top. Cover with the leek mixture. Drizzle with olive oil and garnish with fennel pollen.

Grilled Corn (page 259)

Sungold Tomato Toast (page 20)

Grilled Sturgeon (page 180)

THAI FISH CURRY

Serves 6

In the UK curry is officially more popular than fish and chips. So I ate a lot of it there. It always really impressed me that in the UK it was totally all right to put curry on a fine dining menu. That's how I discovered that there is so much more to it than heat, acidity, butter, and salt. There are so many variations beyond that basic flavour profile, so much nuance. This one is very delicate.

INGREDIENTS

Curry Paste

6 shallots, sliced

80g (½ cup) peeled, chopped ginger

6 cloves garlic, chopped

16g (2 Tbsp) coriander seeds, toasted

2 lime leaves

1½ stalks lemongrass, bruised with the side of a knife and chopped

1 small jalapeno, chopped

30mL (2 Tbsp) canola oil

10g (½ cup) basil leaves

⅓ bunch cilantro

Coconut Curry Base

150g (5¼ oz) solid coconut oil

15mL (1 Tbsp) fish sauce

5g (1 tsp) brown sugar

1.7 L (7½ cups) coconut milk

20g (2 Tbsp) salt

60mL (¼ cup) lime juice

1 small jalapeno, deseeded

Thai Fish Curry

200g (4–5) Japanese eggplants

Salt

Olive oil

200g (1–2) sweet potatoes, unpeeled

750g (26 oz) rockfish or halibut, skin off, boneless, cut in 1.5 to 2cm (¾ to 1 in) cubes

⅓ jalapeno, finely sliced, for garnish

Cilantro sprigs, for garnish

CURRY PASTE

Combine the shallots, ginger, garlic, coriander seeds, lime leaves, lemongrass, and jalapeno pepper in a food processor and blend until the mixture becomes a paste. Transfer to a blender, and mix with the canola oil, basil leaves, and cilantro until smooth.

COCONUT CURRY BASE

Melt the coconut oil in a large pot over medium heat until you see a sheen on the oil. Toast the curry paste, fish sauce, and brown sugar, stirring constantly for even cooking, just until fragrant, about 1 minute. Add the coconut milk and bring to a boil. Lower the heat and allow to simmer for 45 minutes. The liquid should reduce to about 1.5L (6 cups). Transfer 1 cup to a blender and add the jalapeno pepper. Blend on high for 30 seconds. Stir back into the base. Season with salt and lime juice.

THAI FISH
CURRY

Preheat the oven to 212°C (415°F).

Cut the Japanese eggplants in half lengthwise, then slice into 1–1.5cm thick (⅜–½ in) half moons. Toss with a pinch of salt and a drizzle of olive oil, then lay on a baking tray lined with parchment. Roast until golden brown, about 10 minutes. Leave the oven turned on.

Cut the sweet potatoes into 2cm (¾ in) cubes and toss with a dash of olive oil and a pinch of salt. Lay on a baking sheet lined with parchment paper and roast in the oven until cooked through and the edges are browning with some caramelization, about 15 minutes. Set aside.

In a large pot, bring the coconut curry base to a boil. Lower the heat and add the rockfish. Simmer for 3 to 5 minutes, until the fish is just cooked. In the last minute of cooking, add the eggplants and sweet potatoes. Ladle the curry into serving bowls and garnish with jalapeno pepper and cilantro. Serve with steamed jasmine rice.

SYMPHONY OF THE SEA

Serves 6

I spent a lot of time at West trying to come up with elaborate dishes that were really light. For this one, I decided we'd take all the vegetables we could find that could be cut into a brunoise (tiny 3mm (⅛ in) cubes), blanch them, dress them, and spread them in a super-colourful layer over a plate. Then we'd add the best fish and seafood of the season, each cooked its ideal way. Like, seven different types of seafood cooked seven different ways: a grilled scallop, a seared piece of salmon belly, a deep-fried oyster, and so on. Visually, the plate was quite exciting. And in the kitchen? Oh, this dish broke a lot of chefs.

INGREDIENTS

Vegetables

1 medium red beet

1 recipe Tomato Concassé (page 312)

6 green beans, brunoise

½ fennel bulb, brunoise

½ medium kohlrabi, brunoise

½ medium carrot, brunoise

1 medium potato, brunoise

15g (⅓ cup) chopped chives

15g (3 Tbsp) Mayonnaise (page 314 or store-bought)

Pinch salt

Lemon juice

Avocado Purée

2 medium avocados, cut in cubes

15mL (1 Tbsp) lime juice

1.5g (½ tsp) salt

Prawns & Oysters

6 large spot prawns, whole with head on

12 small oysters, shucked

120g (¾ cup) flour

Salt

2 eggs

15mL (1 Tbsp) milk

120g (2 cups) panko crumbs

1L (4 cups) canola oil

16g (2 Tbsp) cornstarch or flour

Scallops & Fish

100mL (7 Tbsp) canola oil

12 medium scallops, cut in half

Salt

6 portions halibut (45g/1½ oz each)

30g (2 Tbsp) butter

6 portions spring salmon (45g/1½ oz each)

Garnishes

½ small green jalapeno, thinly sliced

Mixed microgreens

Lemon juice, for drizzling

Olive oil, for drizzling

Continued . . .

Place the beet in a medium saucepan and cover with salted water by 5cm (2 in). Bring the water to a boil and simmer, covered, until tender when pierced with the tip of a knife, usually 30 to 45 minutes, depending on the size of the beet. Remove from the water and peel while still hot. Allow to cool and cut into 5mm (¼ in) dice.

Bring a medium pot of salted water to a boil. Cook every vegetable separately, I at a time, until tender, starting with the green beans and finishing with the potatoes. When the green beans have cooked, dunk them immediately into an ice bath, then pat dry. Keep the vegetables separate until serving.

When ready to serve, combine all the vegetables (except the beet) with the chives and mayonnaise. Season with a pinch of salt and a squeeze of lemon juice. Set aside at room temperature. Add the beet last and gently incorporate so that it doesn't stain the other vegetables.

Combine the avocados, lime juice, and salt in the bowl of a blender or small food processor and blitz until smooth. Adjust the seasoning as necessary. Transfer to a small piping bag.

Bring a medium pot of salted water to a boil. Separate the spot prawn heads from the tails and set the heads aside. Blanch the tails for I minute, then immediately dunk in an ice bath. This will facilitate peeling the meat. To remove the meat from the shell, turn the prawns on their backs and gently peel back the shell. You can leave the very end of the tail attached for presentation if you like. Set aside.

Place the shucked oysters on a baking tray lined with paper towel. Bring the reserved prawn blanching water to a simmer and drop the oysters in for 10 seconds (this will firm them up and help keep the breading from getting too soggy). Transfer back on the tray to cool.

Prepare a breading station with 3 bowls: I with the flour and 3 pinches of salt combined, I with the eggs and milk gently beaten together, and I with the panko crumbs. Dredge the oysters in the flour mixture and shake off the excess. Using a slotted spoon, dip the oysters in the egg mixture, letting any excess drain off, then roll them around in the panko crumbs. Set aside on a baking tray.

Heat the oil to 195°C (380°F) in a pot large enough that it is not more than half full.

Coat the prawn heads in cornstarch and shake to remove excess. Deep-fry the prawn heads for about 3 minutes until crispy. Transfer to paper towel to soak up excess oil. Season with a pinch of salt.

Drop the oysters in the oil and fry for 2 minutes. Transfer to paper towel to soak up excess oil. Season with a pinch of salt.

Keep the prawns and oysters warm.

SCALLOPS & FISH

Heat a large non-stick pan with 25mL (scant 2 Tbsp) of the oil on high heat. Season the scallops with salt. Sear the scallops, flat side down, for 1 to 2 minutes until golden brown. Add 8g (½ Tbsp) of butter, flip the scallops, and cook for an additional 30 seconds. Remove from the pan and keep warm on a tray lined with paper towel.

Wipe the pan with paper towel and add another 25mL (scant 2 Tbsp) of the oil. Sear the halibut fillets on high heat on 1 side for 1 minute. Turn the heat down to medium and continue cooking for 1 more minute, until the centre is opaque. Flip the fish and add 15g (1 Tbsp) butter and baste for 1 minute. The halibut should be cooked only to medium, as it has a tendency to dry out. Keep warm.

Wipe the pan with a paper towel and add 25mL (scant 2 Tbsp) of oil. Sear the salmon portions on high heat then add 8g (½ Tbsp) of butter and flip the fish. The salmon might take 1 more minute of cooking. Keep warm.

Wipe the pan with a paper towel. Reheat the prawn tails in the remaining 25mL (scant 2 Tbsp) of oil for 30 seconds on each side. Keep warm.

SERVE

Place a layer of the vegetable mixture on the bottom of a plate. Divide the salmon, halibut, scallop pieces, prawn tails, crispy prawn heads, and fried oysters between each plate.

Pipe with dots of avocado purée, and garnish with jalapeno slices and a few microgreens. Drizzle the whole dish with lemon juice and olive oil.

HAWKSWORTH

It began with fish soup. I had learned to make it back in 1992 in my first gig on the fish station at the Canteen. Now, 15 years on, here I was running the pass at West, preparing my BC version as an off-menu special request for my good friend Willie Mitchell—then a defenceman for the Vancouver Canucks—and his wife Megan, who loves cooking and does it very well.

The soup base is rich with the flavours of Southern France: ripe tomatoes and olive oil, wine-soaked fish bones, Pernod, and of course saffron. Once all that was sautéed and simmered, I strained the mix through a fine chinois and added an array of local fish and seafood cooked à la minute: wild salmon, halibut, scallops, mussels, clams, and spot prawns. In place of the usual croutons, there was grilled focaccia, and my rouille was brightened with roasted red pepper and basil along with the expected saffron. I sent the soup out to the Mitchells and their guests in a lidded tureen, had it served to them tableside, and blew their minds.

Later that night, Willie came back to the kitchen to thank me and to ask me to come out to his table to meet his dinner guests. But I was in the middle of placing food orders for the following week, and dealing—okay, fighting—with my dishwasher. So I just said, "N-o-o-o, Willie, please, not tonight. I'm really fine back here." Willie insisted. I grudgingly gave in. Next thing, I was standing by the Mitchells' table, being introduced to developer Bruce Langereis, from Delta Land Development. We talked local food and restaurants. Bruce had never been to West before, but evidently he liked it because right then and there he said, "We're actually looking for a restaurant partner in the hotel."

"What hotel?" I asked.

"We just bought the Hotel Georgia."

Oh, *that* hotel.

It was my dream restaurant location. Often, in those late days at West, on my days off I'd take a walk over to West Georgia and Howe, stand by the newspaper boxes on the southeast corner, and gaze at that grand old hotel across the street. It had everything I wanted. It was central, stately, and elegant, and it looked over a streetscape as compelling as anything in London, Paris, or New York. I could see a future there. But in the meantime, the place had also been run—okay, beaten—into the ground. Its restaurant, the

Georgian Bar and Grill, was closed and boarded up with plywood. I had tried to get a meeting with the hotel's owners, but they had declined. Now I knew why: they had been in the middle of selling to Bruce. And here he was, full of my fish soup and inviting me—unprompted—to come on board. I jumped at it.

Within days, I was in a meeting with Bruce, Delta Land Development Chair Tony Hii, and their project team, listening to their plans for the Georgia: a five-star hotel, a new condo tower—and a great new restaurant. So after much deliberation, I gave Jack three weeks' notice. I expected to be walked right out the door; instead he asked me to stay on for six months while he looked for a new chef, and in the interim, finish the West cookbook that I'd started on. I had deep reservations, but agreed—and lasted five and a half months.

That stretch of 2007 was awkward, but 2008 was a whole lot worse. My new partners had just planned a $250 million hotel development that hinged on condo sales when—wham!—along came a financial crisis so intense that I thought we were headed backward a few thousand years. Annabel and I had just had our son, Heston, and next thing, it felt like the world was ending. Eventually Delta scraped together new financing, and construction never actually stopped—but it was very slow. For two and a half years we were basically in limbo. I had a retainer and went to our office on West Hastings every day, but all I could do was design menus and make lists of staff I wanted to hire. I felt like the guy in that story about the Japanese businessman who's been fired, but instead of sharing the shameful news with his family keeps up appearances by getting into a suit and hopping on the rush hour train each morning, to nowhere. The only good part of the ordeal was that I was around for Heston. I did my best to keep my name in the public eye by doing catering and cooking for charity events, and we weathered the storm. And finally, we got started on the real business of putting Hawksworth Restaurant together.

Alessandro Munge, who was hired to redo the hotel, is a very gifted restaurant designer. We had space for 110 seats, but we wanted to spread them over distinct, intimate spaces with subtly different moods. Studio Munge created three rooms: the bar and lounge; the Pearl Room, with its deco-inspired oval chandelier and Venetian plaster walls; and the Art Room, with its full wall–sized Rodney Graham panel installation. Meanwhile, François Morin and the team from SML Stainless in Quebec City came in to build an equally beautiful kitchen.

While the build-out was going on, I went out and hired really, really good people. It was the thing I did best. For front of house I got Chad Clark, a very polished manager who really understands service and is great with guests. I got sommelier Terry Threlfall, who had worked with me at West, to come home from London, where he was running the multi-award-winning wine program at Michelin-starred Chez Bruce. Bar manager Brad Stanton had great experience, an interest in cocktail history, and a knack for pairing drink and food.

Then there was my head chef, Kristian Eligh. I spotted him working in the kitchen at Diva at the Met—and knew instantly the guy was really, really good, of a calibre way beyond what you usually see. Hawksworth Restaurant put my name on my first business, and every chef who takes that next step and becomes a business owner needs a top-tier head chef to run his kitchen and take care of its day-to-day operations while he deals with everything from payroll and accounting to negotiating service contracts, menu and recipe development, dealing with media, you name it. In my case—from the outset—I was planning more than just the namesake restaurant. At the very least we were going to do a catering arm. It was full bore. I relied on Kristian. We went through every menu and every dish together. He knew the style I was looking for, and I trusted him absolutely to carry it out.

The style we launched Hawksworth with was more colourful, had more contrast in its textures, and was lighter eating than anything I had cooked before. All of that was a direct evolution of the culinary journey I had already undertaken at West. I never wanted to cook fine dining that was for special occasions only; I was always aiming for a cuisine that was refined, but also accessible and light enough that diners could come in for lunch and then back again for dinner that same day if they wanted to.

You could also eat indulgently if you chose. We opened with that classic parfait of foie gras that I learned in the UK and put on the first menu at Ouest. But Asian influences were now as pronounced as French ones in an increasingly international culinary mix. The opening menu had a carpaccio of yellowfin tuna loin with julienned Japanese pear and creamy avocado, seasoned with yuzu and topped with crunchy puffed rice. On the other hand, we had 72-hour sous vide–cooked beef short rib with black pepper jam, green papaya, and diced peanuts.

The range seemed to hit the right note. In our first year, Hawksworth Restaurant took seven different golds at the *Vancouver Magazine* awards, and *Maclean's* magazine named us Canada's Restaurant of the Year. It was a great start. H

MEAT & POULTRY

Roasted Turnips (page 251)

GRILLED QUAIL, CONCORD GRAPE MOSTARDA, TOASTED PISTACHIOS

Serves 6

This is a very delicious dish for summertime grilling. By keeping your quail on the bone, you're going to keep some moisture in there when you grill them. When you do, use high heat—the char of the grill marks adds a hit of flavour that I really like. The mostarda has sweetness, acidity, and some heat too, so it's got a nice balance.

NOTE

If you want to take it the next level, scatter some foraged wild leaves over the platter just before you serve it—like miner's lettuce, or wild arugula. If you are serving this as a main dish on its own, increase the number of quail to six (one per person) and double the quantity of the spice mix.

INGREDIENTS

Marinated Quail

6g (2 tsp) coriander seeds

6g (2 tsp) fennel seeds

3g (1 tsp) peppercorns

1.5g (½ tsp) cardamom seeds

Pinch allspice berries

3 quail (about 340g/12 oz each), cut in half (ask your butcher, if necessary)

15mL (1 Tbsp) canola oil

½ orange, zest

Concord Grape Mostarda

300g (2 cups) concord grapes, stems removed

100mL (7 Tbsp) balsamic vinegar

90mL (6 Tbsp) red wine

30g (2½ Tbsp) brown sugar

15g (1½ Tbsp) mustard seeds

2 star anise pods

1 bay leaf

1 sprig rosemary

Toasted Pistachios

50g (⅓ cup) shelled pistachios

Garnish

Olive oil, for drizzling

MARINATED QUAIL

Heat a small sauté pan over medium heat and toast the coriander, fennel, peppercorns, cardamom, and allspice in a pan until fragrant, about 30 seconds. Allow to cool to room temperature. Transfer to a blender or coffee grinder and blitz until finely grind.

In a large bowl, toss the quail in the spices and the oil and orange zest. Marinate in the fridge overnight.

CONCORD GRAPE MOSTARDA

Combine all the ingredients in a small pot over medium-low heat and simmer gently until the mixture becomes syrupy and thick, stirring frequently to ensure it does not stick.

Remove the rosemary, bay leaf, and star anise. Allow to cool at room temperature.

Continued . . .

TOASTED PISTACHIOS Preheat the oven to 175°C (350°F).

Place the pistachios on a baking tray lined with parchment paper and toast for 6 to 10 minutes. Leave the oven on. Allow to cool, then chop.

SERVE Heat a barbecue or grill pan to smoking point. Grill the quail, skin side down, for 1 to 2 minutes to char the skins with grill marks. Transfer to a baking tray lined with parchment paper and roast in the oven for 5 minutes. Remove from the oven and allow to rest for 5 minutes.

Place the quail on a serving platter and spoon the concord grape mostarda on top. Garnish with the pistachios and a drizzle of olive oil.

SQUAB POT-AU-FEU, PARSLEY DUMPLINGS

Serves 4

Pot-au-feu is an old French dish that should not be forgotten. Traditionally it's a hearty winter meal in one pot that features a few differently textured cuts of braising beef, and sometimes chicken too, with root vegetables, leeks, and celery. At West, we used only squab, roasted on the crown, with light parsley and suet dumplings, delicate young vegetables, and porcini mushrooms. This is a luxurious fall or winter dish—an elevated classic.

NOTE

Of all the different fats that can be used for binding a dumpling mixture, suet traps the most air and delivers the fluffiest texture. You can make the consommé several days in advance. For a splash more colour when serving this dish, soak a few pearl onions in beet juice and peel some of the layers to use as a garnish.

INGREDIENTS

Squabs

4 squabs (450g/1 pound each)

Consommé

450g (1 pound) chicken bones, cut in 5cm (2 in) pieces

50mL (3 Tbsp) canola oil

Salt

2 shallots, sliced

200g (4 cups) button mushrooms, sliced

2L (8 cups) Chicken Stock (page 317)

1 stalk celery, quartered

½ small carrot, quartered

½ small onion, quartered

½ small leek, quartered

1 bay leaf

1 duck breast (200g/7 oz), skinned and cut in large chunks

3 egg whites

Squab Leg Confit

55g (6 Tbsp) salt

15g (1 Tbsp) sugar

3g (1 tsp) peppercorns

2g (¼ tsp) juniper berries

2 sprigs fresh thyme

2 bay leaves

500g (2 cups) rendered duck fat or lard

Parsley Dumplings

125g (1 cup) flour, plus extra for dusting

5g (1 tsp) baking powder

Pinch salt

60g (2 oz) cold suet, shredded using a cheese grater

1 recipe Parsley Purée (page 315)

50mL (3 Tbsp) water (approx.)

Vegetables

4 baby carrots, trimmed

6 baby turnips, scrubbed and cut in half

2 baby zucchinis, cut in 4 on the bias

8 pearl onions

4 Brussels sprouts, leaves taken off the heart

Squab Crowns

60mL (4 Tbsp) canola oil

4 button porcini mushrooms, cut in half

15g (1 Tbsp) butter

Pinch salt

Continued . . .

To prepare the squabs, remove the wings, legs, and back first. Set aside the legs. You will be left with the crowns (the breast on the bone); set these aside also.

Preheat the oven to 175°C (350°F).

Place the squab wings and backs and the chicken bones in a roasting pan with the canola oil. Toss to coat, then lightly season with salt. Roast for 15 minutes, stirring every 5 minutes or so to ensure an even colour.

Add the shallots and half the mushrooms and continue to roast for 15 minutes until everything is a rich golden brown.

Drain through a colander to remove the grease and transfer to a heavy-bottomed pot. Add the chicken stock, celery, carrot, onion, leek, and bay leaf. The chicken stock should cover everything. Bring to a boil, then lower the heat and cook at a slow simmer for 1 hour.

Remove from the heat, let rest for 15 minutes, then pass through a colander. Discard the bones and set the stock aside to cool. Taste and adjust the seasoning if necessary.

Blend the duck breast in a food processor for 30 seconds. Place the egg whites in a large bowl and whisk in the duck meat vigorously for 30 seconds to combine.

Pour the squab stock into a deep, heavy-bottomed pot. Add the duck and egg mixture and stir thoroughly to combine. Set the pot over medium heat and slowly bring to a boil; the mixture must be gently stirred with a wooden spoon almost constantly to keep the egg whites from sticking and burning on the bottom. Stop stirring when the egg white starts to coagulate and a crust starts to form on the surface.

Pierce a small hole in the crust with a spoon or a ladle, and let the stock cook gently for 20 minutes. At this point, the mixture must not be stirred at all, or it will become cloudy. Remove from the heat and ladle the consommé very carefully out of the hole in the crust. Pass it through a fine-mesh sieve lined with cheesecloth. Try not to disturb the crust. You should have approximately 1L (4 cups) of consommé. In a fresh pot, bring the consommé to a boil and reduce by about ¼ to intensify the flavour. Reserve until needed.

Combine the salt, sugar, peppercorns, juniper berries, thyme, and bay leaves to create a cure. Rub the cure all over the reserved squab legs, and refrigerate for 6 to 8 hours. When ready, remove the legs from the fridge and rinse off the cure.

Preheat the oven to 150°C (300°F).

Melt the duck fat in a small pot over low heat. Place the legs in a small roasting pan, making sure they do not overlap, and pour over the melted fat. Cover with a piece of parchment paper and cook until you can easily wiggle the knee joint, 2 to 3 hours. Let the legs cool in the fat, then transfer to a baking tray lined with parchment paper, skin side down. Cover with another piece of parchment paper, then place a second baking tray on top of the legs. Add a small weight on top, so that the legs are gently pressed down and slightly flattened for searing. Refrigerate until ready to use.

Continued . . .

PARSLEY DUMPLINGS

Sift the flour, baking powder, and salt into a bowl. Add the suet and 50g (3 Tbsp) of the parsley purée. Make a well in the centre and gradually add enough cold water to bring the mixture together into a pliable dough, slightly moist but not sticky. On a lightly floured surface, gently knead the dough for 15 seconds, dusting with extra flour as needed. Do not overwork.

With floured hands, roll the dough into small tablespoon-sized balls.

Bring a large skillet of salted water to a boil. Add the dumplings and cook until puffed and cooked through, about 15 minutes.

VEGETABLES

Bring a medium pot of salted water to a boil. Add the carrots and cook until tender. Repeat with the turnips, zucchinis, pearl onions, and Brussels sprouts, blanching everything separately in salted water until tender.

SQUAB CROWNS

Preheat the oven to 200°C (400°F).

Heat 45mL (3 Tbsp) of the canola oil in a heavy-bottomed oven-safe non-stick pan. Place the reserved squab crowns in the pan, breast side down, and slowly colour all sides, about 4 minutes a side. Flip the squab and roast in the oven, breast side up, for 2 more minutes until medium-rare; cook slightly longer for medium. Remove from the oven and let rest for 5 minutes before carving.

Reheat the consommé and adjust the seasoning as needed.

Using the same pan as the squab was in, sear the porcini mushrooms for 2 minutes. Add the butter and salt and sear for another minute.

In a separate pan, heat the remaining canola oil. Remove the squab legs from the baking tray and sear, skin side down, for 2 to 4 minutes until the skin is golden brown.

Serve the squab crowns and legs with all of the vegetables, a few herb dumplings, and a ladle of consommé.

ROASTED CHICKEN, PEPERONATA, MACEDONIAN FETA

Serves 6

(photo on page 212)

At Nightingale we marinate this chicken in yogurt mixed with lots of lemon juice and herbs so it comes out tender and crispy with lots of flavour. The peperonata adds sweetness and acidity; the feta and olives a salty counterpart. I love travelling to Mediterranean countries—I'm sure this dish has been inspired by what I've tasted in Croatia or Greece along the way.

INGREDIENTS

Lemon & Yogurt Marinade

750 mL (3 cups) plain yogurt

150mL (⅔ cup) lemon juice

75mL (5 Tbsp) water

5 cloves garlic, minced

2 sprigs mint, chopped

15g (2 Tbsp) dried oregano

2 lemons, zest

Chicken

2 whole chickens (about 1.1kg/2.5 lb)

Peperonata

1 red bell pepper

1 yellow bell pepper

115g (1 cup) canned piquillo peppers, julienned

40mL (scant 3 Tbsp) sherry vinegar

25mL (scant 2 Tbsp) olive oil

30g (2 Tbsp) Castelvetrano olives, halved and pits removed

12g (1 Tbsp) chopped capers

1 sprig Italian parsley, chopped

Pinch chili flakes

Pinch pepper

Pinch salt

Garnish

150g (1 cup) Macedonian feta, crumbled

75g (about 18) Castelvetrano olives

Olive oil, for drizzling

Pepper

MARINATED CHICKEN

Combine all the marinade ingredients and pour over the chickens. Refrigerate the chickens in the marinade overnight, turning at least once to make sure the marinade is covering all sides.

Remove from the fridge and scrape off any excess marinade. Allow the chickens to sit at room temperature for 30 minutes.

Preheat the oven to 160°C (315°F).

Place the chickens on a wire rack set on top of a baking tray lined with parchment paper. Do not overcrowd. Roast until a meat thermometer inserted into the thigh reads 72°C (160°F). This could take about an hour. While the chickens are cooking, prepare the peperonata.

Remove from the oven and allow to rest until cooled enough to handle.

Continued . . .

PEPERONATA Using an open flame, or barbecue, char the outside of the red and yellow peppers until the skin starts to blister and turn black. Place in a stainless-steel bowl and cover with plastic wrap. Let sit for 5 to 10 minutes, to allow the peppers to steam. This will make it easier to peel the skin off. Remove and discard the peel from the peppers, running under cold water to help as needed. Cut the peppers in half and discard the seeds and pith. Pat dry with paper towel.

Slice the bell peppers into a julienne. Combine all the remaining ingredients and adjust the seasoning to taste.

Transfer everything to a small pot and gently warm over medium heat.

SERVE Carve the chicken legs, and separate the drumstick from the thigh. Carve the breasts and cut each breast in half.

Spoon the peperonata into a serving dish. Place the carved chicken on top. Add the crumbled feta, olives, and a drizzle of olive oil. Season with pepper.

PARMESAN-CRUSTED CHICKEN, POTATO GNOCCHI, ARTICHOKE BARIGOULE

Serves 6

This Hawksworth recipe was adapted from a Jean-Georges Vongerichten recipe that works incredibly well. You make an espuma of egg whites, dip the skinless chicken breast in it, and then dredge one side of it in a mixture of Parmesan and flour. Then roast the breasts Parmesan crust side down only—so while the outside gets crusty and salty, the breast basically steams itself. It comes out perfect. The gnocchi here is a slightly more refined version than what we serve at Nightingale (page 136) and is a wonderful gnocchi recipe for any occasion.

INGREDIENTS

Gnocchi

1–2 medium Yukon Gold potatoes (you need 250g/9 oz of cooked potatoes)

1 egg yolk

4g (1 tsp) salt

70g (½ cup) all-purpose flour

Olive oil, for drizzling

30mL (2 Tbsp) canola oil, for searing

Artichoke Barigoule

190mL (¾ cup) olive oil

60g (2¼ oz) sliced Spanish chorizo

3 large artichokes, turned (see page 210), or high-quality artichoke hearts

2 lemons, halved

1 medium carrot, sliced into discs

½ head fennel, sliced

½ medium onion, chopped

1 stalk celery, cut in diamonds

2 cloves garlic

1 bay leaf

4 sprigs thyme

3g (1 tsp) peppercorns

2g (⅔ tsp) fennel seeds

Pinch saffron

Chicken Stock (page 319 or store bought), as needed to cover

250mL (1 cup) white wine

Xanthan gum

Salt

Red Pepper Garnish

1 red bell pepper

Parmesan Crust

80g (⅔ cup) bread flour

120g (1¼ cups) finely grated Parmesan

50g (½ cup) shaved Parmesan shards (use a vegetable peeler)

10g (1 Tbsp) salt

Chicken

4 egg whites

6 chicken breasts (140–170g/ 5–6 oz each)

75mL (7 Tbsp) canola oil

Serve

8g (2 Tbsp) chopped chives

1 sprig parsley, stem removed

Lemon

Continued . . .

GNOCCHI   Preheat the oven to 175°C (350°F).

Stab the potatoes with a knife or fork to allow the steam to escape while cooking. Place on a wire rack set on top of a baking tray. Cook for 1 hour, then rotate the baking tray and flip the potatoes. Cook until tender, up to another hour.

Once cooked, slice the potatoes in half and press them through a fine mesh sieve. Discard the skin. Weigh out 250g (9 oz) of the potato flesh. Thoroughly incorporate the egg yolk and salt into the potato flesh. Cut the flour into the potatoes using a plastic bench scraper; do not overmix. Once incorporated, transfer the mixture to a cutting board and form it into a ball.

Divide the dough into quarters. On a lightly floured work surface, roll each ball into long thin tubes. Cut each tube into 2.5cm (1 in) lengths. Transfer to a baking tray dusted with flour and refrigerate for 15 to 20 minutes.

Bring a stockpot of heavily salted water to a simmer, but not a rolling boil, which would damage your gnocchi. Gently place the gnocchi into the pot in batches and simmer until cooked through. They are ready once they float to the top. Transfer to a baking tray lined with parchment paper and drizzle with olive oil.

Reserve at least 24 gnocchi for this recipe. Freeze the remainder on a baking tray lined with parchment paper, then transfer to a sealable freezer bag. Freeze for up to 1 month.

ARTICHOKE
BARIGOULE   Heat the olive oil in a large pot over medium heat. Add the chorizo and cook until the fat has rendered and the sausage is crisp. Add the artichoke hearts, lemons, carrots, fennel, onion, celery, garlic, bay leaf, thyme, peppercorns, fennel seeds, and saffron. Cover with the chicken stock and white wine. Bring to a boil, cover the surface of the mixture with a cartouche (disc of parchment paper), then reduce the heat to a slow simmer. Cook for 20 to 25 minutes, until the artichokes are tender when pierced with the tip of a knife.

Strain, reserving the liquid and the solids separately. Pick out about 24 pieces each of the carrots, celery, fennel, and chorizo, plus the artichokes, and reserve.

Blend the strained liquid with the remaining vegetables, adding in only enough xanthan gum (just a touch, using the tip of a knife) to emulsify the mixture to a very smooth, well-blended texture. The mixture should not be grainy. Adjust the seasoning as needed.

Cut each artichoke heart into 8 wedges, for a total of 24.

RED PEPPER   Using an open flame, or barbecue, char the outside of the red pepper until the skin starts to blister and turn black. Place in a stainless-steel bowl and cover with plastic wrap. Let sit for 5 to 10 minutes to steam. This will make it easier to peel. Remove and discard the peel, running the pepper under cold water to help as needed. Cut the pepper in half and discard the seeds and pith. Pat dry with paper towel and cut into diamonds.

PARMESAN
CRUST   Mix all the ingredients by hand in a mixing bowl until well combined.

Continued . . .

Preheat the oven to 200°C (400°F).

Pour the egg whites into an ISI gun and charge with 2 cartridges, or lightly whip them until they form stiff peaks. Place some of the foamy egg whites onto a tray or shallow pan. Dip 1 side of each chicken breast in egg white, then in the Parmesan crust.

Heat the oil in a large heavy-bottomed ovenproof pan, ideally cast iron. Place the breasts, Parmesan crust side down, in the pan and roast in the oven for 11 minutes. Remove from the pan and allow to rest for a few minutes before slicing in half lengthwise. Season with salt.

SERVE Heat a skillet with 30 mL (2 Tbsp) of canola oil over medium-high heat and sauté the gnocchi until golden brown, a few minutes each side. Add the artichoke hearts and pepper diamonds and heat for an additional minute.

Reheat the reserved carrots, celery, fennel, and chorizo in their blended cooking liquid over low heat, then divide between 6 plates. Top with the gnocchi and sauteed vegetables, and garnish with chives, parsley, and a squeeze of lemon. Place the chicken alongside.

TURNING AN ARTICHOKE

INGREDIENTS Artichokes

30mL (2 Tbsp) lemon juice

Pull off the outermost leaves of the artichoke until you get down to the lighter, yellow leaves. Use a serrated knife to cut off the stem so that the artichoke will sit up on a plate. Then cut off the top 1/3 of the artichoke, at the point the remaining leaves meet the heart.

Place the lemon juice in a large bowl of water. While you are working, keep the prepared artichokes in the bowl to keep them from browning.

With a paring knife, carefully trim the top and sides of the artichoke in a turning motion, slowly cutting toward the heart. There's no clear demarcation between leaves and heart—the leaves merge and become the heart—as soon as you don't see spaces between the leaves anymore, you're there. Now, using a spoon, remove the furry choke at the centre of the heart. Scrape away at the choke until you've scooped it all out, switching to a pairing knife if needed to clean out the last bits. You will be left with the artichoke heart.

Cook the artichoke hearts according to the recipe.

1.

2.

3.

4.

5.

6.

Roasted Chicken (page 205)

English Pea & Burrata
Tortellini (page 132)

Tuna, Arugula & Avocado Salad
(page 87)

ROASTED DUCK BREAST, XO SAUCE, CAROLINA GOLD RICE, MACADAMIA PURÉE

Serves 6

Duck is rich, and I wanted to make this dish as light as possible. Instead of a traditional sauce—like a reduction finished with butter—being in Vancouver, where our population is now almost a third Chinese, I thought of XO sauce. It's very tasty and has good texture, a little heat, and some acidity too. It really works.

NOTE

In the restaurant we allow the duck to air dry for a few days, uncovered in the fridge; this helps the bird to retain more moisture when it cooks. You can prepare the XO sauce up to several days before serving; it helps the flavour to develop.

INGREDIENTS

Macadamia Nut Purée

125g (1 cup) macadamia nuts, skin off

Salt

Splash Banyuls or champagne vinegar

XO Sauce

85g (5 Tbsp) brunoised bacon

150mL (⅔ cup) canola oil

30g (⅓ cup) dried shrimp, soaked and drained

30g (⅓ cup) dried scallops, soaked and drained

80g (½ cup) minced garlic

80g (½ cup) minced ginger

20g (1 Tbsp) tomato paste

15mL (1 Tbsp) Sriracha-style chili sauce

Fish sauce

Salt

Rice

1.5L (6 cups) water

3g (1 tsp) salt, plus more for seasoning

240g (1¼ cups) Carolina gold rice

30–45g (2–3 Tbsp) butter, cut in small cubes

2 spring onions, finely sliced

1 sprig cilantro, finely sliced

Duck

3 large duck magrets (400–450g/ 14–16 oz each)

Sea salt

Garnish

6–12 pieces gai choy, cleaned, trimmed, and cut in half

15g (1 Tbsp) butter

Sea salt

MACADAMIA NUT PURÉE

Preheat the oven to 160°C (315°F).

Place the nuts on a baking tray lined with parchment paper and toast until fragrant, 10 to 15 minutes. Allow to cool, then transfer to a bowl. Cover with water (at least 10cm/4 in above the nuts; you should have double the volume of water as nuts) and soak in the fridge overnight.

Continued . . .

The next day, drain the nuts and reserve the water. Blend the nuts on high speed for at least 5 minutes and up to 10 minutes, using as much water as required to form a smooth purée. Season with salt and a splash of vinegar. Set aside at room temperature.

XO SAUCE — Render the bacon until crispy in a medium pan over low heat, using a small amount of oil. Remove the bacon, but keep the fat in the pan. Add a bit more oil to the pan and fry the dried shrimp and scallops until slightly crispy. Remove the shrimp and scallops and return the pan to heat.

Once the pan starts smoking, add the remaining canola oil and caramelize the garlic and ginger. Add the tomato paste and cook for 5 minutes. Return the shrimp, scallops, and bacon to the pan and add the chili sauce and any remaining oil. Let the mixture simmer for 30 minutes on very low heat, stirring often so it doesn't stick to the bottom of the pan.

Adjust the seasoning with fish sauce, salt, and more chili sauce as needed.

RICE — Preheat the oven to 175°C (350°F).

Bring the water and salt to a boil in a heavy-bottomed saucepan set over high heat. Add the rice, stir once, and as soon as the water returns to a boil, reduce the heat to low. Simmer gently, uncovered, stirring occasionally, until the rice is just tender with no hard starch at its centre, about 15 minutes. Drain in a fine-mesh sieve and rinse thoroughly with cool water. Shake the colander to drain excess water.

Distribute the rice evenly on a baking tray lined with parchment paper. Place in the oven and allow the rice to dry for about 5 minutes, gently turning from time to time with a spatula. Dot the rice with the butter and sprinkle with salt. Return the baking sheet to the oven and allow the rice to warm through, occasionally turning, until the butter has melted and the rice is hot, about 5 minutes. Mix in the onions and cilantro and keep the rice warm.

DUCK — Trim the excess fat around the duck magrets. With a sharp knife, score the skin of the magrets in a crosshatch pattern, making the squares as close together as possible without cutting into the meat. Set aside on paper towel to absorb excess moisture.

Season the duck magrets with salt on both sides. Place the duck breasts in a hot non-stick cast-iron pan (skin side down without any oil) over medium-low heat. Cook for 6 to 8 minutes, moving from time to time (but not flipping) to ensure an even colouring and crisping of the skin, while continuously draining out the rendered fat.

Flip the magrets and cook for 3 minutes on the meat side. Remove from the heat and let stand for 5 minutes, loosely covered with a piece of foil. When ready to serve, slice the magrets in 6mm (¼ in) slices. Season with sea salt.

GARNISH — Bring a large pot of salted water to a boil. Blanch the gai choy for 1 minute, then quickly sauté in a hot frying pan with the butter and a pinch of salt. Transfer to paper towel to absorb excess fat.

Gently heat the XO sauce. Divide it between 6 serving plates. Smear the macadamia nut purée on the side. Place a portion of gai choy and rice on each plate. Add the duck slices.

JUNGLE PORK CURRY

Serves 8

I can't remember where exactly I was in the UK when I first tried curry with jackfruit, but I was like, "Wow—what is this vegetable?" Jackfruit was something I didn't know about. It's got such a delicious texture. I really liked how it combined with meat in curry, mostly because of how similar the texture of jackfruit is to meat. So when we wanted a curry on the lunch menu at Hawksworth, that's what we did.

INGREDIENTS

Jungle Pork

18g (2 Tbsp) coriander seeds

18g (2 Tbsp) cumin seeds

18g (2 Tbsp) white peppercorns

7g (1 Tbsp) cloves

5 shallots, chopped

3 stalks lemongrass, chopped

150mL (⅔ cup) grapeseed oil

30g (2 Tbsp) shrimp paste

5 cloves garlic, chopped

20g (2 Tbsp) chopped galangal (or a knob of ginger)

4 lime leaves, stems removed and leaves minced

6 red jalapenos, deseeded and chopped

15g (2½ Tbsp) Hungarian paprika

7g (1 Tbsp) ground nutmeg

2kg (4½ lb) pork cheek or shoulder, cut in large 5–8cm (2–3 in) pieces

Curry

1 onion, finely diced

8 cloves garlic, minced

2½L (10 cups) Chicken Stock (page 317 or store-bought)

500g (2 cups) San Marzano crushed tomatoes

1 can (14oz/400g) jackfruit, cut in large 5–8cm (2–3 in) pieces

1 lime, juice

Salt

Garnish

Pineapple, thinly sliced

Cilantro leaves

JUNGLE PORK

Heat a small sauté pan over medium heat and toast the coriander, cumin seeds, peppercorns, and cloves until fragrant, about 30 seconds. Allow to cool to room temperature.

Combine the toasted spices, shallots, lemongrass, oil, shrimp paste, garlic, galangal, lime leaves, jalapenos, paprika, and nutmeg in the bowl of a food processor and pulse until smooth.

Place the pork in a large bowl, add the paste, and rub thoroughly to coat. Cover and refrigerate for 12 hours, and up to 24 hours.

Continued . . .

CURRY   Scrape any excess paste off the meat, then lightly brown the meat in a large sauté pan or Dutch oven over medium heat, stirring frequently for 15 minutes. You may have to do this in batches. Remove the meat from the pan.

Add the onion and garlic to the pan and sauté until lightly browned. Return the meat to the pan.

Add the stock and the tomatoes and stir well. If the pork pieces are not completely covered, add up to 1L (4 cups) of water until they are, then stir again. Simmer uncovered on the lowest possible heat until the meat is tender when pierced with a knife, about 2 hours. In the last 30 minutes of cooking, add the jackfruit.

Add the lime juice and season with salt.

SERVE   Serve with basmati rice, and garnish with pineapple slices and cilantro.

ROASTED LAMB CHOPS, TRUFFLE MOUSSE, SMOKED CARROTS, POMME PURÉE

Serves 6

We did a lot of variations on this recipe at West. Sometimes we used lamb mousse with some shredded braised lamb folded in. Other times we did chicken mousse with wild mushrooms. My favourite was chicken mousse with lots of truffle. However you do it, the key is to start with a really nice quality lamb chop. It's old school, and lots of work, but so delicious.

INGREDIENTS

Caul Fat

12 pieces caul fat, 13 × 13cm (5 × 5 in) each

Smoked Carrots

24 medium carrots, trimmed

2 handfuls apple wood chips, for smoking

Olive oil

Salt

Chicken Mousse

200g (7 oz) skinless, boneless chicken breast, cut in small chunks

1 egg white

Pinch salt

Pinch cayenne

100mL (7 Tbsp) heavy cream

15g (⅓ cup) chopped chives

1 small fresh black truffle, chopped

A few drops good-quality white truffle oil

Pomme Purée

1kg (2.2 lb) large Yukon Gold potatoes, unpeeled

225g (1 cup) unsalted cold butter, cut in cubes

100mL (7 Tbsp) cream

1 sprig thyme

1 clove garlic, crushed

Salt

Lamb

3 racks lamb, frenched and cut into 4 double lamb chops each

30mL (2 Tbsp) canola oil

30g (2 Tbsp) butter

Sea salt

Chervil, for garnish

CAUL FAT

Submerge the caul fat in cold water and soak it in the refrigerator overnight, and up to a few days. The water should be changed several times. Alternatively, run cold water continuously over the caul fat until it is completely white.

Continued . . .

SMOKED CARROTS

Bring a shallow pot of salted water to a boil. Add the carrots, cover, and cook until tender, about 20 minutes. Transfer to the tray of a smoker and smoke with the apple wood chips for 20 minutes. (If you don't have a smoker you can use your barbecue: place the chips under the grill and light them (but not the grill), then close the lid and let smoke for 20 minutes.)

Remove from the smoker, drizzle with olive oil, and sprinkle with salt. Transfer to a dehydrator (or an oven at 95°C/200°F) for 4 to 6 hours, until shriveled and shrunk in size by almost half, intensifying their flavour.

CHICKEN MOUSSE

Place the chicken, egg white, salt, and cayenne in a food processor. With the machine running slowly, add half the cream. Mix until smooth and combined. Press the mixture through a fine mesh sieve into a large bowl and reserve over an ice bath. Gradually add the second half of the cream, beating with a rubber spatula to incorporate some air and lighten the mousse. Gently fold in the chives, truffle, and truffle oil. Refrigerate.

POMME PURÉE

Preheat the oven to 175°C (350°F).

Stab the potatoes with a knife multiple times to prepare for roasting. Place on a wire rack over a baking tray lined with parchment paper and cook until soft (this could take up to an hour), rotating the potatoes once after about 30 minutes.

In a small pot, bring the butter, cream, thyme, and garlic to a boil. Strain through a fine-mesh sieve and keep it warm but not boiling.

Press each potato through a fine mesh sieve or potato ricer to separate the flesh from the skin. Discard the skins. Transfer the potatoes to a large bowl.

Start incorporating the hot cream into the potatoes a little at a time, folding with a rubber spatula after each addition, until loose and soft but not soupy. Press once more through a fine mesh sieve and season with salt.

LAMB

Preheat the oven to 175°C (350°F).

Using an offset spatula or a spoon, place 15mL (1 Tbsp) chicken mousse on top of each lamb chop. Add a single layer of caul fat over each chop, and fold back around the bone and under the chop. Trim the excess as required. Set the chops on a baking tray lined with parchment paper.

Heat the oil in a large sauté pan on medium heat. Place the lamb chops in the pan, folded caul fat side down to seal it (you may have to do this in batches so as not to over-crowd the pan). Sear for 3 minutes. Place all 12 chops back in the pan to capture all of the flavours (or on a baking tray if your pan is not big enough), and set in the oven for 6 minutes.

Reheat the smoked carrots in the oven on a baking tray lined with parchment paper. Reheat the pomme purée in a pot and adjust the seasoning and consistency with a little more hot cream or milk as needed.

Continued . . .

Remove the lamb from the oven. Place the sauté pan with the chops back over medium heat, add the butter, and baste the chops until nicely browned on all sides, 3 to 4 minutes in total. This should cook the lamb to medium. Let rest for 3 to 4 minutes, then season with the sea salt.

Place a quenelle of pomme purée on each of 6 serving plates. Add the carrots and lamb chops. Garnish with the chervil.

BRAISED VEAL CHEEKS, ROSEMARY POLENTA, BRAISED SALSIFY, CHARRED SHALLOTS

Serves 6

Cheeks are widely used for braises in Europe, but you see a lot less of them here. I think everyone should get on the cheek train. They have so much flavour, and they're full of collagen; they are very tender when you braise them right. We serve them with soft polenta and roasted salsify. This is rich and luxurious comfort food.

NOTE

Braised dishes get better with age. After a day or two, their flavours have had a chance to mature and develop together.

INGREDIENTS

Veal Cheeks

1½kg (3.3 lb) veal cheeks, trimmed

500mL (2 cups) dry white wine

2 stalks celery, finely chopped

1 carrot, chopped

1 white onion, coarsely chopped

1 bouquet garni (1 sprig thyme and 1 bay leaf tied with butchers' twine)

3g (1 tsp) peppercorns

30mL (2 Tbsp) canola oil

Salt and pepper

1–1½L (4 to 6 cups) Veal Stock (page 317)

Rosemary Polenta

525mL (2 cups plus 2 Tbsp) Chicken Stock (page 317 or store-bought) or water

825mL (3⅓ cups) milk

1 clove garlic, finely chopped

2 pinches salt

175g (generous 1 cup) yellow or white cornmeal

90g (6 Tbsp) butter, cubed

60g (½ cup plus 1 Tbsp) grated Parmesan

50g (4 Tbsp) mascarpone cheese

1 sprig rosemary, stem removed, finely chopped

Braised Salsify & Charred Shallots

3 medium shallots, unpeeled

15mL (1 Tbsp) canola oil

12 salsify (10cm/4 in each)

Lemon juice, as needed

25mL (scant 2 Tbsp) olive oil

Salt

Water or chicken stock, as needed

1 sprig thyme

15g (1 Tbsp) butter

Pickled Shimeji Mushrooms

15mL (1 Tbsp) canola oil

1 bay leaf

1 sprig thyme

1 sprig rosemary

1 package (150g) shimeji mushrooms, trimmed

Pinch salt

75mL (5 Tbsp) white wine

75mL (5 Tbsp) white wine vinegar

Serve

45g (3 Tbsp) butter

15mL (1 Tbsp) sherry vinegar

Salt

Pepper

18 parsley leaves

Continued . . .

PICKLED
SHIMEJI
MUSHROOMS

Heat the oil in a small pot over medium heat until just below smoking point. Carefully add the bay leaf, thyme, and rosemary and crackle in the oil to infuse. Add the mushrooms and salt, and sweat briefly, for 90 seconds, stirring constantly. Add the white wine and white wine vinegar, and bring just to a simmer.

Transfer to a stainless-steel bowl and cool immediately. The mixture will have a slight thickness due to the natural slime of the mushrooms. Remove and discard the herbs. Allow the mushrooms to pickle for at least 2 hours and up to 1 week in the fridge.

VEAL CHEEKS

Place the veal cheeks in a large bowl. Add the wine, celery, carrots, onions, bouquet garni, and peppercorns. Toss gently to combine, making sure the meat is coated in the wine. Cover with plastic wrap and refrigerate for at least 8 hours and up to overnight.

Remove the veal cheeks from the marinade, pat dry with a paper towel, and set aside. Strain the marinade into a bowl and reserve the liquid along with the solids, setting aside the bouquet garni.

Preheat the oven to 120°C (250°F).

Heat the oil in a large ovenproof heavy-bottomed sauté pan or cast-iron Dutch oven over medium heat. Season the cheeks with salt and pepper. Sear the cheeks for 2 to 3 minutes on each side, or until evenly browned. Remove the cheeks and set aside. Add the solids from the marinade and cook for 3 to 5 minutes, or until they begin to soften and caramelize.

Return the cheeks to the skillet. Add the marinating liquid and bring to a boil. Reduce the heat to medium and simmer for 10 minutes, or until the liquid has reduced by half. Add the bouquet garni and veal stock. The stock should just cover the cheeks.

Bring to a boil once more and cover the cheeks with a cartouche (disc of parchment paper) and the pan with a lid or a piece of foil. Place in the oven and cook for 2 to 3 hours or until the meat is fork-tender.

ROSEMARY
POLENTA

Bring the chicken stock and milk to a boil in a medium pot set over high heat. Add the garlic and salt. Reduce the heat to medium and very slowly whisk in the cornmeal, whisking constantly to ensure no lumps. Switch to a wooden spoon, and simmer on low heat, stirring often. Cook for 10 to 12 minutes, scraping the bottom of the pan thoroughly while stirring.

Once tender, remove the pot from the heat and add the butter a little at a time while stirring until incorporated. Add the Parmesan, mascarpone, and rosemary. Season to taste.

SALSIFY &
SHALLOTS

Cut the shallots in half. Leave the skin on and the root attached. Heat the canola oil in an ovenproof frying pan and sear the shallots, flat side down, until roasted darkly but not burned. Turn face up and place into the oven at 175°C (350°F) until soft, 10 to 15 minutes. Remove from the oven and set aside.

Peel and trim the ends from the salsify. To prevent browning, submerge the salsify in a bowl of cold water with a squeeze of lemon juice.

Continued . . .

Heat the olive oil in a large sauté pan over medium-high heat. Cook the salsify, stirring occasionally, until they begin to turn translucent, about 4 minutes. Season with salt and add enough water or chicken stock to reach halfway up the salsify. Add the thyme and butter. Cover and simmer over low heat until tender, 8 to 12 minutes, depending on the thickness and age of the roots. Drain and set aside.

SERVE   Remove the veal cheeks from the oven and then the sauté pan and set aside. Keep the oven on.

Strain the braising liquid into a large pot. Discard the leftover solids. Bring the braising liquid to a boil, lower the heat, and simmer until reduced by half. This could take up to 30 minutes. Skim any visible fat from the surface. Add 30g (2 Tbsp) of the butter and swirl the pan in a constant circling motion, or whisk, until well incorporated. Stir in the sherry vinegar. Season with salt and pepper. Add the cheeks back to the pan and heat just until warmed through.

Strain the mushrooms from the pickling liquid. Transfer to a baking sheet lined with parchment paper and heat in the oven for a few minutes. Reheat the shallots in the same way.

Slowly reheat the polenta and adjust the taste and consistency with a little milk if necessary. When the polenta sits for a while, it gets thicker.

Reheat the salsify in the rest of the butter until the butter starts to foam and the salsify are lightly coloured and golden brown. Season with pepper.

Divide the polenta between 6 serving dishes and top with the veal cheeks. Drizzle with some sauce and garnish with the roasted salsify, shallots, pickled mushrooms, and parsley leaves.

THE HAWKSWORTH BURGER

Serves 10

The burger itself is a great place for all sorts of great-quality kitchen trim: pieces of chuck, rib-eye, and sometimes even leftover tenderloin—all really nice cuts of beef. When we were trying to figure out how to make a unique statement with it, my head chef at Hawksworth, Kristian Eligh, suggested putting an onion ring on top of the beef. From there, off we went, with the tomato jam and barbecue sauce and a house bun. We've been selling 30 a day for seven years.

INGREDIENTS

Burger Buns

215g (1¾ cups) pastry flour

325g (2½ cups) bread flour

40g (3 Tbsp) sugar

9g (1 Tbsp) salt

150mL (⅔ cup) water

150mL (⅔ cup) milk

14g (1 Tbsp plus 2½ tsp) fresh yeast or 7g (2 tsp) active dry yeast

65mL (¼ cup) olive oil

50g (3½ Tbsp) butter, in pieces

Egg, for brushing

Black and white sesame seeds, for sprinkling

Beef Patties

Vegetable oil

150g (1 cup) minced onion

150g (1 cup) Garlic Confit (page 312)

1kg (2¼ lb) beef chuck, ground

500g (1 lb) boneless beef short rib, ground

150g (5½ oz) beef fat cap, ground

Salt and pepper

Olive oil, for brushing

Tempura Onion Rings

500g (3⅔ cups) rice flour

6g (1 tsp) baking powder

5g (1 tsp) baking soda

1.5g (½ tsp) salt

500mL (2 cups) ice-cold (or sparkling) water

30mL (2 Tbsp) sherry vinegar

30mL (2 Tbsp) sesame oil

30mL (2 Tbsp) grapeseed oil

2L (8 cups) canola oil

10 slices red onion (2cm/¾ in rings)

Flour, for dusting

Salt

Burgers

1 recipe Barbecue Sauce (page 313)

1 recipe Tomato Jam (page 311)

Lettuce, as needed, washed and dried

Sliced tomato, as needed

10 slices aged Canadian cheddar

Bacon strips, as needed, cooked

Pickles, sliced, as needed

Continued . . .

BURGER BUNS

Combine the pastry flour, bread flour, sugar, and salt in the bowl of a stand mixer fitted with the hook attachment.

Combine the water, milk, and yeast in a bowl and blend with an immersion blender to dissolve the yeast. Add the oil and blend to incorporate.

Pour the yeast mixture into the stand mixer and add the butter. Mix at medium speed for 7 to 9 minutes to form a supple elastic dough. Cover with plastic wrap and leave to rise in the fridge until doubled in size, overnight.

Divide the dough into 10 equal 100g (3½ oz) pieces. Round each into a ball by rolling against the countertop with your hands. Place the balls on a baking tray lined with parchment paper and leave in a warm draft-free area to rise until 1½ times their original size; the time will vary depending on the heat of the area.

Preheat the oven to 175°C (350°F).

Lightly beat the egg and brush it on the tops of the buns, using a pastry brush. Sprinkle with the sesame seeds. Bake the buns until deep golden brown, 16 to 18 minutes.

BEEF PATTIES

Heat the vegetable oil in a large sauté pan over medium heat and sweat the minced onion and garlic until totally translucent, about 5 minutes. Use a slotted spoon to remove the onion and garlic from the oil and transfer to paper towel to soak up excess oil. Allow to cool.

Grind all the meat and fat in a meat grinder or have your butcher do this for you. Place in a mixing bowl and add the onion and garlic. Season generously with salt and pepper and mix by hand until combined.

Divide the meat into 10 equal portions and pack, 1 at a time, into a 10cm (4 in) ring mould to form 10 patties. Place the patties on a baking tray lined with parchment paper and brush liberally with olive oil to avoid oxidation. Wrap the tray in plastic wrap and refrigerate for at least 4 hours before cooking.

TEMPURA ONION RINGS

Whisk together the rice flour, baking powder, baking soda, and salt. Add the water, vinegar, sesame oil, and grapeseed oil and whisk until smooth. Pour the batter into an ISI gun and charge with 3 cartridges. If you do not have an ISI gun, use sparkling water in place of the cold water and keep the mixture in the bowl.

Heat the canola oil to 175°C (350°F) in a pot large enough that it is not more than half full.

Place the onion rings in a bowl, and lightly flour them, shaking off any excess. Squeeze some of the tempura batter out of the ISI gun. Using a fork, roll a few pieces of onion around at a time, to fully coat each piece with batter.

Fry the onions in batches until crispy and golden brown, 3 to 5 minutes per ring. Transfer to a paper towel to soak up excess oil. Season with salt.

Continued . . .

Preheat the oven to 200°C (400°F).

Using a non-stick skillet or cast-iron pan on high heat, sear each patty on both sides until dark brown and crisp. Place the patties on a baking tray lined with parchment paper and finish cooking in the oven to your desired doneness. I recommend medium (an internal temperature of 60°C–63°C/140°F–145°F).

Slice the burger buns in half and lightly toast under the broiler. Build your burgers, starting with the barbecue sauce and tomato jam, and then add the patty and the onion ring. Fill it with your favourite toppings. At Hawksworth, we serve our burgers with lettuce, tomato, aged Canadian cheddar, crispy bacon, pickle, and a side of fries.

48-HOUR BEEF SHORT RIBS, COMPRESSED MELON, BLACK PEPPER JAM, GREEN PAPAYA SALAD

Serves 6

Beef short ribs are such a great application for sous vide cooking. You get very little moisture loss so the meat turns out incredibly juicy. It gets soft, then you chill it to set it up, and grill it or roast it to finish. It's a rich, fatty cut, so instead of saucing it with a reduction we glaze them and serve them with black pepper jam with loads of shallots, and a bright, refreshing green papaya salad. When we put this on the menu at West as a starter, we couldn't keep up. We had to bring it back on the opening menu at Hawksworth.

INGREDIENTS

Beef Short Ribs

1.3kg (3 lb) bone-in beef short ribs

2 sprigs thyme, stems removed

3 cloves garlic, crushed

Salt

Pepper

Compressed Melon

100mL (7 Tbsp) water

100g (½ cup) sugar

½ honeydew melon, in 18 cubes 2cm (¾ in) each

3 juniper berries

Black Pepper Jam

30mL (2 Tbsp) grapeseed or canola oil

½ onion, chopped

2 shallots, coarsely chopped

2 knobs ginger, peeled and chopped

15 cloves garlic, chopped

1½ bunches scallions, sliced

15g (1 Tbsp) dried fermented black beans

½ Thai chili, seeded and coarsely chopped

10g (1½ Tbsp) pepper

125mL (½ cup) soy sauce

125mL (½ cup) water

100mL (7 Tbsp) hoisin sauce

Sugar

Green Papaya Salad

65mL (¼ cup) water

50g (¼ cup) palm sugar

2 lime leaves

½ fresh jalapeno or red Thai chili, seeds removed

15mL (1 Tbsp) fish sauce

250mL (1 cup) fresh lime juice

1 shallot, finely chopped

Salt

⅓ green papaya, peeled and sliced into very fine julienne

Beef Short Ribs Glaze

100mL (7 Tbsp) hoisin sauce

50mL (3 Tbsp) yuzu juice

30mL (2 Tbsp) light soy sauce

¼ orange, juice

Garnish

Sea salt

12 leaves Thai basil

Continued . . .

BEEF SHORT RIBS

Rub the beef short ribs with the thyme, garlic, salt, and pepper, then cover and refrigerate for 5 hours. Transfer to 1 or more vacuum-seal pouches. Seal with a vacuum sealer and cook in a water bath at 63°C (145°F) with a sous vide immersion circulator for 48 hours.

Remove from the water bath, cool the ribs, and remove from the bags. Trim the excess fat and bones and portion in 170g (6 oz) rectangles.

COMPRESSED MELON

Bring the water to a boil in a small pot over high heat. Whisk in the sugar until it dissolves, to create a syrup. Cool rapidly over an ice bath.

Place the cubed honeydew melon in a vacuum-seal pouch with the syrup and juniper berries. (You can also use a regular ziplock bag but the flavour will be less intense.) Seal with a vacuum sealer and refrigerate for 2 hours.

BLACK PEPPER JAM

Heat the oil in a skillet over medium to high heat. Add the onion, shallots, ginger, and garlic and cook until golden brown, stirring frequently. Add the scallions, black beans, chili, and pepper, and cook, stirring, until fragrant, about 5 minutes longer. Add the soy sauce, water, and hoisin sauce and reduce by ⅓. Cook until the mixture is thick and jammy and coats the back of a spoon.

Adjust the seasoning and balance with sugar as required. While the mixture is still hot, blend it in a food processor until smooth but not puréed.

GREEN PAPAYA SALAD

Combine the water with the palm sugar, lime leaves, and chili in a small pot. Bring to a boil and cook until the sugar has dissolved. Blend for 1 minute with an immersion blender until combined. Strain through a fine-mesh sieve.

Add the fish sauce, lime juice, and shallot and stir to combine. Season with salt. Refrigerate until cool. When ready to serve, mix the papaya with the dressing.

BEEF SHORT RIBS GLAZE

Whisk all the ingredients together until combined.

SERVE

Preheat the oven to 150°C (300°F).

Cover or brush the short rib pieces with half of the glaze and heat in the oven until hot through, about 10 minutes. Halfway through cooking, brush with the remaining glaze. Cut each rib rectangle in half.

Smear some of the black pepper jam on each of 6 serving plates and place the short ribs on top. Season with sea salt. Add the melon and papaya salad, and garnish with the basil leaves.

GRILLED HANGER STEAK, RED ONION AGRODOLCE, GORGONZOLA BUTTER

Serves 6
(photo on page 248)

Hanger steak is an interesting cut. It's the diaphragm muscle, so there's only one per animal and it has a lot more flavour than a piece of tenderloin. It has great texture too—as long as you don't overcook it and you let it rest properly before you slice it. Gorgonzola butter works really well with it, and the sweet and sour onion cuts through its richness.

INGREDIENTS

Red Onion Agrodolce

45mL (3 Tbsp) olive oil

550g (6 cups) sliced red onion

9g (1 Tbsp) salt

160mL (⅔ cup) red wine

90mL (6 Tbsp) red wine vinegar

35g (scant 3 Tbsp) sugar

Gorgonzola Butter

115g (½ cup) butter, room temperature

35g (⅓ cup) gorgonzola dolce, room temperature

5g (2 Tbsp) finely chopped parsley

Pinch salt

15g (2 tsp) Garlic Confit (page 314)

Grilled Hanger Steak

1kg (2¼ lb) angus hanger steak

Salt and pepper

Olive oil, for drizzling

Sea salt

15g (2½ Tbsp) finely grated fresh horseradish, for garnish (optional)

RED ONION AGRODOLCE

Heat the oil in a sauté pan over medium heat and sauté the onions and salt until most of the moisture has evaporated and the onions are starting to stick to the bottom of the pan, 10 to 15 minutes. Stir often. Add the wine, wine vinegar, and sugar and bring the mixture to a boil. Reduce the heat and simmer until thickened to a jam-like consistency.

GORGONZOLA BUTTER

Place all the ingredients in a mixing bowl and whisk until smooth.

Spread a piece of plastic wrap over the work surface. Spoon the butter onto the plastic wrap and use a scraper or rubber spatula to shape it into a log, 3cm (1¼ in) in diameter. Roll the plastic wrap tightly around the log. Refrigerate until firm.

Remove the gorgonzola butter from the fridge and unwrap. Slice into thin rounds.

STEAK

Season the steak with salt and pepper. Heat up a grill pan or barbecue. Grill for 4 to 5 minutes on each side (for medium-rare) and get a nice charring on all sides. Allow the steak to rest on a wire rack for 10 minutes.

SERVE

Reheat the agrodolce and spoon onto a plate or serving platter. Slice the steak into 1cm thick (½ in) slices. Drizzle with olive oil and season with sea salt. Arrange the steak on top of the agrodolce and add the butter slices on top of the steak. You can lightly blowtorch or very quickly broil at this point to start the butter melting.

Garnish with the freshly grated horseradish, if using.

NIGHTINGALE

I knew even from when Hawksworth first opened that I was going to do something else—a second big restaurant—I just wasn't sure what. There was no way I was going to open a second Hawksworth in Vancouver. So it made sense to do something casual and less expensive. I wanted to serve larger numbers of customers—but without burning out cooks, the way the intense kitchens at places like Hawksworth or West have a way of doing.

I was still trying to figure out the concept when I went on a quick visit to Los Angeles, where Willie Mitchell was then playing for the Kings. Megan had a place she wanted to show me for lunch. It was Gjelina, in Venice Beach. The vibe was totally local, relaxed, and casual, and the food was really, really simple—but perfectly executed, seasonal, and delicious. I was just like, "This is unbelievable." I mean, I'd been doing all that delicate tweezery food for so long. Then I saw Travis Lett's army of guys in the back, just turning out simple, unfussy, beautiful food. It struck a nerve and shook me up.

There was nothing like it back in Vancouver. A lot of the reason why had to do with the quality of the produce that's locally available. In California the vegetables are so good, and the growing season that much longer. They've got fresh local asparagus at their farmers' markets in March instead of June. It's easy to forget what a massive difference great vegetables make to the final dish when you're cooking simply. But trust me: they do. You can't serve charred carrots with tahini and cilantro and call it a dish when you're using generic carrots; it tastes like nothing. But make it with properly grown organic carrots, full of flavour and their own natural sweetness, and it's going to be fantastic.

Before we started on the new project, we had to be sure that we had the suppliers in place to do it right. Then we began the hunt for our location. Realtor Stephen Moscovich found us a soaring high-ceilinged space in the MNP Tower on West Hastings Street, a building I had always loved for its European-style grandeur. So we set Studio Munge loose again to design our two-storied space. It was Annabel who—riffing off the hawk in our surname—came up with the friendlier alternative of a nightingale, the perfect moniker for the accessible restaurant we were planning.

For chef, I picked Phil Scarfone, who had been with me since opening day at Hawksworth, where he started on the garnish section. We worked together closely on menu development for a bigger, equally demanding, but different sort of restaurant. The hardest thing about the cooking at Nightingale has always been restraint. We never wanted it to be fancy—just delicious. Each dish concept has to be stripped down to basics, until it has only the necessary elements: texture, flavour, contrasts, and balance. The mandate is for the food to be simple, healthful, and light. A typical Nightingale menu has around 20 items that are vegetarian, and nearly half of those are vegan. The vegetarian offering is key; Nightingale is intended as a showcase for great BC produce, prepared in a way that is flavourful, satisfying, and full of textural contrasts. But it's a big menu of 40 or 50 items. There are going to be some exceptions. We always have three big items like steak, or osso bucco, or whole fish. We always have two or three items that are out there—like veal tongue tonnato—to keep things interesting for regulars. But we still generally keep our sauces bright, light, and herbaceous—as in chimichurri and salsa verde.

Our number-one job is sourcing. We spend the winter poring over heirloom seed catalogues with our main producer, Zaklan Heritage Farm, get them to grow something new for us—like puntarella, or spigarello, or some obscure strain of arugula—and then we buy all of it. Their whole crop.

We were slammed at the start and got busier fast, and it keeps going. We average 700 covers a day. There's 12, sometimes 14 chefs. When I was a teenager, I dreamed of opening a pizzeria. It took a while, but now—finally—I'm selling 150 pizzas a day. Over a week, we'll do 500 orders of fried chicken and 175 hanger steaks. We put on roasted cauliflower dressed up with sunflower seeds and sultanas and dusted with turmeric, and seven days later we've done 500 orders. The numbers are mad.

We opened Nightingale because that's the way I now like to eat—but it has proved enough of an asset to the bottom line that the Hawksworth brand can now expand in ways I used to only dream of. There's still Hawksworth, of course, the namesake fine dining showcase. There are two casual cafés called Bel. And an alliance with Air Canada to provide them with hundreds of inflight menu items for first class passengers, both in the air and on the ground with two full service first class airport lounges, at YYZ and YVR. And at YVR, we will be adding Hawksworth Kitchen, an airport restaurant offering the general public a taste of something from all our restaurants—from Bel Café to Hawksworth, and Nightingale pizza, too. We also enjoy the process of working closely with our local farms and suppliers so much that we're hoping to branch out and do it ourselves, with a Hawksworth Farm hopefully in operation one day. Meanwhile, the Hawksworth Restaurant group now has over 300 employees, and counting. H

VEGETABLES

GRILLED BROCCOLINI, CILANTRO DRESSING, ZA'ATAR

Serves 6

(photo on page 80)

Broccolini has been around for 20 years, but it sometimes feels like it came out of nowhere. Ever since my son, Heston, tried it, he won't touch broccoli anymore: only broccolini.

NOTE

Za'atar is traditionally made with dried herbs such as marjoram or thyme (the Arabic word za'atar, pronounced ZAH-tahr, also means "thyme"). Here we add oregano, which goes extremely well with the nuttiness of sesame. If you don't want to blend your own, coax extra fragrance from a store-bought mix by lightly toasting it.

INGREDIENTS

Cilantro Dressing
100g (½ cup) tahini
65mL (¼ cup) white wine vinegar
65mL (¼ cup) water
55mL (4 Tbsp) canola oil
10mL (2 tsp) sesame oil
10g (1 Tbsp) salt
½ bunch cilantro, large stems removed
Pinch cayenne

Za'atar
10g (1 Tbsp) coriander seeds
10g (1 Tbsp) cumin seeds
3g (1 tsp) fennel seeds
8g (1¼ tsp) sumac
55g (6 Tbsp) white sesame seeds
2.5g (¾ tsp) salt
3g (2 tsp) dried oregano

Broccolini
3 bunches broccolini, trimmed

CILANTRO DRESSING

Blend the tahini, vinegar, water, canola oil, sesame oil, and salt together until smooth. Add the cilantro and cayenne and blend again until smooth.

ZA'ATAR

Preheat the oven to 175°C (350°F).

Heat a small sauté pan over medium heat and toast the coriander seeds until aromatic and crackling, about 30 seconds. Remove from the pan and set aside to cool. Repeat this process with the cumin and then fennel seeds. Pulse the coriander, cumin, fennel, and sumac in a coffee grinder or food processor until ground but still slightly coarse.

Toast the sesame seeds in the oven on a baking tray lined with parchment paper until golden, 4 to 5 minutes. Pulse in a coffee grinder or food processor until ground but still slightly coarse.

In a mixing bowl, combine the ground spices and sesame seeds with the salt and oregano.

BROCCOLINI

Bring a large pot of salted water to a rapid boil. Blanch the broccolini for 1 minute and refresh in ice water. Pat dry.

Heat up a grill pan on high heat. Grill the broccolini for 1 minute on each side. Transfer to a stainless-steel bowl and smother the broccolini with dressing. Plate and sprinkle with za'atar.

ROASTED CAULIFLOWER,
GREEN HARISSA, SUNFLOWER SEEDS

Serves 6

(photo on page 257)

This vividly green and brightly flavoured variation on harissa—with fresh herbs and jalapeno—adds vibrancy to sweet roasted cauliflower. The end result is at least as delicious as that creamy cauliflower gratin you grew up with, and a whole lot healthier, too.

NOTE

For a more colourful version, use purple or orange cauliflower or even Romanesco—or a mix. The green harissa can be made a few days in advance. Store it in the fridge with plastic wrap pressed right on the surface. Try the sauce with other roasted vegetables, or as a rub for baked or grilled fish.

INGREDIENTS

Harissa

8 jalapeno peppers, stems removed

10g (1 Tbsp) coriander seeds

10g (1 Tbsp) cumin seeds

300mL (1¼ cups) olive oil

65g (1⅓ cups) coarsely chopped cilantro

65g (1⅓ cups) coarsely chopped parsley

5 scallions, chopped

3 cloves garlic, coarsely chopped

1 shallot, coarsely chopped

15mL (1 Tbsp) sherry vinegar

8g (1 Tbsp) salt

Sunflower Seeds

30mL (2 Tbsp) olive oil

50g (⅓ cup) sunflower seeds

Salt

Cauliflower

1 very large head cauliflower, cut in golf ball–sized florets, cleaned and patted dry

Olive oil, for drizzling

Salt and pepper

HARISSA

Preheat the oven to 230°C (450°F). Split 5 of the jalapeno peppers and remove the seeds. Place them on a baking tray lined with parchment paper. Roast until blistered and golden brown, about 6 minutes. Set aside to cool. Leave the oven on for the cauliflower.

Toast the coriander and cumin until fragrant and light brown in a heavy-bottomed skillet over medium heat, about 1 minute. Set aside to cool.

Place the cooled jalapenos and spices in a blender or food processor with the remaining raw jalapenos, oil, cilantro, parsley, scallions, garlic, shallots, sherry vinegar, and salt. Blitz until smooth but with small visible specks, like a pesto. Set aside.

SUNFLOWER SEEDS

In a separate sauté pan or skillet, heat the oil over medium heat. Add the sunflower seeds and stir until rich golden brown, about 5 minutes. Season with salt. Set aside to cool.

CAULIFLOWER

Drizzle the cauliflower with olive oil, and sprinkle with salt and pepper. Place on a baking tray lined with parchment paper and bake until dark golden brown at the edges, 15 to 20 minutes, turning once or twice during the cooking. Place the cauliflower in a serving dish. Generously spoon over some of the harissa and sprinkle with toasted sunflower seeds.

ROASTED BRUSSELS SPROUTS, PICKLED GRAPES & PINE NUTS

Serves 6

(photo on page 257)

When I was growing up, Brussels sprouts were always overcooked and soft and sort of horrifying. A hard roast is the simple cure. These are halved, roasted, and caramelized, and they're dense with flavour. So we added some vinegar-pickled grapes for balance and colour—and just like that, Nightingale sells 40 pounds of Brussels sprouts a day!

INGREDIENTS

Pickled Grapes

125mL (½ cup) white wine vinegar

65mL (¼ cup) water

40g (3 Tbsp) sugar

1 bay leaf

Pinch peppercorns

Pinch coriander seeds

Pinch salt

120g (¾ cup) red grapes, halved

Brussels Sprouts

50g (6 Tbsp) pine nuts

30mL (2 Tbsp) olive oil

500–600g (6 cups) Brussels sprouts, trimmed and halved

Handful parsley leaves, stems removed

PICKLED GRAPES

Place the vinegar, water, sugar, bay leaf, peppercorns, coriander, and salt in a pot and bring the mixture to a boil. Transfer to a heatproof container and chill in an ice bath immediately. Once cool, strain out the spices and bay leaf. Pour the cold pickling liquid over the grapes. Cover and chill in the fridge to pickle for at least 4 hours.

BRUSSELS SPROUTS

Preheat the oven to 190°C (375°F). Place the pine nuts on a baking tray lined with parchment paper and toast until golden brown, 5 to 10 minutes. Set aside to cool.

Turn the oven up to 200°C (400°F). When the pine nuts are cool, gently pulse them in a food processor until coarsely chopped.

Place a large heavy-bottomed, ovenproof skillet, ideally cast iron, over medium to high heat and heat enough olive oil to thinly coat the pan. Place the Brussels sprouts in the pan, in batches if necessary, cut side facing down, and cook until nicely caramelized, 3 to 4 minutes. Transfer to a baking tray lined with parchment paper, cut side up. Roast in the oven until the sprouts are tender all the way through, about 6 minutes. When the sprouts come out of the oven, throw in the parsley leaves and pickled grapes and gently toss to combine.

Place the sprouts in a serving platter and sprinkle with the toasted pine nuts.

CARROTS, SIKIL PAK, PUFFED QUINOA

Serves 6

(photo on page 249)

Sikil pak is a spicy Mayan condiment that's thickened with ground pepitas. Its fragrant heat and the sweetness of caramelized roast carrots are great together.

INGREDIENTS

Puffed Quinoa

30g (3 Tbsp) raw white quinoa

500mL (2 cups) canola oil

Salt

Sikil Pak

100g (¾ cup) pumpkin seeds

5mL (1 tsp) canola oil

35mL (2 Tbsp) olive oil

½ white onion, sliced

½ small jalapeno, deseeded and sliced

2 cloves garlic, finely chopped

175mL (¾ cup) water

125mL (½ cup) lime juice

5g (½ Tbsp) salt

6g (1 tsp) cumin seeds, toasted and ground

3.5g (2 tsp) smoked paprika

Pinch dried oregano

Pinch chili flakes

Carrots

36 multicoloured baby carrots (or 1 bunch regular carrots)

Olive oil

Salt

Micro cilantro, for garnish

PUFFED QUINOA

Cook the quinoa according to package instructions, then dehydrate at 55°C (130°F) for 4 to 6 hours. You can also leave the quinoa overnight in your oven on the lowest setting with the door cracked open. Do not overdry.

Heat the oil to 175°C (350°F) in a pot large enough that it is not more than half full. Sprinkle in the quinoa and cook quickly until doubled in size (less than 30 seconds). Remove with a spider or metal sieve. Transfer to paper towel and sprinkle with salt.

SIKIL PAK

Preheat the oven to 190°C (375°F).

Combine the pumpkin seeds and canola oil and spread on a baking tray lined with parchment paper. Toast in the oven, tossing halfway through, until golden brown, about 6 minutes. Allow to cool.

Heat the olive oil in a large skillet over medium heat. Add the onion, jalapeno, and garlic and shallow-fry over medium heat until the vegetables are just starting to colour, 5 to 8 minutes. Allow to cool slightly.

Transfer the cooked onion mixture and toasted pumpkin seeds to a food processor. Add the water, lime juice, salt, cumin, paprika, oregano, and chili flakes. Blend on high for 4 minutes, scraping down the sides as needed, to ensure an evenly smooth texture.

CARROTS

Preheat the oven to 220°C (425°F). Drizzle the carrots with olive oil and season with salt. Roast on a baking tray lined with parchment paper for 10 minutes, then reduce the heat to 165°C (325°F) and cook until tender, about 10 more minutes. Transfer to a serving tray. Spoon with sikil pak and sprinkle with crispy puffed quinoa and micro cilantro.

Grilled Hanger Steak (page 234)

Sweet Potato, Charred Scallion Dip (page 258)

Carrots, Sikil Pak,
Crispy Quinoa (page 247)

GRILLED RAMPS, SAUCE GRIBICHE

Serves 6

(photo on page 40)

Ramps are the first delicate wild flavour of springtime. If you miss their short season, you can always make this side dish with asparagus—for which sauce gribiche is a classic accompaniment.

INGREDIENTS

Sauce Gribiche

1 egg

2 egg yolks

15g (1 Tbsp) Dijon mustard

1 lemon, juice

225mL (scant cup) canola oil

40mL (scant 3 Tbsp) cold water

Salt

50g (5 Tbsp) capers, finely chopped

45g (5 Tbsp) cornichons, finely chopped

8g (3 Tbsp) chopped chives

8g (3 Tbsp) flat-leaf parsley, chiffonade

1 small shallot, finely chopped

Pickled Mustard Seeds

Pinch peppercorns

Pinch chili flakes

Pinch coriander seeds

Pinch fennel seeds

200mL (¾ cup) white wine vinegar

75mL (5 Tbsp) water

15g (1 Tbsp) sugar

40g (¼ cup) mustard seeds

Grilled Ramps

3–5 bunches ramps

Olive oil, for drizzling

Salt

Parsley leaves, for garnish

SAUCE GRIBICHE

Bring a pot of water to a boil, add the egg, and cook for about 9½ minutes until hard-boiled. Allow to cool, then peel and finely chop.

Place the egg yolks, mustard, and lemon juice in a food processor and blitz for 30 seconds. Slowly pour in the canola oil in a very fine stream, alternating with a fine stream of water, allowing the mixture to emulsify. Season with salt. Transfer to a bowl and fold in the remaining ingredients including the finely chopped egg.

PICKLED MUSTARD SEEDS

Place the peppercorns, chili flakes, coriander seeds, and fennel seeds in a cheesecloth sachet secured with string. In a small pot, heat the vinegar, water, sugar, and mustard seeds, and add the sachet. Allow to simmer slowly until the mustard seeds are tender, 15 to 20 minutes. Allow the mixture to cool and then remove the sachet and set aside.

GRILLED RAMPS

Coat the ramps with a drizzle of olive oil, leaving the bulbs and leaves attached. If the bulbs are large, you can slice them down the middle to butterfly them open.

Heat a grill pan or a barbecue on high. Place the bulbs only on the grill for 1 minute on each side, then flip to the leaves and grill for just 10 seconds.

Place the ramps on a serving dish and add a generous spoonful of sauce gribiche in the centre. Garnish with pickled mustard seeds and parsley leaves.

ROASTED TURNIPS & TURNIP GREENS, BAGNA CAUDA

Serves 6

(photo on page 198)

Harukei turnips have great flavour and delicious greens. In this recipe, you separate them, roast the turnips and then add their greens back in at the end. Tossing the greens with the hot turnips and a good dressing, they come out just wilted—exactly as you want them.

INGREDIENTS

Bagna Cauda Vinaigrette

2 shallots, brunoise

60g (8–10) anchovy fillets, chopped

150mL (⅔ cup) good-quality olive oil

4 cloves garlic, minced

Roasted Turnips & Turnip Greens

15–20 golf ball–sized white turnips, halved

40mL (scant 3 Tbsp) white wine vinegar

20 large turnip leaves, cut in 4cm wide (1½ in) ribbons

BAGNA CAUDA VINAIGRETTE

Mix together all the ingredients.

TURNIPS

Preheat the oven to 215°C (420°F).

Place the cut turnips on a baking tray lined with parchment paper. Roast for 15 minutes, turning halfway through for even colour on all sides.

As soon as the turnips come out of the oven, place in a stainless-steel bowl and add the vinegar. Toss in the greens so that the warm turnips wilt the greens.

Transfer to a serving platter and spoon the bagna cauda vinaigrette on top.

MAITAKE MUSHROOMS, BROWN BUTTER, HAZELNUT

Serves 6

The maitake—or hen-of-the-woods—is both delicious and unusually nutritious. At Nightingale, we treat these mushrooms simply, sautéing them and then serving them with the nutty, brown butter they were cooked in. Add hazelnuts and pecorino, and all those flavours meld into one.

NOTE

Hen-of-the-woods mushrooms are now widely cultivated and so increasingly easy to find. But if you still cannot track any down, substitute clusters of oyster mushrooms.

INGREDIENTS

45g (⅓ cup) coarsely chopped hazelnuts

3 clusters maitake mushrooms, approximately 125g (4½ oz) each

150g (⅔ cup) cold butter, cubed

Salt

50g (½ cup) finely grated pecorino

Preheat the oven to 180°C (350°F). Place the hazelnuts on a baking tray lined with parchment paper and toast until golden brown, 5 to 10 minutes. Set aside to cool.

Split each mushroom cluster into 6 large wedges.

Heat the butter in a heavy-bottomed or cast-iron pan on medium to high heat. When the butter starts to foam, add the mushrooms and season with salt. Turn the heat down and cook for 5 to 8 minutes, rotating the mushrooms so they cook evenly on each side. At this point, the butter should have turned dark brown but not be burned.

Place the mushrooms in a serving dish. Drizzle with some, but not all, of the brown butter from the pan. Garnish with toasted hazelnuts and pecorino.

ROASTED EGGPLANT, HUMMUS, DUKKAH & PICKLED ONIONS

Serves 6

(photo on page 58)

Roasted eggplant has such a luscious texture. The hummus adds to its rich creaminess, the dukkah gives crunch and a little spice, and the pickled onions and torn mint brighten it all up.

INGREDIENTS

Puffed Rice

500mL (2 cups) canola oil

30g (3 Tbsp) wild rice

Salt

Dukkah

20g (2 Tbsp) hazelnuts, toasted

20g (2 Tbsp) pine nuts, toasted

Pinch toasted and ground coriander seeds

9g (3 tsp) white sesame seeds, toasted

9g (3 tsp) black sesame seeds, toasted

Pinch cumin seeds, toasted and ground

Pinch Baharat Spice (page 319)

Pinch salt

Hummus

125g (¾ cup) drained canned chickpeas

1 clove garlic

3 cloves Garlic Confit (page 312)

15mL (1 Tbsp) olive oil

10mL (2 tsp) lemon juice

Pinch salt

8g (1½ tsp) tahini

5g (1½ tsp) sesame seeds, toasted

40mL (scant 3 Tbsp) water

Pickled Red Onions

75mL (5 Tbsp) white wine vinegar

50mL (3 Tbsp) water

25g (2 Tbsp) sugar

Pinch salt

1 bay leaf

Pinch pepper

Pinch coriander seeds, toasted

½ red onion, sliced 2.5cm (1 in) thick

Roasted Eggplants

9 small round Indian purple eggplants cut in half, or 4 long Japanese eggplants cut in 6mm (¼ in) pieces

60mL (¼ cup) olive oil

2 pinches salt

Pinch dried oregano

Pinch chopped rosemary

20mL (1⅓ Tbsp) sherry vinegar

Garnish

18 leaves fresh mint, torn

PUFFED RICE

Heat the oil to 220°C (425°F) in a pot large enough that it is not more than half full. Sprinkle the wild rice into the oil. The rice will puff up in a few seconds. Remove with a spider or metal sieve. Transfer to paper towel to soak up excess oil. Sprinkle with salt.

DUKKAH

Roughly chop the hazelnuts and pine nuts. Combine with the puffed rice in a mixing bowl and toss with the rest of the ingredients until everything is incorporated. Season with more salt if needed.

Run the chickpeas under cold water for 5 minutes.

Combine the chickpeas, garlic, garlic confit, oil, lemon juice, salt, tahini, and sesame seeds in a blender or food processor and purée until smooth, adding water as necessary. Season to taste with salt.

PICKLED RED ONIONS
Bring the vinegar, water, sugar, salt, bay leaf, pepper, and coriander to a boil in a pot. Set the onion in a bowl and pour the liquid over top while hot. Let sit until completely cooled down.

EGGPLANTS
Preheat the oven to 175°C (350°F).

Score the flesh of the eggplants with a knife, cutting halfway into the flesh but not through the skin, creating a crosshatch pattern with scores about 1cm (⅜ in) apart.

Toss the eggplants, oil, salt, oregano, and rosemary thoroughly together. Arrange the eggplants in a single layer, flat side down, on a baking tray lined with parchment paper. Roast for 15 to 20 minutes. Remove from the oven and drizzle with the sherry vinegar.

Spread a layer of hummus on the flat face of each eggplant piece. Return the eggplant pieces back in the oven for a few minutes to reheat.

Garnish with pickled red onions, dukkah, and mint leaves.

Delicata Squash Salad (page 83)

Roasted Cauliflower (page 243)

Roasted Brussels Sprouts (page 246)

SWEET POTATO, CHARRED SCALLION DIP

Serves 6

(photo on page 248)

This is a very simple play on your classic steakhouse baked potato with all the fixings. We just use a sweet potato instead, ramp up the flavour with charred scallions in place of chives, and add crispy dehydrated prosciutto instead of bacon.

INGREDIENTS

Charred Scallion Dip

3 scallions, green and white parts separated

250g (1 cup) sour cream or crème fraîche

125mL (½ cup) buttermilk

½ lemon, juice

8g (3 Tbsp) chopped parsley

Pinch salt

Pinch pepper

Crispy Prosciutto

300g (10½ oz) slab prosciutto

Sweet Potatoes

6 sweet potatoes, unpeeled

1 jalapeno, deseeded, brunoised

2 scallions, green parts only, julienned

Pepper

CHARRED SCALLION DIP

Heat up a grill pan or barbecue on high. Char the white parts of the scallions on the grill until tender. Do not char the greens or they will become bitter. Cool down immediately.

Finely chop the charred and raw scallions, and mix with the sour cream, buttermilk, lemon juice, parsley, salt, and pepper in a stainless-steel bowl.

CRISPY PROSCIUTTO

Cut the prosciutto into chunks. Put through a meat grinder using the medium die, or chop finely using a food processor or by hand.

Fry the prosciutto in a skillet on low heat until crispy, stirring from time to time. Drain the fat and transfer to paper towel to absorb excess oil. Set aside.

SWEET POTATOES

Preheat the oven to 175°C (350°F).

Bake the sweet potatoes on a baking tray lined with parchment paper for 30 to 40 minutes, until tender when pierced with a knife.

Cut the potatoes in half and transfer to a serving tray. Spoon the scallion dip overtop. Garnish with jalapenos, crispy prosciutto, julienned scallions, and pepper.

GRILLED CORN, BLACK TRUFFLE CREMA

Serves 6

(photo on page 182)

Here we put together two of our favourite ingredients—one high-end, one low—and the result is decadent, delicious, and fun.

INGREDIENTS

Black Truffle Crema

250g (1 cup) sour cream

110mL (7 Tbsp) buttermilk

6g (⅓ of a truffle) black truffle, finely grated on a Microplane

2 pinches salt

2.5mL (½ tsp) truffle oil

Grilled Corn

6 ears corn, husk on

100g (1 cup) finely grated Parmesan

2 scallions, white and green parts, chopped

1 jalapeno, deseeded, brunoise

Pepper

BLACK TRUFFLE CREMA

Mix together all the ingredients.

GRILLED CORN

Preheat the oven to 200°C (400°F). Bake the corn in the husk for 12 minutes. Remove from the oven and allow to cool enough to shuck.

Preheat a grill pan or barbecue. Quickly char the shucked corn on all sides.

Cut each cob into 3 pieces. Generously roll each piece in the truffle crema. Then sprinkle with grated Parmesan, scallions, and jalapeno. Season with pepper.

DESSERTS

DARK CHOCOLATE CHUNK COOKIES

Makes 24

This is the chocolate and chocolate and more chocolate cookie that we serve at Bel Café. They are messy, gooey, bitter, sweet, and delicious.

NOTE

Always use good-quality chocolate in your cookies. For this recipe we use Valrhona Guanaja 70%.

INGREDIENTS

250g (2 cups) cake flour

80g (⅔ cup) cocoa powder

7g (2 tsp) salt

3g (½ tsp) baking soda

2 eggs

180mL (¾ cup) water

5mL (1 tsp) vanilla extract

200g (¾ cup plus 2 Tbsp) butter, softened

200g (1 cup) sugar

30g (2½ Tbsp) dark brown sugar

125g (½ cup plus 2 Tbsp) golden brown sugar

480g (1 lb plus 1 oz) Valrhona Guanaja 70% dark chocolate pieces

Preheat the oven to 165°C (325°F).

Sift together the flour, cocoa powder, salt, and baking soda and set aside.

Use a hand whisk to combine the eggs, water, and vanilla.

In the bowl of a stand mixer fitted with the paddle attachment, cream together the butter and the sugars at medium speed, until light and fluffy. Add the egg mixture and blend to incorporate, scraping down the sides of the bowl as necessary. Add the dry ingredients and chocolate pieces and mix just long enough to form a dough.

Scoop the dough into 24 equal portions and place on a baking tray lined with parchment paper. Bake for about 10 minutes until just set. Remove from the oven and allow to cool. Store in an airtight container for up to 3 days.

PEANUT BUTTER & JAM ICE CREAM SANDWICHES

Makes 12 — These peanut butter cookies are sold at Bel Café and are an amazing take on everyone's favourite sandwich. We roll them in chopped freshly roasted peanuts for added crunch.

NOTE — *If tartaric acid is unavailable, replace with 5g (1¼ tsp) citric acid. If vanilla bean is unavailable, use good-quality paste or extract instead.*

INGREDIENTS

Raspberry Pâte de Fruits
2.5mL (½ tsp) tartaric acid
2.5mL (½ tsp) water
255g (1¼ cups) sugar
4.5g (1¼ tsp) yellow pectin
230g (1 cup) raspberry purée
45g (3 Tbsp) glucose
10mL (2 tsp) lemon juice

Peanut Butter Cookies
160g (1¼ cups) pastry flour
110g (¾ cup) bread flour
2.5g (½ tsp) baking soda
2.5g (¾ tsp) salt
180g (generous ¾ cup) butter
180g (¾ cup) smooth unsweetened
    peanut butter
180g (¾ cup plus 2 Tbsp) sugar
180g (¾ cup plus 2 Tbsp) golden
    yellow sugar
1½ eggs, room temperature

Roasted Peanuts
500g (3½ cups) whole blanched peanuts
30mL (2 Tbsp) peanut oil
2.5g (¾ tsp) sea salt

Caramel Ice Cream
575mL (2⅓ cups) milk
300mL (1¼ cups) cream
3.5g (1 tsp) salt
¼ vanilla bean, split and scraped
360g (1¾ cups) sugar
70g (⅓ cup) butter
7 egg yolks

RASPBERRY
PÂTE DE
FRUITS

Place twelve 10cm (4 in) flan rings on a baking tray lined with parchment paper, and lightly spray with non-stick cooking spray (you can do this in batches if you have fewer flan rings).

Combine the acid and water in a microwave-safe container. Warm in the microwave on medium power for 30 seconds, stir to dissolve, then set aside.

Sift the sugar and pectin together.

Heat the purée and glucose in a large saucepan over medium heat until the mixture reads 40°C (104°F) on a candy thermometer. Then slowly whisk in the sugar mixture. Continue cooking until the mixture reaches 107°C (225°F). Whisk in the acid solution, then the lemon juice. Divide the hot mixture between the rings. Set aside to cool and set. Remove from the rings when fully set.

PEANUT BUTTER COOKIES

Sift together the pastry flour, bread flour, baking soda, and salt.

In the bowl of a stand mixer fitted with the paddle attachment, cream together the butter, peanut butter, and sugars at medium speed, until combined. Add the eggs and blend to incorporate, scraping the sides of the bowl as needed. Add the dry ingredients and mix just long enough to form a dough.

Scoop the dough into 24 equal portions and place on a baking sheet lined with parchment paper. Refrigerate until firm.

Preheat the oven to 185°C (365°F). Lightly dust your hand with flour and press down on the cookies. Bake until golden, 8 to 10 minutes. Remove from the oven and allow to cool, then cut with a 10cm (4 in) circle cookie cutter to create perfect circles.

ROASTED PEANUTS

Preheat the oven to 150°C (300°F).

Toss the peanuts with the oil and salt. Transfer to a baking tray lined with parchment paper and roast until golden brown, tossing once or twice. Remove from the oven and allow to cool, then coarsely chop and set aside.

CARAMEL ICE CREAM

Warm the milk, cream, salt, and vanilla in a saucepan until the mixture reaches 40°C (104°F). Set aside.

Place a thick-bottomed saucepan with high sides over medium heat. Add the sugar in 3 additions, allowing it to melt in between, stirring constantly with a wooden spoon. Continue to cook until a dark amber colour is reached, then deglaze with the cream mixture. Be careful as the cream will bubble vigorously. Transfer to a bowl and whisk in the butter. Allow to cool to 40°C (104°F).

Whisk the egg yolks into the hot caramel and cream mixture, whisking constantly. Transfer back to the thick-bottomed saucepan. Cook over medium heat, stirring constantly, until the mixture has thickened and reaches 85°C (185°F). Strain through a fine-mesh sieve. Chill in a bowl set over an ice bath.

Freeze according to the manufacturer's instructions for your ice cream machine.

Place 12 (ideally acetate-lined) 10cm (4 in) flan rings on a baking tray lined with parchment paper, and pipe the ice cream into each ring. Place the tray in the freezer until the ice cream has frozen solid.

ICE CREAM SANDWICHES

Press one of the raspberry pâte de fruits onto one cookie. Press a ring of frozen ice cream onto another cookie, and then sandwich the two halves together. Roll the edge of the cookie around in the chopped roasted peanuts. Repeat with the remaining cookies. Serve immediately, or store, sealed, in the freezer for up to 1 month.

RASPBERRY CRUMBLE MUFFINS

Makes 12

This muffin base is richer and more cake-like than most, inspired by raspberry cheese-cake. You fold in frozen cubes of cream cheese and fresh raspberries, then bake it with a crumble topping. It has a rich, gooey centre and goes great with a cup of coffee.

NOTE

Any berry may be substituted for the raspberry.

INGREDIENTS

Crumble	*Muffins*
180g (1¼ cups) bread flour	135g (¾ cup plus 1 Tbsp) bread flour
120g (scant 1 cup) pastry flour	230g (1¾ cups) pastry flour
150g (¾ cup) sugar	22g (1⅓ Tbsp) baking powder
Pinch salt	5g (1½ tsp) salt
3g (½ tsp) baking powder	300mL (1¼ cups) buttermilk
200g (¾ cup plus 2 Tbsp) butter, diced, cold	255mL (generous 1 cup) canola oil
	2 eggs
	230g (1 cup plus 2 Tbsp) golden brown sugar
	120g (½ cup) cream cheese, cut in 1cm (⅜ in) cubes, chilled
	120g (1 cup) fresh raspberries

CRUMBLE

Sift together all of the ingredients except for the butter. Transfer to the bowl of a stand mixer fitted with the paddle attachment and add the butter. Mix at medium speed until a crumbly consistency forms. Transfer to a baking tray lined with parchment paper and chill until firm.

MUFFINS

Preheat the oven to 175°C (350°F).

Sift together the bread flour, pastry flour, baking powder, and salt.

In the bowl of a stand mixer fitted with the paddle attachment, mix together the buttermilk, oil, and eggs. Add the sugar and mix to combine. Add the other dry ingredients and mix just until combined. Fold in the chilled cream cheese and raspberries with a rubber spatula just until dispersed throughout the batter.

Divide equally into 12 paper-lined muffin cups and top each with about 50g (2 Tbsp) of the crumble.

Bake for 25 minutes, or until a cake tester inserted into a muffin comes out clean. Remove from the oven and allow to cool on a wire rack. Store in an airtight container for up to 2 days.

DOUBLE LEMON TART, CONFIT LEMON ZEST

Serves 10 (one 20cm/8 in tart)

This is hands-down my favourite dessert. It's so refreshing, it's sublime. I'm a sucker for citrus-based desserts, and this really is the best.

NOTE

When available, Meyer lemons can be substituted for a more floral and less acidic flavour.

INGREDIENTS

Tart Pastry

300g (2⅓ cups) pastry flour

300g (2⅓ cups) bread flour

5g (1⅓ tsp) salt

200g (1 cup) sugar

400g (1¾ cups) butter, softened

1 egg

Lemon Curd

125g (½ cup plus 2 Tbsp) sugar

2 lemons, zest

225mL (¾ cup plus 3 Tbsp) lemon juice

3 eggs

6 egg yolks

135g (½ cup plus 1 Tbsp) butter, softened

Lemon Filling

235g (1 cup plus 3 Tbsp) sugar

2 lemons, zest

4 eggs

8 egg yolks

250mL (1 cup) cream

180mL (¾ cup) lemon juice

Confit Lemon Zest

1 lemon

125g (½ cup plus 2 Tbsp) sugar

250mL (1 cup) water

5g (1 tsp) glucose

TART PASTRY

Sift together the pastry flour, bread flour, and salt.

In a stand mixer fitted with the paddle attachment, cream together the sugar and butter until incorporated. Scrape down the sides of the bowl as needed. Add the dry ingredients and blend until a crumbly dough forms. Add the egg and blend to form a soft dough. Wrap in plastic wrap and refrigerate overnight.

LEMON CURD

Combine the sugar and zest in a stainless-steel bowl, and rub to release the oils. Mix in the lemon juice, eggs, and egg yolks.

Set the bowl over a pot filled with a few inches of water and whisk constantly over low heat, until the mixture thickens into a curd and reaches 83°C (181°F). Remove from the heat and cool to 45°C (113°F).

Add the butter in 3 additions, and blend with an immersion blender until smooth, then pass through a fine-mesh sieve. Transfer to a sealable container and cover the surface directly with plastic wrap. Refrigerate overnight.

Continued . . .

TART SHELL   On a lightly floured surface, roll the pastry to 3mm (⅛ in) thickness. Line a 20cm (8 in) flan ring with the pastry, and trim the edges. Refrigerate for 1 hour.

Preheat the oven to 165°C (325°F).

Line the pastry with parchment paper and fill with baking weights. Bake until golden, 16 to 18 minutes.

LEMON FILLING   Combine the sugar and lemon zest, and rub to release the oils. Whisk in the eggs and yolks, then the cream, then the lemon juice. Strain through a fine-mesh sieve.

CONFIT LEMON ZEST   Using a vegetable peeler, remove the lemon zest in long, thin strips. Carefully remove any excess pith and then julienne the zest. Blanch for 1 minute in a pot of boiling water, then strain using a fine-mesh sieve.

Bring the sugar, water, and glucose to a simmer in a saucepan, stirring to completely dissolve the sugar. Add the blanched zest, bring back to a simmer, and cook until translucent, about 30 minutes. Transfer to a sealable container. Allow to cool, then refrigerate.

SERVE   Preheat the oven to 150°C (300°F).

Place the baked tart shell on a baking tray lined with parchment paper, and remove the parchment paper and baking weights from inside it.

Fill the shell with the lemon filling and bake until just set, about 20 to 25 minutes (the tart should be set but still a little wobbly). Remove from the oven and allow to cool.

Top the cooled tart with the lemon curd and garnish with confit lemon zest pieces.

CARAMEL POTS DE CRÈME WITH WHIPPED CRÈME FRAÎCHE

Serves 6

This was one of the original desserts on the Nightingale menu and it's still going strong. So simple, but so good.

NOTE

If vanilla bean is unavailable, use good-quality paste or essence.

INGREDIENTS

Crème Fraîche

300mL (1¼ cups) heavy cream
100mL (7 Tbsp) buttermilk

Pots de Crème

415mL (1⅔ cups) cream
160mL (⅔ cup) milk
5g (1½ tsp) salt
¼ vanilla bean, split and scraped
100g (½ cup) sugar
6 egg yolks

Vanilla Breton

60g (½ cup plus 1 Tbsp) pecans
200g (1½ cups) pastry flour
12g (scant Tbsp) baking powder
3g (1 tsp) salt
¼ vanilla bean, split and scraped
130g (⅔ cup) sugar
130g (½ cup plus 1 Tbsp) butter
3 egg yolks

Butterscotch Sauce

45g (3 Tbsp) butter
145g (¾ cup) brown sugar
120mL (½ cup) cream

Whipped Crème Fraîche

200mL (¾ cup) cream
15g (2 Tbsp) icing sugar

CRÈME FRAÎCHE

Combine the cream and buttermilk in a stainless-steel bowl. Cover with cheesecloth and leave to culture and thicken in a warm spot in your kitchen for 24 hours, then refrigerate overnight.

POTS DE CRÈME

Bring the cream, milk, salt, and vanilla to a simmer in a pot over low heat.

Place a thick-bottomed pan with tall sides over medium heat. Add the sugar in 3 additions, stirring continuously with a wooden spoon, allowing it to melt between additions. Cook until dark amber in colour, then add the cream. Be careful as the mixture will bubble violently. Remove from the heat and allow to cool to 40°C (105°F).

Place the egg yolks in a large bowl. Slowly pour the hot caramel and cream into the egg yolks while constantly whisking to create a custard. Refrigerate overnight.

Continued . . .

VANILLA
BRETON

Grind the pecans to a fine powder in a food processor.

Sift together the flour, baking powder, and salt. Stir in the pecan powder.

Rub the vanilla into the sugar to free the seeds, then sift together.

In the bowl of a stand mixer fitted with the paddle attachment, cream the sugar with the butter on medium speed, then add the egg yolks in 3 additions. Scrape down the sides of the bowl as needed. Add the dry ingredients and blend to form a soft dough. Wrap in plastic wrap and refrigerate until firm.

BAKING

Preheat the oven to 135°C (275°F).

Strain the refrigerated custard through a fine-mesh sieve. Fill six 240mL (8 oz) jars with the custard to the halfway point. Place the jars in a shallow baking dish and fill the dish ⅓ full with simmering water. Transfer to the oven and cook until the custards are just set and jiggle when gently shaken, about 30 to 40 minutes.

Remove the baking dish from the oven, then the jars from the dish, and allow to cool. Cover with plastic wrap and refrigerate.

Increase the heat of the oven to 175°C (350°F).

On a lightly floured work surface, roll the chilled pastry into a rectangle that is 0.5cm (¼ in) thick. Transfer to a baking tray lined with parchment paper. Bake until golden, about 20 minutes. Allow to cool.

BUTTERSCOTCH
SAUCE

Melt the butter in a pot over medium heat. Add the sugar and about 50mL (3 Tbsp) of the cream. Stir to dissolve, then bring to a simmer and continue to cook for 3 minutes. Remove from the heat, and whisk in the remaining cream. Chill over an ice bath, stirring occasionally.

WHIPPED
CRÈME
FRAÎCHE

In the bowl of a stand mixer fitted with the whisk attachment, combine the cream, 90mL (about ⅓ cup) of the crème fraîche, and the icing sugar. Whip until the cream holds medium peaks. Refrigerate the remaining crème fraîche for up to 1 week.

SERVE

Spoon the whipped crème fraîche into the custard pots. Top with shards of Breton pastry. Drizzle with butterscotch sauce.

CANDY CAP ICE CREAM, WALNUT WAFER, MAPLE CRUMBLE

Serves 6

Candy cap mushrooms are an incredible product. When they're fresh you have no idea, but when they're dried they have the most amazing maple scent that will fill up your whole kitchen. This dessert has a wonderful toasted flavour, a little like tonka bean. Add maple, walnut praline, and toffee, and you have a dish perfect for fall and winter.

NOTE

Dried candy cap mushrooms can be found at specialty grocers or online. If vanilla bean is unavailable, use good-quality paste or essence.

Be vigilant when you're cooking the sugar syrup for the sponge toffee. The baking soda acts as an accelerant for the Maillard reaction so you've got to be careful not to go too far. All you want is a hint of colour—not dark caramel.

INGREDIENTS

Candy Cap Ice Cream

15g (1 cup) dried candy cap mushrooms

240g (1¼ cups) sugar

½ vanilla bean, split and scraped

17 egg yolks

800mL (3¼ cups) milk

300mL (1¼ cups) cream

35g (3 Tbsp) trimoline

Dulcey Namelaka

1½ sheets gelatin

170g (6 oz) Valrhona Dulcey 32% caramelized white chocolate pieces

100mL (7 Tbsp) milk

5g (1 tsp) glucose

200mL (¾ cup plus 2 Tbsp) cream

Creamy Walnut Praline

110g (1 cup) walnut pieces

35mL (2 Tbsp) water

80g (⅓ cup plus 1 Tbsp) sugar

20mL (1⅓ Tbsp) grapeseed oil

225mL (¾ cup plus 3 Tbsp) cream

300g (10½ oz) Valrhona Almond Praline 60%

Crispy Vanilla Milk

50g (¼ cup) sugar

¼ vanilla bean, split and scraped

1.25g (¼ tsp) iota carrageenan powder

1g (¼ tsp) guar gum powder

250mL (1 cup) skim milk

Maple Gel

6g (1½ tsp) agar powder

1.5g (⅜ tsp) locust bean gum powder

300mL (1¼ cups) maple syrup

125mL (½ cup) water

Maple Crumble

100g (¾ cup) pastry flour

75g (½ cup) bread flour

75g (⅓ cup) maple sugar

3g (½ tsp) baking powder

1.5g (½ tsp) salt

115g (½ cup) butter, cold

Walnut Wafer

20g (1½ Tbsp) sugar

20mL (1⅓ Tbsp) water

65g (½ cup) walnuts

25g (¼ cup) almond flour

Continued . . .

Sponge Toffee

375g (1¾ cups plus 2 Tbsp) sugar   125g (½ cup) glucose

15g (1 Tbsp) baking soda   65mL (¼ cup) water

CANDY CAP ICE CREAM

Coarsely grind the candy cap mushrooms in a spice grinder.

Combine the sugar and vanilla and rub to release the seeds. Whisk in the egg yolks.

Bring the milk, cream, and trimoline to a simmer in a pot over low heat. Remove from the heat and slowly pour in the egg yolk mixture, whisking constantly to temper the eggs. Return to the stove and cook until the mixture has thickened and reaches 83°C (181°F).

Strain using a fine-mesh sieve. Whisk in the ground mushrooms, then cool over an ice bath. Transfer to a storage container and refrigerate overnight.

The next day, freeze and churn the ice cream in an ice cream machine according to the manufacturer's directions. Freeze until ready to use.

DULCEY NAMELAKA

Place the gelatin sheets in a bowl of cold water.

Place the chocolate in a stainless-steel bowl set over a pot filled with a few inches of water. Heat over low heat until half the chocolate is melted.

In a separate pot, bring the milk and glucose to a simmer, then remove from the heat. Remove the gelatin sheets from the water and add to the milk mixture, whisking to dissolve.

Slowly add the milk mixture to the chocolate, stirring with a rubber spatula, to form a ganache. Blend in the cream using an immersion blender until very smooth. Transfer to a storage container, cover with plastic wrap, and refrigerate overnight.

CREAMY WALNUT PRALINE

Preheat the oven to 160°C (315°F).

Place the walnuts on a baking tray lined with parchment paper and roast until fragrant, about 15 minutes.

Heat the water and sugar in a pot over medium heat, without stirring, until the sugar is a dark amber colour, 10 to 12 minutes. Stir in the roasted nuts, then pour the mixture onto a baking tray lined with parchment paper and allow to cool. Break into small pieces and transfer to a blender. Add the oil, and purée until a smooth, fluid paste forms.

Bring the cream to a simmer in a pot over low heat.

Combine the walnut paste and almond praline pastes in a food processor. With the machine running, pour in the hot cream in a slow stream, blending to emulsify and form a smooth, glossy paste. Transfer to a storage container, cover with plastic wrap, and allow to cool. Refrigerate overnight.

CRISPY
VANILLA MILK

Combine the sugar and vanilla, and rub the vanilla to release the seeds, then sift. Add the carrageenan and guar gum and whisk in the milk. Transfer to a pot and bring to a boil over medium heat.

Transfer to the bowl of a stand mixer fitted with the whisk attachment. Whip on medium to high speed until medium to firm peaks form.

Line a dehydrator tray with a plastic sheet. Spread the whipped milk out in an even layer, and dry overnight at 52°C (125°F). Flip and return to the dehydrator until the centre is crisp. Break into irregular shards and reserve in a storage container.

MAPLE GEL

Sift together the agar and locust bean gum.

Place the syrup and water in a blender. With the machine running, adjust the speed so a vortex forms, and slowly add the agar mixture. Blend for 1 minute, then transfer to a pot over medium heat. Bring to a full boil and continue cooking for 1 minute, then transfer to a storage container and allow to cool to room temperature. Refrigerate to set.

Once set, chop into pieces and purée in a blender at high speed until a smooth gel forms. Chill over ice, stirring occasionally.

MAPLE
CRUMBLE

Sift together the dry ingredients into the bowl of a stand mixer fitted with the paddle attachment. Dice the butter into 1cm (½ in) cubes, add to the mixer, and mix until a crumbly consistency forms. Spread onto a baking tray lined with parchment paper and refrigerate to chill.

Preheat the oven to 135°C (275°F).

Bake the crumble until just golden, about 20 minutes. Allow to cool, then break up any large chunks. Return to the oven and bake for another 10 minutes. Cool and store in a sealable container.

WALNUT
WAFER

Bring the sugar and water to a boil in a pot over medium heat while whisking to dissolve the sugar. Chill over an ice bath.

Coarsely chop the walnuts in a food processor. Combine the walnuts and almond flour in a large bowl and mix in the cold syrup to form a paste. Wrap in plastic wrap and refrigerate for 30 minutes.

Preheat the oven to 135°C (275°F).

Remove the plastic wrap and place the paste between 2 layers of parchment paper. Use a rolling pin to roll it out as thin as possible, then transfer to a baking tray. Bake for 8 minutes. Allow to cool, then break into irregular shards. Store in a sealable container.

Continued . . .

SPONGE
TOFFEE
Sift together 50g (¼ cup) of the sugar with the baking soda.

Bring the remaining sugar and the glucose and water to a boil in a pot over medium heat and cook until the centre just starts to colour. Remove from the heat and add the sugar and baking soda mixture. Quickly stir to incorporate, then pour onto a silicone mat. Allow to cool, then break into irregular shards. Store in a sealable container.

SERVE
Place the fluid maple gel in a squeeze bottle. Fill a piping bag fitted with a plain tip with a 1.5cm (½ in) opening with the dulcey namelaka. Fill another piping bag of the same size with the creamy walnut praline.

Pipe alternating mounds of namelaka and praline into each of 6 shallow serving bowls. Sprinkle the maple crumble into each bowl. Combine the crispy vanilla milk, walnut wafer, and sponge toffee, and mound in the centre of each bowl. Randomly add dots of maple gel around the bowls. Finish with 1 large quenelle of candy cap ice cream.

DARK CHOCOLATE FONDANT, BURNED ORANGE COMPOTE & HAZELNUT

Serves 6

We had this dessert on the opening menu at Hawksworth and it was super-popular—so we kept it on for quite some time. People still ask for it now. The flavours are clean, the base is nice and crunchy, and there's that rich layer of fondant. Dark chocolate, orange, and hazelnut is such a classic combination.

NOTE

Always use good-quality chocolate; we like Valrhona Opalys 33%, Jivara 40%, and Guanaja 70%.

INGREDIENTS

Mandarin Sorbet
100g (½ cup) sugar
55g (¼ cup) glucose powder
4.4g (1⅛ tsp) sorbet stabilizer powder
300mL (1¼ cups) water
27.5g (2 Tbsp) invert sugar
550mL (2¼ cups) mandarin juice

Burned Orange Compote
50g (¼ cup) sugar
300mL (1¼ cups) orange juice
1 orange, zest
¼ cinnamon stick, crushed
¼ vanilla bean, split and scraped
2 oranges
7.5g (1 Tbsp) Ultra-Sperse 3

Orange Puffs
125mL (½ cup) mandarin juice
125mL (½ cup) water
4g (1 tsp) Methocel F50
200g (1 cup) sugar
½ mandarin orange, zest

Fondant Base
65g (2⅓ oz) Valrhona Jivara 40% milk chocolate pieces
65g (2⅓ oz) Valrhona Opalys 33% white chocolate pieces
225g (1 cup) 50% hazelnut paste
160g (2 cups) feuilletine

Chocolate Fondant
100g (7 Tbsp) pasteurized egg yolks
100g (¾ cup) icing sugar, sifted
290g (10¼ oz) Valrhona Guanaja 70% dark chocolate pieces
125mL (½ cup) cream
80g (5½ Tbsp) butter, softened
100mL (7 Tbsp) water, at 80°C (176°F)

Soft Praline
125mL (½ cup) cream
250g (1 cup) 50% hazelnut paste

Simple Syrup
200mL (¾ cup) water
100g (½ cup) sugar

Continued . . .

Orange Fluid Gel

6g (1½ tsp) agar powder

1.5g (⅜ tsp) locust bean gum powder

375mL (1½ cups plus 1 Tbsp) orange
  juice

½ orange, zest

Garnish & Serve

250g (2 cups) hazelnuts

Lemon balm

MANDARIN
SORBET

Whisk together the sugar, glucose powder, and stabilizer.

Heat the water and invert sugar in a pot over medium heat until it reaches 40°C (105°F). Take the pan off the heat, and using an immersion blender, slowly mix in the stabilizer mixture. Return to the heat and bring to a boil while whisking constantly. Remove from the heat and strain. Refrigerate overnight.

The next day, add the orange juice. Then freeze and churn the sorbet base in an ice cream machine according to the manufacturer's instructions. Freeze until ready to use.

BURNED
ORANGE
COMPOTE

Place a thick-bottomed pot with tall sides over medium heat. Add the sugar in 3 additions, stirring continuously with a wooden spoon, allowing it to melt between additions. Cook until dark amber in colour, then add the orange juice. Be careful, the mixture will bubble violently. Add the orange zest, cinnamon, and vanilla and bring to a simmer. Allow to cool, then chill overnight.

Slice the top and bottom off the oranges, and cut away the peel and pith. Remove the segments of citrus flesh; you need 18 orange segments.

Strain the chilled liquid using a fine-mesh sieve and place in a tall narrow container. Add the Ultra-Sperse 3 and blend to combine using an immersion blender. Toss the segments with the liquid until they are coated.

ORANGE
PUFFS

Combine the juice and water in a blender. With the machine running, adjust the speed to form a vortex and slowly add the Methocel F50. Blend to combine, then transfer to a small pot and bring to a boil over medium heat. Transfer to a storage container, allow to cool, then refrigerate for at least 8 hours.

Line a dehydrator tray with a plastic sheet. In the bowl of a stand mixer fitted with the whisk attachment, combine the chilled liquid with the sugar and whip until it holds stiff peaks. Fold in the zest. Spread the mixture in an even layer over the plastic sheet. Dry overnight at 52°C (125°F).

FONDANT
BASE

Place the chocolate pieces in a stainless-steel bowl set over a pot with a few inches of water in it. Heat over low heat until the chocolate is melted. Remove from the heat and stir in the hazelnut paste then the feuilletine. Spread evenly over a baking tray lined with a silicone mat. Cover with plastic wrap and refrigerate until the chocolate fondant is ready.

CHOCOLATE FONDANT

In the bowl of a stand mixer fitted with the whisk attachment, combine the egg yolks and icing sugar and whip on high speed until doubled in volume.

Place the chocolate pieces in a stainless-steel bowl and set the bowl over a pot with a few inches of water in it. Heat over low heat until the chocolate is melted.

Bring the cream to a simmer in a pot over medium heat. Remove from the heat and slowly add the cream to the chocolate, stirring with a rubber spatula, to form a ganache.

Add the ganache to the yolk mixture and whisk to combine, scraping down the sides of the bowl as needed. Add the butter and whisk to combine. With the mixer running, slowly stream in the hot water, and mix until very smooth and emulsified. Pour over the prepared fondant base, spread to an even layer, and return to the fridge. Chill for I hour. Then cover with plastic wrap and freeze until firm.

SOFT PRALINE

Bring the cream to a simmer. Place the hazelnut paste in a food processor, and with the machine running, slowly stream in the hot cream, blending to emulsify and form a smooth, glossy paste. Transfer to a storage container, cover with plastic wrap, and allow to cool. Refrigerate until firm.

SIMPLE SYRUP

Bring the water and sugar to a boil in a pot over medium heat, while whisking to dissolve the sugar. Allow to cool, transfer to a storage container, and refrigerate.

ORANGE FLUID GEL

Whisk together the agar and locust bean gum. Place the orange juice and 125mL (½ cup) of the simple syrup in a blender. With the machine running, adjust the speed to form a vortex, and slowly add the agar mixture. Blend for 1 minute. Transfer to a saucepan. Bring to a boil over medium heat and continue cooking for 1 minute. Add the orange zest.

Transfer to a storage container and allow to cool to room temperature. Refrigerate to set.

Once set, remove from the container and dice into pieces. Purée in a blender at high speed until a smooth gel forms. Chill over ice, stirring occasionally. When ready to serve, transfer to a squeeze bottle.

GARNISH

Preheat the oven to 160°C (315°F). Place the nuts on a baking tray lined with parchment paper and roast until fragrant, 15 to 20 minutes.

Allow to cool. Then place in a sandwich bag and crack with a rolling pin or mallet.

SERVE

Remove the fondant from the freezer and allow to come to room temperature. Cut into four 11 × 14cm (4¼ × 5½ in) strips. Wrap 3 of the strips tightly in plastic wrap and then aluminum foil and freeze for up to 2 months. Using an offset spatula, spread a thin layer of praline over the surface of the remaining strip, then cut into six 2cm wide (¾ in) bars.

Using a pastry brush, stroke the soft praline across each serving plate. Place the fondant bars on each plate and add dots of orange fluid gel and orange compote segments, crushed orange puffs, and toasted hazelnuts. Add a quenelle of sorbet and garnish with a few leaves of lemon balm.

CONDENSED MILK ICE CREAM, RED BERRIES, VANILLA

Serves 6

We use local, seasonal produce as much as possible, and get inspired every day when a truck full of it shows up at the kitchen. In mid-June, Matthew Atkinson from Very Berry arrives with sweet, beautiful BC strawberries that are impossible to resist. The range of textures in this dessert, from the Breton pastry to the shards of crispy milk, are brightened with the fruity acidity of the raspberry cream and strawberry fluid gel, and, of course, fresh berries.

INGREDIENTS

Raspberry Crème

¾ sheet gelatin

50g (¼ cup) sugar

125g (½ cup) raspberry purée

2 eggs

110g (½ cup) butter

Crispy Vanilla Milk

50g (¼ cup) sugar

¼ vanilla bean, split and scraped

1.25g (¼ tsp) iota carrageenan powder

1g (¼ tsp) guar gum powder

250mL (1 cup) skim milk

Condensed Milk Ice Cream

40g (¼ cup) milk powder

4.5g (1 tsp) ice cream stabilizer powder

20g (1½ Tbsp) sugar

15g (1 Tbsp) glucose powder

600mL (scant 2½ cups) milk

4 egg yolks

200g (⅔ cup) sweetened condensed milk

130mL (½ cup) cream

Simple Syrup

200mL (¾ cup) water

100g (½ cup) sugar

Strawberry Gel

6g (1½ tsp) agar powder

2g (½ tsp) locust bean gum powder

300g (1¼ cups) strawberry purée

Breton Pastry Shards

140g (1 cup plus 1 Tbsp) pastry flour

12g (scant Tbsp) baking powder

3g (1 tsp) salt

130g (⅔ cup) sugar

¼ vanilla bean, split and scraped

130g (½ cup plus 1 Tbsp) butter

3 egg yolks

Sponge Toffee

375g (1¾ cups plus 2 Tbsp) sugar

15g (1 Tbsp) baking soda

125g (½ cup) glucose

65mL (¼ cup) water

Serve

Fresh strawberries

Fresh raspberries

Peppermint sprigs

Continued . . .

RASPBERRY
CRÈME

Place the gelatin sheets in a bowl of cold water.

In a stainless-steel bowl, combine the sugar, raspberry purée, and eggs and whisk to combine. Place the bowl over a pot with a few inches of water set over low heat. Whisking constantly, cook the mixture until thickened and it reaches 85°C (185°F). Remove from the heat and allow to cool to 50°C (122°F).

Remove the gelatin sheets from the water. Add them to the raspberry mixture and whisk to combine.

Using an immersion blender, add the butter in 3 additions, blending after each addition. Blend until smooth, and then pass through a fine-mesh sieve. Transfer to a sealable container and cover the surface directly with plastic wrap. Refrigerate overnight.

CRISPY
VANILLA MILK

In a stainless-steel bowl, combine the sugar and vanilla. Rub the vanilla to release the seeds and then sift together. Combine the carrageenan and guar gum with the sugar mixture, then whisk the mixture into the milk. Transfer to a pot and bring to a boil over medium heat.

Transfer to the bowl of a stand mixer fitted with the whisk attachment. Whip on medium to high speed until medium to firm peaks form.

Line a dehydrator tray with a plastic sheet. Spread the whipped milk in an even layer on the tray. Dry overnight at 52°C (125°F). Flip and return to the dehydrator until the centre is crisp. Break into irregular shards and reserve in a storage container.

CONDENSED
MILK ICE
CREAM

Sift together the milk powder, stabilizer, sugar, and glucose powder. Bring the milk to 40°C (105°F) over medium heat. Add the dry ingredients, whisking to combine.

Slowly pour this hot mixture into the egg yolks and sugar mixture in a large bowl, while constantly whisking to temper the eggs. Return to the stove and cook until thickened and it reaches 85°C (185°F).

Strain using a fine-mesh sieve, then cool over an ice bath to 40°C (105°F). Add the condensed milk and cream and whisk to combine. Transfer to a storage container and refrigerate overnight.

The next day, freeze and churn the ice cream base in an ice cream machine according to the manufacturer's directions. Freeze until ready to use.

SIMPLE SYRUP

In a saucepan, combine the water and sugar and cook over medium heat to bring to a boil, while whisking to dissolve the sugar. Allow to cool, transfer to a storage container, and refrigerate.

STRAWBERRY
GEL

In a stainless-steel bowl, whisk together the agar and locust bean gum.

Place 200mL (¾ cup) of the simple syrup and the strawberry purée in a blender, adjust the speed to form a vortex, and slowly add the agar mixture. Blend for 1 minute, then transfer to a saucepan. Cook the mixture over medium heat. Bring to a full boil, and continue cooking for 1 minute. Transfer to a storage container and allow to cool to room temperature. Refrigerate to set.

Once set, remove from the container and dice into pieces. Place in a blender and purée at high speed until a smooth gel is formed. Chill over ice, stirring occasionally. When ready to serve, transfer the fluid gel to a squeeze bottle.

BRETON
PASTRY
SHARDS

Sift together the flour, baking powder, and salt.

In the bowl of a stand mixer fitted with a paddle attachment, cream the sugar, vanilla and butter, then add the egg yolks in 3 additions, scraping down the sides of the bowl as needed. Add the dry ingredients and blend to form a soft dough. Wrap in plastic wrap and chill until firm.

Preheat the oven to 175°C (350°F).

On a lightly floured work surface, roll the chilled pastry into a rectangle 0.5cm (¼ in) thick. Transfer to a baking tray lined with parchment paper. Bake until golden brown and crispy, about 25 minutes. Allow to cool, then break it into irregular shards and reserve in a sealable storage container.

SPONGE
TOFFEE

Sift together 50g (¼ cup) of the sugar and the baking soda using a fine mesh sieve.

In a saucepan, combine the remaining sugar with the glucose and water. Bring to a boil over medium heat and continue cooking until the centre just starts to colour. Remove from the heat and add the sugar and baking soda mixture. Quickly stir to incorporate and then pour the toffee onto a silicone mat. Allow to cool and then break into irregular shards. Reserve in a sealable storage container.

SERVE

Using a mini offset spatula or the back of 'a spoon, stroke the raspberry crème across the bottom of 6 shallow serving bowls. Add the crispy vanilla milk, Breton pastry pieces, and sponge toffee, then the strawberry gel. Add the berries, a quenelle of ice cream on top, and garnish with peppermint.

PANNA COTTA, MANGO & GARAM MASALA

Serves 6

We wanted to make a dessert for Hawksworth with garam masala, a sweet spice blend that just has the best flavour. That got us started with the mango and yogurt. Then we were inspired by the puffed grains you find sold at Indian street markets, and so added the puffed rice and quinoa to give texture.

INGREDIENTS

Mango Sorbet

170g (¾ cup plus 2 Tbsp) sugar

50g (3 Tbsp plus 1 tsp) glucose powder

5g (1¼ tsp) sorbet stabilizer powder

375mL (1½ cups plus 1 Tbsp) water

12.5g (1 Tbsp) invert sugar

500g (2 cups) mango purée

Mango Transparent

80g (6 Tbsp) isomalt powder

60g (½ cup) icing sugar

60g (½ cup) maltodextrin

250g (1 cup) mango purée

Simple Syrup

300mL (1¼ cups) water

150g (¾ cup) sugar

Coriander Fluid Gel

3g (1 tsp) coriander seeds

6g (1½ tsp) agar powder

1.5g (⅜ tsp) locust bean gum powder

300mL (1¼ cups) water

Panna Cotta

2¾ sheets gelatin

275mL (generous 1 cup) yogurt

140mL (½ cup plus 1 Tbsp) cream

140mL (½ cup plus 1 Tbsp) buttermilk

65g (3 Tbsp) buckwheat honey

¼ vanilla bean, split and scraped

Mango Gelée

1½ sheets gelatin

120g (½ cup) mango purée

20mL (1⅓ Tbsp) passion fruit juice

Puffed Rice

1.25L (5 cups) water

2.5g (¾ tsp) salt

125g (⅔ cup) short-grain rice

500mL (2 cups) canola oil

Puffed Quinoa

1.25L (5 cups) water

2.5g (¾ tsp) salt

125g (¾ cup) red quinoa

Puffed Wild Rice

50g (¼ cup) wild rice

Garam Masala

6g (2 tsp) cumin seeds

6g (2 tsp) coriander seeds

5g (1½ tsp) cardamom seeds from inside
a green pod

5g (1 tsp) dried fenugreek

5g (2 tsp) ground cinnamon

0.5g (¼ tsp) ground cloves

1.5g (⅔ tsp) ground nutmeg

1 small bay leaf

Garnish

3 medjool dates

Micro cilantro

Continued . . .

MANGO SORBET

Whisk together the sugar, glucose powder, and stabilizer. Combine the water and invert sugar in a saucepan over medium heat and heat to 40°C (105°F).

Using an immersion blender, slowly add the dry ingredients to incorporate. Continue whisking over medium heat to bring to a boil. Remove from the heat, strain using a fine-mesh sieve, then cool over an ice bath. Refrigerate overnight.

The next day, add the mango purée to the chilled base. Then freeze and churn the ice cream base in an ice cream machine according to the manufacturer's directions. Freeze until ready to use.

MANGO TRANSPARENT

Sift together the isomalt, icing sugar, and maltodextrin. Add the mango purée and whisk to combine everything.

Line a dehydrator tray with a plastic sheet. Spread the mango mixture in an even layer on the tray. Dry overnight at 52°C (125°F). Flip and return to the dehydrator until the centre is crisp. Break into irregular shards and store in a sealable container.

SIMPLE SYRUP

Bring the water and sugar to a boil over medium heat, whisking to dissolve the sugar. Allow to cool, transfer to a storage container, and refrigerate.

CORIANDER FLUID GEL

In a sauté pan over medium heat, toast the coriander seeds until fragrant. Allow the seeds to cool, place in a resealable bag, and crush by hitting with a rolling pin or mallet.

In a stainless-steel bowl, whisk together the agar and locust bean gum.

Place the water and 200mL (¾ cup) of the simple syrup in a blender. Adjust the speed to form a vortex and slowly add the agar mixture. Blend for 1 minute, then transfer to a saucepan over medium heat. Add the toasted crushed seeds. Bring the mixture to a full boil, then continue cooking for 1 minute. Transfer to a storage container and allow to cool to room temperature. Refrigerate to set.

Once set, remove from the container and dice the gel into pieces. Place in a blender and purée at high speed until a smooth gel is formed. Chill over ice, stirring occasionally. When ready to serve, transfer the gel to a squeeze bottle.

PANNA COTTA

Place the gelatin sheets in a bowl of cold water.

Whisk together the yogurt, cream, buttermilk, honey, and vanilla. Measure 120mL (½ cup) of this mixture into a stainless-steel bowl. Set the bowl over a pot with a few inches of water set over low heat. Keeping the bowl over the water bath and constantly whisking, cook the mixture until it has thickened and reaches 40°C (105°F). Remove from the heat.

Remove the gelatin sheets from the water and add to the warm cream, whisking to dissolve. Add the remaining cream mixture and whisk to incorporate. Strain using a fine-mesh sieve.

Divide between six 350mL (12 fl oz) glasses. Refrigerate until set, about 40 minutes.

MANGO GELÉE   Place the gelatin sheets in a bowl of cold water.

In a saucepan, warm 80mL (⅓ cup) of the simple syrup to 40°C (105°F). Remove the gelatin sheets from the water and add them to the warm syrup, whisking to dissolve. Add the mango purée and passion fruit juice, using an immersion blender to blend. Strain through a fine-mesh sieve. Gently pour 30mL (2 Tbsp) over each panna cotta and return to the fridge to chill until set, about 30 minutes.

PUFFED RICE   Combine the water and salt in a saucepan. Using a fine-mesh sieve, rinse the rice under cold running water until the water runs clear. Add to the saucepan and bring to a simmer over medium heat. Cook until very, very soft almost to the point of falling apart, about 30 to 40 minutes. Strain and rinse under cold water to remove any excess starch.

Line a dehydrator tray with a single layer of cheesecloth. Spread the rice in an even layer on the tray. Dry for 2 hours at 52°C (125°F).

In a large pot, heat the oil to 220°C (425°F). The pot should be large enough that it is not more than half full.

Using a fine-mesh sieve, plunge the dehydrated rice into the oil and fry until it puffs. Drain the puffed rice on paper towel. Keep the oil for the quinoa and wild rice.

PUFFED
QUINOA   Combine the water and salt in a saucepan. Using a fine-mesh sieve, rinse the quinoa under cold running water until the water runs clear. Add to the water and bring to a simmer over medium heat. Cook until very tender, almost to the point of falling apart, about 30 to 40 minutes. Strain and rinse under cold water to remove any excess starch.

Line a dehydrator tray with a single layer of cheesecloth. Spread the quinoa in an even layer on the tray. Dry for 2 hours at 52°C (125°F).

Heat the same pot of oil to 220°C (425°F).

Using a fine-mesh sieve, plunge the dehydrated quinoa into the oil and fry until it puffs. Drain the puffed quinoa on paper towel. Keep the oil for the wild rice.

PUFFED
WILD RICE   Heat the same pot of oil to 220°C (425°F).

Using a fine-mesh sieve, plunge the wild rice into the oil until it puffs, just a few seconds. Drain the puffed rice on paper towel.

Continued . . .

GARAM MASALA

Preheat the oven to 150°C (300°F).

Combine all the ingredients then spread over a baking tray and toast in the oven until very fragrant, about 12 minutes. Remove from the oven and allow to cool. Alternatively, toast the spices in a sauté pan over medium heat, shaking continuously, until they begin to release aromas, about 8 minutes. Use a spice mill to process to a fine powder.

Combine the puffed rice, quinoa, and wild rice. Dust with the masala and toss to combine.

SERVE

Cut the dates in half lengthwise, and then cut each half into 3 slivers.

Place 4 dots of coriander gel on the surface of each panna cotta. Add the puffed grains. Place a quenelle of mango sorbet in the centre of the grains, then the date slivers and shards of mango transparent. Garnish with the herbs.

DARK CHOCOLATE ALMOND FINANCIERS, CHOCOLATE CHANTILLY MOUSSE, RASPBERRY

Serves 6

Valrhona makes a Grand Cru dark chocolate called Manjari, which is bright and acidic and works really well with raspberries. So, we turn that into a dark chocolate mousse. Then we make a sort of gluten-free financier, cook it in a really small savarin mould, glaze it with dark chocolate, and sprinkle it with cocoa nibs. Then we add some chocolate curls and raspberry gel, cubes of raspberry jelly, and fresh raspberries, too. The result is all sorts of delicious variations on a great combination.

NOTE

You will need savarin molds (8 x 2cm/3¼ x ¾ in size) and one quarter baking tray (23 × 33cm/ 9 × 13 in) to make this dish. Always use good-quality chocolate—for this recipe we use Valrhona Guanaja 70%, Manjari 64%, and Opalys 33%.

INGREDIENTS

Raspberry Crème

¾ sheet gelatin

125g (½ cup) raspberry purée

2 eggs

50g (¼ cup) sugar

60g (¼ cup) butter, softened

Dark Chocolate Almond Financiers

30g (1 oz) Valrhona Guanaja 70% dark chocolate pieces

200g (1 cup) sugar

150g (1½ cups) finely ground blanched almonds

15g (2 Tbsp) cornstarch

10g (2 Tbsp) cocoa powder

3g (1 tsp) salt

5 egg whites

30mL (2 Tbsp) heavy cream

Manjari Chantilly Mousse

⅓ sheet gelatin

80g (3 oz) Valrhona Manjari 64% dark chocolate pieces

45mL (3 Tbsp) milk

125mL (½ cup) heavy cream

Dark Chocolate Glaze

6 sheets gelatin

350g (1¾ cups) sugar

125mL (½ cup) water

100g (1¼ cups) cocoa powder, sifted

175mL (⅔ cup) heavy cream

Dark Chocolate Coating

100g (⅔ cup) whole almonds

500g (1 lb 2 oz) Valrhona Manjari 64% dark chocolate pieces

30mL (2 Tbsp) coconut oil

Raspberry Confit

2 sheets gelatin

100g (½ cup) sugar

14g (1 Tbsp) NH pectin

430g (1¾ cups) raspberry purée

90g (⅓ cup) glucose

Continued . . .

Raspberry Fluid Gel

6g (1½ tsp) agar powder

1.5g (⅜ tsp) locust bean gum

50g (¼ cup) sugar

175mL (⅔ cup) water

300g (1¼ cups) raspberry purée

Gluten-Free Crumble

155g (1¼ cups) rice flour

155g (1¼ cups) sorghum flour

155g (1¼ cups) tapioca starch

30g (6 Tbsp) cocoa powder

6g (1 tsp) baking powder

1.8g (½ tsp) xanthan gum

175g (¾ cup plus 1 Tbsp) brown sugar

285g (1¼ cups) butter, diced, cold

Raspberry Opalys Curls

250g (9 oz) Valrhona Opalys 33% white chocolate pieces

25mL (scant 2 Tbsp) coconut oil

5g (2 Tbsp) freeze-dried raspberries, crushed

Garnish

Lemon balm

Freeze-dried raspberries

RASPBERRY CRÈME

Place the gelatin sheets in a bowl of ice water.

In a stainless-steel mixing bowl, combine the raspberry purée, eggs, and sugar, and set over a pot filled with a few inches of water. Heat over low heat, whisking constantly, until the mixture thickens into a curd and reaches 83°C (181°F). Remove from the heat and incorporate the butter using an immersion blender to form a smooth consistency. Chill overnight.

DARK CHOCOLATE ALMOND FINANCIERS

Preheat the oven to 160°C (315°F).

In a bowl set over simmering water, melt the chocolate. Set aside to cool while you make the batter.

Sift together the sugar, ground almonds, cornstarch, cocoa powder, and salt.

Whisk together the egg whites and cream.

In the bowl of a stand mixer fitted with the paddle attachment, on medium speed, combine the dry ingredients and egg white mixture. Mix to form a smooth batter.

Using a whisk, blend about ⅕ the batter into the warm chocolate. Once a smooth, uniform texture is reached, add the remaining batter and stir to incorporate.

Pipe 25g (1 oz) of batter into each of the 24 savarin forms (you can also do this in batches). Bake until puffed and set, about 13 minutes. Remove from the oven and allow to cool. Once cool, remove from the forms. You only need 6 of the financiers for this recipe, so wrap the remaining in plastic wrap and freeze for up to 1 month.

Pipe a thin, even layer of raspberry crème onto 6 of the financiers. Transfer to a baking tray, cover loosely with plastic wrap, and freeze until cool and the crème is set, about 1 hour.

MANJARI CHANTILLY MOUSSE

Place the gelatin in a bowl of ice water.

Place the chocolate in a stainless-steel bowl and set over a pot with a few inches of water in it. Heat over low heat until the chocolate is melted.

Bring the milk and softened gelatin sheets to a simmer in a pot.

Combine the melted chocolate and hot milk, using a whisk to form a smooth ganache. Cool to 40°C (104°F).

In the bowl of a stand mixer fitted with the whisk attachment, whip the cream until it holds soft peaks. Gently fold in the ganache.

Transfer the mousse to a piping bag, and pipe a little into in each of 6 savarin forms. Top with an inverted financier and press so that the financier is coated in the mousse. Freeze.

DARK CHOCOLATE GLAZE

Place the gelatin sheets in a bowl of ice water.

Heat the sugar and water in a saucepan set over medium heat until 103°C (217°F). Add the cocoa powder, using an immersion blender to process it to a smooth consistency. Add the soft gelatin sheets, stirring to dissolve them. Briefly use an immersion blender to combine. Add the cream, and briefly blend again.

DARK CHOCOLATE COATING

Preheat the oven to 135°C (275°F).

Spread the almonds on a baking tray and toast for 20 minutes. Cool, and then coarsely chop.

Place the chocolate in a stainless-steel bowl and set over a pot with a few inches of water in it. Heat over low heat until the chocolate is melted. Stir the coconut oil and toasted nuts into the chocolate.

RASPBERRY CONFIT

Place the gelatin sheets in a bowl of ice water.

Sift together the sugar and pectin.

Heat the raspberry purée and glucose in a saucepan set over low heat until 40°C (104°F). Add the sugar while constantly whisking. Bring to a boil. Remove from the heat and add the softened gelatin sheets. Pour onto a quarter baking tray lined with plastic wrap and chill in the refrigerator until firm.

RASPBERRY FLUID GEL

Whisk together the agar and locust bean gum.

Heat the sugar and water to a simmer in a saucepan set over medium heat. Remove from the heat.

Place the purée and syrup in a blender and adjust the speed to form a vortex. Slowly add the agar mixture. Blend for 1 minute. Transfer to a saucepan. Bring to a boil over medium heat and continue cooking for 1 minute.

Transfer to a storage container and allow to cool to room temperature. Refrigerate to set.

Once set, remove from the container and dice into pieces. Place in a blender and purée at high speed until a smooth gel is formed. Chill over ice, stirring occasionally. When ready to serve, transfer the fluid gel to a squeeze bottle.

Continued . . .

GLUTEN-FREE CRUMBLE

Preheat the oven to 160°C (315°F).

Sift together the rice flour, sorghum flour, tapioca starch, cocoa powder, baking powder, and xanthan gum using a fine-mesh sieve.

In the bowl of a stand mixer fitted with the paddle attachment, combine the dry ingredients with the sugar and butter. Blend to form a crumbly texture. Spread out on a baking tray lined with parchment paper and chill.

Bake the crumble for 30 minutes. Allow to cool, then crush.

RASPBERRY OPALYS CURLS

Place ¾ of the chocolate in a stainless-steel bowl and set over a pot with a few inches of water. Heat over low heat, stirring occasionally, until the chocolate is melted. Remove from the heat and add the remaining chocolate, stirring until smooth. Add the coconut oil and freeze-dried raspberries. Stir to incorporate. Pour into a tall plastic storage container (you want to create a block of chocolate) and let stand until completely set. Using a mandoline or sharp vegetable peeler, shave thin curls from the chocolate block.

SERVE

Using a microwave at half power, heat the dark chocolate glaze to 30°C (86°F). Place the frozen savarin moulds on a glazing rack. Pour the glaze evenly over the savarins and allow the excess to drip off. Return to the freezer to set the glaze.

Wash the lemon balm and gently dry with paper towel.

Cut small cubes of raspberry confit.

Coarsely chop the dark chocolate coating. Using a microwave at half power, heat the coating to 30°C (86°F), pausing occasionally to stir until smooth. Dip ⅓ of the glazed financier into the coating.

Dust each of 6 plates with crushed freeze-dried raspberries. Place the financiers off-centre on the plates, and garnish with gluten-free crumble. Place dots of raspberry gel and cubes of raspberry confit on the plates, and finish with raspberry Opalys curls and lemon balm.

COCKTAILS

When we were preparing to launch Hawksworth and turned our thoughts to its bar, we were very mindful of our historic setting. The original hotel was launched in the Roaring Twenties, the early glory years of the cocktail bar, and we wanted to pay tribute to that with something more substantial than a mere appreciative nod. We aimed to do it with an elegant and sophisticated setting, gracious service, and a cocktail program rooted in a classic style of mixology, executed with the best modern ingredients and the latest techniques.

The Nightingale bar subscribes to the same program. The atmosphere there may be far more casual, but the cocktails served up draw on the structures established in a more formal past. The cocktail menu focuses on classics from different eras, modernized for our own with an emphasis on seasonality in the mixes and garnishes.

The drink recipes included here are mostly classics—and sometimes very local classics (see the Hotel Georgia on page 304, updated from a dusty, yellowing bar guide found on site)—conceived for the contemporary palate, and executed with a sense of fun, whimsy, and pleasure. Which is what bars are supposed to be all about.

Our wine program, on the other hand, is deeply serious. Nearly a third of our very sizeable wine purchases are acquired with the strict intention of long-term cellaring. Which is to say that the Hawksworth cellar is impractically large, and not very economical, so that our team of sommeliers can always be in the luxurious position of serving the right wine at its right time to the right person. Nonetheless, our emphasis is on value. Whether local vintages from BC, or wines from farther afield in both New World and Old, we are on a constant quest to uncover the unexpected—the best little-known producers in the finest wine regions—to be able to serve our customers top quality wines that they are unlikely to encounter elsewhere. H

ANCIENT RUIN

Serves 1

NOTE   *This was created by former Hawksworth bartender Alex Black in 2013 and based loosely on the classic 20th-century cocktail.*

INGREDIENTS

Half serrano pepper, deseeded and finely julienned

45mL (1½ fl oz) Los Siete Misterios Doba-Yej mezcal

15mL (½ fl oz) crème de cacao

30mL (1 fl oz) lemon juice

8mL (¼ fl oz) agave syrup

Tonka bean, for garnish

Add the pepper to the mezcal and infuse at room temperature for 4 hours. Strain and rebottle.

Shake the infused mezcal with the crème de cacao, lemon juice, agave syrup, and some ice. Strain into a chilled coupette. Garnish with freshly grated tonka bean.

CRANBERRY GINGER *(photo on page 302)*

Serves 1

INGREDIENTS

60mL (2 fl oz) Bremner's cranberry juice

15mL (½ fl oz) orgeat syrup

15mL (½ fl oz) lemon juice

295mL (10 fl oz) ginger beer

Add the cranberry juice, orgeat syrup, and lemon juice to a tall Collins glass and fill with ice. Top with the ginger beer.

GIN CROOKED

NOTE | *This was created in 2017 by bar manager Luke O'Toole for a regular guest. It became so popular that we had to add it to the menu permanently.*

INGREDIENTS

45mL (1½ fl oz) Hayman's Old Tom gin

25mL (¾ fl oz) Pierre Ferrand Dry Curaçao

8mL (¼ fl oz) Luxardo Maraschino liqueur

8 dashes Dillon's ginger bitters

Grapefruit twist, for garnish

Stir all the ingredients with ice. Strain into a chilled coupette. Garnish with the grapefruit twist.

CASCADE FASHIONED (*photo on page 303*)

Serves 1

INGREDIENTS

Cedar Whiskey

1 bottle (750mL) Wild Turkey 101 bourbon

10g (2 Tbsp) cedar chips

Cascade Fashioned

1 small piece lemon peel

1 small piece orange peel

1 dash Angostura bitters

1 dash Ms. Better's Cyprus Bowl bitters

1 brown sugar cube

50mL (1¾ fl oz) Cedar Whiskey (left)

8mL (¼ fl oz) Long Table gin

Douglas fir tip, for garnish

CEDAR WHISKEY | Combine the bourbon and cedar chips in a container and leave for 10 hours to infuse. Strain and funnel back into the bourbon bottle. Store as you would a regular whiskey.

CASCADE FASHIONED | Add the lemon peel, orange peel, Angostura bitters, Cyprus Bowl bitters, and the sugar cube to a cocktail mixing glass. Muddle together to break down the sugar cube.

Add 50mL (1¾ fl oz) of the cedar whiskey and the Long Table gin. Fill with ice and stir to dilute. Strain into a rocks glass filled with ice. Garnish with the Douglas fir tip.

Cranberry Ginger (page 300)

Tempest (page 307)

White Negroni (page 307)

Nightingale Martini (page 306)

Cacade Fashioned (page 301)

HOTEL GEORGIA

Serves 1

NOTE

This was adapted by original Hawksworth bar manager Brad Stanton from a recipe that appears in Ted Saucier's Bottoms Up *(published in 1951).*

INGREDIENTS

45mL (1½ fl oz) Beefeater gin

30mL (1 fl oz) lemon juice

15mL (½ fl oz) orgeat syrup

1 egg white

4 dashes orange blossom water

Freshly grated nutmeg, for garnish

Add all the ingredients except the nutmeg into a cocktail shaker. Shake with ice until well chilled. Strain to remove the ice. Shake without ice for a second time to whip air into the egg white.

Strain into a chilled coupette. Garnish with the nutmeg.

PAPER PLANE

Serves 1

NOTE

I can often be found drinking this cocktail in the Hawksworth lounge; it's a favourite of mine, and of many of our regular guests. It was created in 2007 by Sam Ross at the Violet Hour in Chicago.

INGREDIENTS

25mL (¾ fl oz) Aperol

25mL (¾ fl oz) Bulleit bourbon

25mL (¾ fl oz) Montenegro Amaro

25mL (¾ fl oz) lemon juice

Shake all ingredients with ice. Strain into a chilled coupette.

Hotel Georgia (page 304)

Paper Plane (page 304)

Night Moves (page 306)

Poperin Pear (page 307)

NIGHT MOVES *(photo on page 305)*   *Serves 1*

NOTE

This was created by former head bartender Cooper Tardivel in 2013 and named after the 1976 Bob Seger track.

INGREDIENTS

45mL (1½ fl oz) Ron Zacapa 23-year-old rum

25mL (¾ fl oz) Taylor Fladgate white port

15mL (½ fl oz) Amaro Averna

4 dashes Angostura bitters

Maraschino cherry, for garnish

Stir all the ingredients except the cherry over ice. Strain into a chilled coupette. Garnish with a maraschino cherry.

NIGHTINGALE MARTINI *(photo on page 303)*   *Serves 1*

INGREDIENTS

Nightingale Vermouth

6g (3 Tbsp) loose-leaf green tea (such as TWG Sencha Prestige)

2g (1 Tbsp) loose-leaf white tea (such as TWG White Mortal)

350mL (12 fl oz) Maidenii dry vermouth

350mL (12 fl oz) Lillet Blanc

Nightingale Martini

60mL (2 fl oz) Botanist gin

15mL (½ fl oz) Nightingale Vermouth (left)

Spritz of Bruichladdich Port Charlotte (Islay whisky), from a spray bottle

Spritz of St. Germain elderflower liqueur, from a spray bottle

3 concord or red grapes, skewered, for garnish

NIGHTINGALE VERMOUTH

Add both teas to a container with the dry vermouth and Lillet Blanc and allow to infuse for 7 hours, then strain. Refrigerate for up to 1 month.

NIGHTINGALE MARTINI

Add the gin and Nightingale vermouth to a cocktail mixing glass. Fill with ice and stir to dilute.

Spritz a chilled martini or coupe glass with Islay whisky. Strain the cocktail into the glass. Spritz with elderflower liqueur. Garnish with the grapes.

POPERIN PEAR   *(photo on page 305)*   *Serves 1*

(photo on page 305)

NOTE

This was created in 2014 by Hawksworth head bartender Cooper Tardivel and named for a line in Shakespeare's Romeo and Juliet.

INGREDIENTS

30mL (1 fl oz) unfiltered apple juice

25mL (¾ fl oz) Bombay gin

25mL (¾ fl oz) Grey Goose La Poire vodka

25mL (¾ fl oz) yellow chartreuse

15mL (½ fl oz) lemon juice

11g (¼ fl oz) honey

Shake all ingredients with ice. Strain into a chilled coupette.

WHITE NEGRONI   *(photo on page 302)*   *Serves 1*

(photo on page 302)

INGREDIENTS

30mL (1 fl oz) Botanist gin

30mL (1 fl oz) Maidenii dry vermouth

30mL (1 fl oz) Luxardo Bitter Bianco

3 dashes Scrappy's grapefruit bitters

1 small piece grapefruit peel, for garnish

Add all ingredients except the grapefruit peel into a cocktail mixing glass. Fill with ice and stir to dilute. Strain into a small rocks glass filled with ice. Garnish with the grapefruit peel.

TEMPEST   *(photo on page 302)*   *Serves 1*

(photo on page 302)

INGREDIENTS

45mL (1½ fl oz) Monkey Shoulder whisky

15mL (½ fl oz) Bruichladdich Port Charlotte (Islay whisky)

15mL (½ fl oz) Maidenii classic vermouth

15mL (½ fl oz) Amaro Averna

3 bar spoons Fernet-Branca

3 dashes Apothecary Cacao Coffee bitters

1 small piece orange peel, for garnish

Add all ingredients except the orange peel into a cocktail mixing glass. Fill with ice and stir to dilute. Strain into a chilled martini or coupe glass. Garnish with orange peel.

GLOSSARY

PIZZA DOUGH

Makes enough for 3 pizzas

INGREDIENTS

Poolish

125mL (½ cup) water, room temperature

65g (½ cup) Primitiva (type I) flour

65g (½ cup) Italian 00 flour

0.18g (¹⁄₁₆ tsp) active dry yeast

Pizza Dough

70g (2½ oz) sourdough starter

230g (1¾ cups) Italian 00 flour

40g (⅓ cup) semolina flour

85mL (⅓ cup) water, 21°C (70°F)

0.3g (⅛ tsp) active dry yeast

8g (1 Tbsp) salt

7mL (1½ tsp) olive oil

POOLISH

In a bowl, combine the water, flours, and yeast. Mix just until combined but do not over-mix. Cover with plastic wrap and refrigerate to slow down the yeast. Let sit overnight, ideally 16 to 20 hours.

PIZZA DOUGH

In the bowl of a stand mixer fitted with the hook attachment, mix the poolish and sourdough starter with the flours and 80mL (⅓ cup) of the water for 4 minutes on low speed.

Stop the machine, and add the yeast at the centre where the hook is in the dough. Without mixing or removing the dough hook, cover the dough and let it rest for 20 minutes.

Use your hands to turn the dough twice in the bowl to incorporate the yeast. Once the yeast has been folded inside, slowly add the 5mL (1 tsp) of remaining water and the salt around the edge of the bowl, alternating one and then the other. The water helps dissolve the salt, reducing the risk of coarse salt breaking the gluten strands. Mix the dough for 3 minutes on low speed, then 2 minutes on medium speed. Cover with plastic wrap and let rest for 1 hour.

Slowly add the oil while mixing on low speed. Once the oil is thoroughly incorporated, mix for 1 additional minute on medium speed. Then mix for 3 seconds on high.

Portion the dough into 3 pieces and shape into round balls. Wrap each in plastic wrap and refrigerate until ready to use.

Remove from the fridge and let it sit at room temperature for a minimum of 2 to 3 hours before use.

PASTA DOUGH

Makes enough for 6 portions

NOTE

When working with pasta—in balls, or sheets—always keep it covered with plastic wrap or a kitchen towel as it dries out (and becomes unworkable) quickly.

INGREDIENTS

300g (2⅓ cups) Italian 00 flour

3 egg yolks

2 eggs

Pinch salt

Dash olive oil

Combine all the ingredients in the bowl of a food processor and pulse until the dough comes together into a large ball. Remove and knead by hand for at least 4 to 5 minutes.

Wrap tightly in plastic wrap and refrigerate for 30 minutes.

Unwrap the dough and divide into quarters. Work with 1 piece at a time and keep the other pieces covered with plastic wrap or a slightly damp tea towel. Run each quarter of dough through a pasta roller on progressively thinner settings until you have a sheet of paper-thin pasta. You should be able to see your fingers through it.

As the sheet of pasta comes off the pasta machine, lay it on a floured board and cut it into rectangular sheets about 30cm (12 in) long. Sprinkle flour lightly on each sheet after you cut it, and continue stacking the pasta sheets on top of each other. Keep them covered with a lightly dampened towel. Work quickly, as the fresh pasta will dry out.

ANCHOVY BREADCRUMBS

Makes 250g (1 cup)

INGREDIENTS

150g (1½ cups) grated baguette (about ⅓ of a baguette)

40g (3 Tbsp) chopped anchovy fillets

45mL (3 Tbsp) olive oil

20g (1 cup) basil leaves, chopped

Combine all the ingredients in a large pot and heat over medium heat, stirring constantly and breaking up all large chunks of anchovy and basil. Cook until golden brown, about 2 minutes. Transfer to a baking sheet lined with paper towel. Let stand for 30 minutes.

PIZZA TOMATO SAUCE

Makes 250mL (1 cup)

INGREDIENTS

340g (1½ cups) canned San Marzano
    tomatoes

30mL (2 Tbsp) olive oil

½ white onion, small dice

2 cloves garlic, sliced

Pinch salt

2 pinches dried oregano

Purée the tomatoes using an immersion blender until smooth.

Heat the olive oil in a medium pot over medium heat and sweat the onion, garlic, and salt, stirring frequently, until translucent, about 5 minutes. Add the tomatoes and oregano, reduce the heat, and cook over very low heat for 1 to 1½ hours, stirring frequently right to the bottom, as this sauce will scorch easily if left unattended. If you can, elevate the pot above the heat with a wire rack so it simmers really slowly, without burning the bottom.

Adjust the seasoning as needed and allow to cool before using. Refrigerate for up to 4 days.

ROASTED TOMATO SAUCE

Makes 375mL (1½ cups)

INGREDIENTS

6 Roma tomatoes

30mL (2 Tbsp) olive oil

2 cloves garlic

10 basil leaves

½ white onion, cut in small dice

Pinch salt

340g (1½ cups) canned San Marzano
    tomatoes

50mL (3 Tbsp) water

Preheat the oven to 230°C (450°F).

Toss the Roma tomatoes with half the olive oil and place on a baking tray lined with parchment paper. Roast until caramelized, about 25 minutes.

Meanwhile, add the remaining olive oil and the garlic to a pot and shallow-fry over medium heat until the garlic is bubbly and fragrant with a nice golden-brown colour. Add the basil and allow to crackle and infuse for 1 minute. Add the onions and salt. Reduce the heat to low and cook until soft, about 15 minutes. Stir frequently and do not allow the onions to colour. Add the roasted tomatoes and their roasting juices.

Add the canned tomatoes and water. Blend with an immersion blender for a few minutes until smooth. Bring to a slow simmer and cook for 1 to 1½ hours over low heat. Stir frequently right to the bottom, as the tomatoes will scorch easily if left unattended. If you can, elevate the pot above the heat with a wire rack so it simmers really slowly, without burning the bottom. Remove from the heat and purée in a high-speed blender or using an immersion blender on high for 90 seconds. Refrigerate for up to 4 days.

TOMATO JAM

INGREDIENTS

75mL (5 Tbsp) olive oil

3 shallots, finely chopped

2 cloves garlic, finely chopped

2 sprigs tarragon

1 sprig basil

1 sprig thyme

20g (1 Tbsp) tomato paste

10 Roma tomatoes, peeled and diced

80mL (⅓ cup) sherry vinegar

⅓ jalapeno, deseeded and finely chopped

50g (¼ cup) sugar

Preheat the oven to 150°C (300°F).

Heat the olive oil in a large ovenproof sauté pan over medium heat. Sauté the shallot and garlic until translucent, about 5 minutes.

Tie the tarragon, basil, and thyme together in a piece of cheesecloth secured with string to make a sachet. Add the sachet to the pan, along with the tomato paste, tomatoes, vinegar, and jalapeno and cook in the oven until it reaches a jam-like consistency, 1 to 2 hours.

Remove from the oven and return to the stove. Add the sugar and bring to a boil. Refrigerate for up to 5 days.

SEMI-DRIED TOMATOES

INGREDIENTS

125g (1 cup) cherry tomatoes (about 10)

2 cloves garlic, thinly sliced

30mL (2 Tbsp) olive oil

1 sprig thyme, leaves only

Pinch salt

Pinch sugar

Cut the cherry tomatoes in half, lengthwise, and toss with the garlic, olive oil, thyme, salt, and sugar. Transfer the tomatoes to a baking tray lined with parchment paper, cut sides up. (Do not use an aluminum baking sheet; the acid in the tomato will react with the metal.)

Place in a dehydrator (or an oven at 95°C/200°F) for 2 to 4 hours, until semi-dried and just starting to blister. Refrigerate for up to 1 week.

TOMATO CONCASSÉ

Makes 25g (2 Tbsp)

INGREDIENTS   2 Roma tomatoes

Cut an X on the bottom of each tomato. Bring a pot of water to a boil and blanch the tomatoes for 20 seconds and then immediately drop in an ice bath.

Peel the tomatoes. Cut each in half and discard the seeds and insides. Dice the outside flesh into 5mm (¼ in) dice.

GARLIC CONFIT

Makes 1 head garlic

INGREDIENTS   1 head garlic, unpeeled
65mL (¼ cup) olive oil
Salt

Preheat the oven to 175°C (350°F).

Slice 6mm (¼ in) off the top of the head of garlic, exposing the cloves. Place the head of garlic in the centre of a piece of aluminum foil. Drizzle with olive oil and sprinkle with salt, then seal the packet. Bake for 40 minutes. Remove from the oven and allow to cool. Serve whole or squeeze the flesh out of every clove to use in other recipes. Store in an airtight container, drizzled with olive oil, for up to 1 week.

GARLIC BUTTER

Makes 125mL (½ cup)

NOTE   *Having espelette pepper on hand for a fruity and mildly spicy finish is great, but a few extra twists of the pepper mill or some chili flakes will work here too.*

INGREDIENTS   100g (7 Tbsp) salted butter

2 cloves garlic, finely chopped

Pinch espelette pepper or red chili flakes
   or ½ Thai chili, deseeded, finely
   diced (optional)

1 lemon, zest and juice

15g (⅓ cup) chopped chives

Melt the butter in a pan over low heat. Add the garlic, espelette pepper (if using), lemon juice and zest, and chives. Keep warm.

TARTARE SAUCE

Makes 250mL (1 cup)

INGREDIENTS

200mL (¾ cup) mayonnaise

30g (3 Tbsp) drained chopped capers

35g (3 Tbsp) drained chopped gherkins

1 small shallot, finely chopped

¼ lemon, juice

8g (3 Tbsp) chopped parsley

Salt

Pepper

Mix all the ingredients together in a bowl. Refrigerate for up to 1 week.

COCKTAIL SAUCE

Makes 125 mL (½ cup)

INGREDIENTS

100g (6 Tbsp) tomato ketchup

25g (1 Tbsp) prepared horseradish

3 dashes Tabasco or other hot sauce

3 dashes Worcestershire sauce

½ lemon, juice

Mix all the ingredients together in a bowl. Refrigerate for up to 1 week.

BARBECUE SAUCE

Makes 500mL (2 cups)

INGREDIENTS

20mL (1⅓ Tbsp) vegetable oil

1 onion, minced

3 cloves garlic, coarsely chopped

290mL (1¼ cup) ketchup

290mL (1¼ cup) cider vinegar

200mL (¾ cup) water

180g (¾ cup plus 2 Tbsp) brown sugar

50mL (3 Tbsp) Worcestershire sauce

1 ancho chili, toasted

18g (2 Tbsp) salt

6g (1 Tbsp) herbes de Provence

6g (1 Tbsp) smoked sweet paprika

6g (1 Tbsp) pepper

Heat the oil in a medium pot over medium heat and sauté the onion and garlic until slightly browned, about 5 minutes. Add the remaining ingredients and simmer until thickened to a sauce consistency, stirring occasionally. Allow to cool. Transfer to a blender and blend until smooth, then strain through a fine-mesh sieve. Refrigerate for up to 1 week.

ROASTED TOMATO VINAIGRETTE

125mL (½ cup)

INGREDIENTS

60mL (4 Tbsp) olive oil

1 clove garlic, sliced

2 shallots, sliced

25 cherry tomatoes

15g (1 Tbsp) tomato paste

30mL (2 Tbsp) sherry vinegar

Salt

Sugar

Preheat the oven to 190°C (375°F).

Heat 15mL (1 Tbsp) of the olive oil in a medium ovenproof sauté pan over low heat and sweat the garlic and shallots until soft and translucent, about 2 minutes. Stir in the tomatoes and tomato paste. Cook until the tomatoes are blistered and caramelized, about 15 minutes.

Remove the tomatoes from the pan. Deglaze the pan with the sherry vinegar and scrape with a wooden spoon to collect all the bits from the pan. Blend everything in a blender, adding the remaining olive oil slowly in a steady stream to allow the mixture to emulsify. Season with the salt and sugar as needed. Refrigerate for up to 1 week.

MAYONNAISE

Makes 125mL (½ cup)

INGREDIENTS

1 egg yolk, room temperature

15g (1 Tbsp) Dijon mustard

Pinch salt

1 lemon, juice

125mL (½ cup) neutral-flavoured oil, such as grapeseed or canola

Place the egg yolk, Dijon mustard and salt in a mixing bowl with high sides. Pour the lemon juice into the bowl and whisk the mixture well. Slowly, a few drops at a time, pour the oil into the bowl while whisking constantly. Once the mayonnaise has started to thicken, pour in the rest of the oil in a slow and steady stream. If the oil starts to build up, stop pouring and whisk the mayonnaise briskly until the oil is incorporated. Refrigerate for up to 1 week.

PARSLEY PURÉE

Makes 45mL (3 Tbsp)

INGREDIENTS

40g (1¼ cups) packed parsley leaves,
    stems removed

40g (1¼ cups) baby spinach, stems
    removed

Salt

Bring a large pot of salted water to a rolling boil. Drop the parsley and spinach into the water and cook until the parsley is soft and starts to disintegrate, 1 to 2 minutes. Drain and immediately dunk in an ice bath. Squeeze excess water out.

Blitz the parsley and spinach in a blender on high speed until smooth. Pass through a fine-mesh sieve. Allow to cool over ice and then season with salt.

TUNA CONFIT OIL

Makes 250mL (1 cup)

INGREDIENTS

2 cloves garlic, smashed

15g (2 Tbsp) chopped jalapeno

2 strips lemon peel

2 strips orange peel

1 sprig rosemary

2 sprigs thyme

3g (1 tsp) fennel seeds

3g (1 tsp) peppercorns

250mL (1 cup) canola oil

Combine all the ingredients in a medium pot and bring up to a slow simmer over medium heat. Reduce the heat to low and cook for 20 minutes. Remove from the heat and allow all the aromatics and flavours to infuse for 2 hours. Strain through a fine-mesh sieve; discard the solids and reserve the oil. Refrigerate in a sealed jar for up to 1 month.

VEGETABLE NAGE

INGREDIENTS

1 large onion

2 stalks celery, including some leaves

2 large carrots

1 bunch scallions, chopped

8 cloves garlic, minced

8 sprigs parsley

6 sprigs thyme

2 bay leaves

Pinch salt

2L (8 cups) water

Combine all the ingredients in a large pot and bring to a boil over high heat. Reduce the heat and simmer for 20 minutes. Strain, pushing through a fine-mesh sieve. Allow to cool. Refrigerate for up to 1 week or freeze for up to 3 months.

FISH STOCK

INGREDIENTS

900g (2 lb) bones from white fish (such as ling cod or halibut)

1 leek, white part only, sliced

½ stalk celery, sliced

½ onion, small dice

¼ fennel bulb, sliced

2 cloves garlic, crushed

1 sprig thyme

1 bay leaf

80mL (⅓ cup) white wine

10 white peppercorns, crushed

½ lemon, sliced

2 sprigs parsley

Rinse the fish bones for 5 to 10 minutes under cold running water.

In a large stockpot, combine the bones, leek, celery, onion, fennel, garlic, thyme, bay leaf, and wine. Add enough water to cover, then bring to a simmer. Skim the impurities off the surface and add the peppercorns. Simmer for 20 minutes, skimming the surface every 5 minutes. Add the lemon and parsley, remove from the heat, and steep for 10 minutes.

Strain, pressing through a fine-mesh sieve. Allow to cool. Refrigerate for up to 1 week or freeze for up to 3 months.

VEAL STOCK

Makes 1L (4 cups)

INGREDIENTS

3.5kg (8 lb) veal bones, in 5–8cm (2–3 in) pieces

150g (½ cup) tomato paste

6 stalks celery, coarsely chopped

3 carrots, coarsely chopped

1 large onion, coarsely chopped

Small handful peppercorns

4 bay leaves

3 sprigs thyme

Preheat the oven to 220°C (425°F).

Spread the bones in a roasting pan and roast for about 30 minutes, turning once. Remove from the oven and smear a thin layer of tomato paste over the bones. Add the celery, carrots, and onion, and roast for another 15 to 20 minutes, until the vegetables begin to caramelize.

Transfer to a large stockpot. Deglaze the roasting pan with water (or red wine) and add to the stockpot. Add the peppercorns, bay leaves, and thyme. Cover with cold water.

Over medium heat, slowly bring the mixture to a very gentle simmer; do not boil. Let simmer gently for at least 4 hours, and up to 12, skimming the surface every 30 minutes. If the bones become exposed, add more water and lower the heat.

Remove the bones and discard. Strain, pushing through a fine-mesh sieve. Chill quickly over an ice bath, then refrigerate. Skim off any fat that has solidified on the top before using. Refrigerate for up to 1 week or freeze for up to 3 months.

CHICKEN STOCK

Makes 2L (8 cups)

INGREDIENTS

1.8kg (4 lb) chicken bones

2 stalks celery, coarsely chopped

½ onion, coarsely chopped

2 small carrots, coarsely chopped

2 cloves garlic, crushed

1 sprig thyme

1 bay leaf

2.5L (10 cups) cold water

In a large stockpot, combine the bones, vegetables, and herbs and cover with the water. Bring to a boil and simmer for 4 to 6 hours. Strain, pushing through a fine-mesh sieve. Allow to cool. Refrigerate for up to 1 week or freeze for up to 3 months.

CHICKEN VELOUTÉ

400mL (1⅔ cups)

INGREDIENTS

15mL (1 Tbsp) canola oil

100g (2 cups) button mushrooms, roughly sliced

2 shallots, roughly sliced

1 clove garlic, sliced

1 sprig thyme

165mL (¾ cup) white wine

165mL (¾ cup) Noilly Prat (dry vermouth)

500mL (2 cups) Chicken Stock (page 317 or store-bought)

250mL (1 cup) cream

Salt

Heat the oil in a large sauté pan over medium heat and sweat the mushrooms, shallots, garlic, and thyme until translucent with very little to no colour, 4 to 5 minutes.

Add the wine and vermouth and reduce until all liquids have evaporated. Add the chicken stock and simmer on medium until reduced by half. Add the cream, bring to a boil, and reduce to a simmer. Reduce the liquid for 15 more minutes. Strain, pressing through a fine-mesh sieve. Season to taste with salt. Refrigerate for up to 3 days.

MADEIRA JUS

Makes 125mL (½ cup)

INGREDIENTS

450g (1 lb) chicken or quail bones (depending on recipe), broken into 5cm (2 in) pieces (optional)

15mL (1 Tbsp) vegetable oil

50g (1 cup) button mushrooms, sliced

2 medium shallots, sliced

3g (1 tsp) peppercorns

1 clove garlic

1 bay leaf

150mL (⅔ cup) Madeira

300mL (1¼ cups) Veal Stock (page 317)

100mL (7 Tbsp) Chicken Stock (page 317)

15g (1 Tbsp) butter

Preheat the oven to 165°C (325°F).

Lightly drizzle the bones with vegetable oil and place in a roasting pan lined with parchment paper. Roast for 30 to 40 minutes until golden brown, tossing halfway through to ensure even colour on all sides.

Sweat the mushrooms and shallots in a heavy-bottomed skillet, until lightly brown, 3 to 5 minutes. Add the bones, peppercorns, garlic, and bay leaf. Deglaze with the Madeira and reduce until syrupy and glaze-like. Add the veal stock and chicken stock and bring to a boil. Lower the heat and slow simmer until the liquid is reduced by ⅔. Pass through a fine-mesh sieve without pressing. Then whisk in the butter. Refrigerate for up to 1 week.

BASIL CHIPS

Makes 18 chips

INGREDIENTS

Olive oil

18 basil leaves

Salt

Cover a large plate with a layer of plastic wrap. Drizzle with just a touch of olive oil and brush with a pastry brush to cover the surface entirely. Place the basil leaves on top, and brush each with a drop of olive oil. Season with salt. Cover with another piece of plastic wrap. Microwave for 1 minute, then check to see if the leaves are dry. Test by letting one cool completely on a cold surface and seeing if it becomes crispy and translucent. If still soft, microwave for another 30 seconds. Do not overcook, or the leaves will turn brown.

BAHARAT SPICE

Makes about 100g (about 1 cup)

INGREDIENTS

20g (3 Tbsp) pepper

16g (scant 2 Tbsp) coriander seeds

16g (scant 2 Tbsp) cumin seeds

8g (scant Tbsp) allspice berries

4g (1 tsp) cardamom seeds

Pinch cloves

2 whole cinnamon sticks

Pinch grated nutmeg

18g (3 Tbsp) sweet paprika

Heat a small sauté pan over medium heat and toast all the spices except the paprika until fragrant. Process in a spice grinder with the paprika. Store with your spices. It lasts forever.

ACKNOWLEDGMENTS

This book would not have been possible without Stéphanie Noël, who as a young chef signed up to join my opening team at Ouest and has worked with me on and off for 20 years since. Stéphanie took on the job of rewriting all of our restaurant recipes pretty much single-handedly. It's a shocking amount of work and I am extremely grateful that she undertook it.

The other chef I need to single out here is Phil Scarfone, who joined my opening team at Hawksworth back in 2011, and after a tour of the stations in that kitchen, launched Nightingale in 2016. This cookbook would not be what it is without Phil's recipes from that restaurant. Allan Tam has now taken the reigns at Nightingale and I am sincerely grateful to him also.

Neither would the recipes from Hawksworth be what they are without the unique contribution of Kristian Eligh, who launched Hawksworth with me, and worked at my side for nearly a decade afterwards. I have never worked with another chef so closely, and so easily, with the confidence that we understood things the same way. Kristian's contribution cannot be overstated. Antonio Sotomayo now leads the team at Hawksworth and I thank him for all of his incredible work.

Wayne Kozinko has helmed our pastry kitchen since the launch of Hawksworth. He is a superb pastry chef, highly skilled and always imaginative. He is also super-consistent, steady as a rock. As his role has expanded to overseeing production of all our catering desserts, the Air Canada dessert file, and all those daily croissants and other pastries and cookies for Bel Café, his consistency still never wavers.

As for the many terrific bartenders who have contributed to our cocktail program over the years, Cooper Tardivel still stands out years after he left us for setting the stage for the success that followed. Several have taken up the reins since. And nowadays, Josh Nidzgorski is taking us to new heights in that role. Bryant Mao oversees the wine program at both restaurants, and he is absolutely at the top of the game.

There is, of course, more to cookbooks than recipes. There are all those words. So for putting mine on paper in the right order I need to thank Jacob Richler, who I met nearly 20 years ago, when as a restaurant critic he dropped in one evening to size up my cooking. Fortunately, he liked what he tasted. I don't usually much care for critics, but I have learned over the years that Jacob and I see eye to eye. He usually puts it better than I do, so I'm very glad that he wanted to write this book with us.

Clinton Hussey is my number-one go-to food photographer. There's no one better. What an eye. And he's easy to work with, too. Thank you for everything, Clinton, to you, and your team.

All that said, there would still be no book at all if it weren't for Lindsay Paterson, Robert McCullough, and their team at Appetite, who had the vision to put these recipes, words, and photographs together in a book that I sincerely hope you enjoy as much as I do.

This cookbook would also not exist were it not for Hawksworth Restaurant. So with that in mind I want to thank my great friends Willie and Megan Mitchell, who—one night at West—introduced me to my future business partner, Bruce Langeréis of Delta Land Development. Bruce has been integral to our success, as has Tony Hii. Thank you, Bruce and Tony, for all your support.

And sincere thanks to all of our staff (past, present, and future). There are too many names to mention, and I'm incredibly grateful to you all.

Finally, I need to thank my wife, Annabel, and our son, Heston. They are my support and my inspiration. They make everything possible, and mean more to me than I could possibly explain here. Thank you.

INDEX

Appetite by Random House® and colophon are registered trademarks of Penguin Random House LLC.

Library and Archives Canada Cataloguing in Publication is available upon request.
ISBN: 978-0-525-61009-0
eBook ISBN: 978-0-525-61010-6

Photography by Clinton Hussey
Photography on pages vii, 3, 5, 44, 47, 116-117, 239 c/o Hawksworth Restaurant Group; on pages viii, 6, 10-11, 95, 116, 148, 149, 154, 196-197, 235, 236, 244, 296-297 by EVAAN; on page 192 c/o Rosewood Hotel Georgia

Back cover illustration by Brian Boulton
Book and case design by Kelly Hill

Printed and bound in China

Published in Canada by Appetite by Random House®, a division of Penguin Random House Canada Limited.

www.penguinrandomhouse.ca

10   9   8   7   6   5   4   3   2   1

appetite
by RANDOM HOUSE

Penguin
Random
House

CHEF DAVID HAWKSWORTH is widely regarded as one of North America's greatest chefs. He was born and raised in Vancouver, then spent a decade training at Michelin-starred restaurants in the UK, such as Le Manoir aux Quat'Saisons, L'Escargot, and The Square. He returned to Canada in 2000 and took his first Head Chef position, at Ouest (later renamed West), in Vancouver. In 2008 he became the youngest chef inducted into the BC Restaurant Hall of Fame.

Chef Hawksworth opened his eponymous restaurant in 2011, at the Rosewood Hotel Georgia. It was awarded the 2012 and 2013 *Vancouver Magazine* Restaurant of the Year and Chef of the Year awards, followed by five consecutive wins for Best Upscale Dining. Shortly after opening it was named in *enRoute* magazine's top three Best New Restaurants, and as *Maclean's* magazine's Restaurant of the Year. Chef Hawksworth opened his second restaurant in 2013, the sensationally popular Nightingale. He also operates two locations of Bel Café, Hawksworth Catering, the Hawksworth Young Chef Scholarship Foundation, and an exclusive culinary partnership with Air Canada. He lives in Vancouver with his wife and son.

Hawksworth: The Cookbook is a celebration of Chef Hawksworth's career to date.

CHEF STÉPHANIE NOËL has worked at leading restaurants and resorts in Canada and France, including Laurie Raphaël, West, West Coast Fishing Lodge, Long Beach Lodge, La Réserve de Beaulieu, and Restaurant Septime. She is Development Chef at the Hawksworth Group.

JACOB RICHLER is the founding editor of *Canada's 100 Best Restaurants*, a former *National Post* restaurant critic, a National Magazine Award-winning food columnist, author of *My Canada Includes Foie Gras*, and co-author of three previous cookbooks (with Susur Lee and Mark McEwan).

CLINTON HUSSEY is a multi-award-winning commercial photographer, born and raised in Vancouver.

www.hawksworthrestaurant.com

⃝ @chefhawksworth   ⃝ @hawksworthrest   ⃝ @nightingalerest   ⃝ @belcafeyvr

Book and cover photography: Clinton Hussey
Back cover illustration: Brian Boulton
Book and cover design: Kelly Hill

appetite
by RANDOM HOUSE

www.penguinrandomhouse.ca